D1571967

OPERATIONAL RISK MANAGEMENT

Also by Imad A. Moosa

INTERNATIONAL PARTY CONDITIONS
EXCHANGE RATE FORECASTING
FOREIGN DIRECT INVESTMENT
INTERNATIONAL FINANCIAL OPERATIONS
EXCHANGE RATE REGIMES

Operational Risk Management

Imad A. Moosa
Professor of Finance
Monash University

First published 2007 by
PALGRAVE MACMILLAN
Houndmills, Basingstoke, Hampshire RG21 6XS and
175 Fifth Avenue, New York, N.Y. 10010
Companies and representatives throughout the world

PALGRAVE MACMILLAN is the global academic imprint of the Palgrave
Macmillan division of St. Martin's Press, LLC and of Palgrave Macmillan Ltd.
Macmillan® is a registered trademark in the United States, United Kingdom
and other countries. Palgrave is a registered trademark in the European
Union and other countries.

ISBN-13: 978–0–230–50644–2   hardback
ISBN-10: 0–230–50644–5   hardback

This book is printed on paper suitable for recycling and made from fully
managed and sustained forest sources. Logging, pulping and manufacturing
processes are expected to conform to the environmental regulations of the
country of origin.

A catalogue record for this book is available from the British Library.

A catalog record for this book is available from the Library of Congress.

10   9   8   7   6   5   4   3   2   1
16   15   14   13   12   11   10   09   08   07

Printed and bound in Great Britain by
Antony Rowe Ltd, Chippenham and Eastbourne

To Nisreen and Danny

Contents

List of Figures

List of Tables

List of Abbreviations

AC	Agency and Custody
AIG	Accord Implementation Group
AM	Asset management
AMA	Advanced measurement approach
ANZ	Australia New Zealand (Bank)
APRA	Australian Prudential Regulatory Authority
AUD	Australian dollar
BBA	British Bankers' Association
BCBS	Basel Committee on Banking Supervision
BCCI	Bank for Credit and Commerce International
BDSF	Business distruptin and system failure
BEF	Belgian franc
BIA	Basic indicators approach
BIS	Bank for International Settlements
CAD	Canadian dollar
CAPM	Capital asset pricing model
CB	Commercial banking
CF	Corporate finance
CFO	Chief financial officer
CPBP	Clients, products, and business practices
CRD	Capital requirements directive
DEM	German mark
DPA	Damage to physical assets
DSV	Downside semi-variance
EAD	Exposure at default
EDAM	Execution, delivery, and asset management
EF	External fraud
EL	Expected loss
EPWS	Employment practices and workplace safety
ERM	Enterprise-wide risk management
ETL	Expected tail loss
EU	European Union

EUR	Euro
EVS	Extreme value simulation
EVT	Extreme value theory
FDIC	Federal Deposit Insurance Corporation
G10	The group of ten countries
GARCH	Generalized autoregressive conditional heteroscedasticity
GBP	British pound
GOLD	Global operational loss database
HR	Human resources
IF	Internal fraud
IIF	Institute of International Finance
IMA	Internal measurement approach
IOSCO	International Organisation of Securities Commissions
IRB	Internal-based ratings approach
ISDA	International Swaps and Derivatives Association
IT	Information technology
JPY	Japanese yen
KRD	Key risk driver
KRI	Key risk indicator
LDA	Loss distribution approach
LEVER	Loss estimated by validating experts in risk
LGD	Loss given default
MAD	Mean absolute deviation
MIS	Management information system
MPL	Maximum possible loss
MRC	Minimum regulatory capital
OECD	Organisation for Economic Co-operation and Development
PD	Probability of default
PML	Probable maximum loss
PS	Payment and settlements
QIS	Quantitative impact study
RAROC	Risk-adjusted return on capital
RB	Retail banking
RBC	Risk-based capital
RDCA	Risk drivers and controls approach
RG	Retail brokerage
RMA	Risk management association
RORAC	Return on risk-adjusted capital
SBA	Scenario-based approach
SCA	Scorecard approach
SEC	Securities and Exchange Commission
STA	Standardized approach
TS	Trading and sales
UL	Unexpected loss
VAR	Value at risk

Preface

My interest in operational risk can be traced back to the ten years or so I spent in investment banking before I took the heroic decision to move to academia. That was during the 1980s when the term "operational risk" had not yet surfaced. In hindsight, however, I do realize that the financial institution I worked for was engulfed by operational risk and indeed suffered operational losses on more than one occasion. I recall, for example, a young trader who, in the learning process, incurred a loss of $100,000 on his first deal, not because the market turned against him but because of an error of documentation. It was certainly an operational loss event, not a market loss event. I also recall the chief foreign exchange dealer, who lost huge amounts resulting from taking wrong positions at the wrong time. That was a market loss event, which triggered some legal issues arising from the termination of the dealer's services (that was operational risk). Therefore, when I came across the term "operational risk" in the late 1990s, I certainly had a feel of what that meant, having seen a large number of episodes involving operational losses, and because I realized that banking involved significant operational risk.

Having moved to academia, I became interested in risk management in general and in the measurement and management of foreign exchange risk in particular. Hence, my interest centered on market risk. For some reason, I never got interested in credit risk, although this field was (and is) developing at a rapid pace. I jumped from market risk straight to operational risk, as the latter sounded rather challenging and also because it became the kind of risk that captures the headlines, as corporate scandals surfaced regularly. The advent of the Basel II Accord has also given prominence to, and reinforced my interest in, operational risk. Hence, I decided to write this book.

The book is written for Palgrave's Finance and Capital Markets series, and so the target readership is mainly professionals, some of whom may not have an advanced knowledge of statistics. This is why I decided to make the book as user friendly as possible. Having said that, there is a simplified formal treatment of some topics, particularly the measurement of operational risk (there is certainly a limit to simplification). The book can also be useful for those pursuing research on operational risk, since it includes a comprehensive and up-to-date survey of all aspects of operational risk.

The book falls into nine chapters. The first chapter contains a general introduction to the concept of risk and a comprehensive classification of risk, as well as a discussion of the measurement of risk. Chapter 2 provides an introduction to the Basel accords and the historical development of the Basel Committee. More attention is given in Chapter 2 to the Basel I Accord, but Chapter 3 is devoted entirely to a comprehensive description and evaluation of the Basel II Accord.

Chapter 4 is devoted to the concept of operational risk: its characteristics, definitions, and some misconceptions. It is argued that operational risk is not one-sided, not idiosyncratic, not indistinguishable from other risks, and that it is not transferable via insurance. Chapter 5 is about the identification of operational risk and the classification of operational loss events, including the description of some events that have been captured by the media.

Chapters 6 and 7 deal with the modeling and measurement of operational risk, starting with the presentation of some general principles in Chapter 6. Specifically, Chapter 6 examines the problems of measuring and modeling operational risk, presents a taxonomy of operational risk models, and describes some of the tools and techniques used for this purpose, including Bayesian estimation, reliability theory and the LEVER method. Chapter 7 is more specific, as it deals with the implementation of the AMA, including the loss distribution approach, the internal measurement approach, the scenario-based approach, and the scorecard approach.

Chapter 8 is about the management of operational risk, including a description of the operational risk management framework and the factors that make a successful risk management framework. Also considered in Chapter 8 is the role of insurance in operational risk management. The verdict on Basel II is presented in Chapter 9, which also reconsiders the definition of operational risk, its measurement and misconceptions about it. Basel II is evaluated in terms of its general provisions and from the perspective that it is a form of banking regulation.

Writing this book would not have been possible if it was not for the help and encouragement I received from family, friends, and colleagues. My utmost gratitude must go to my wife and children who had to bear the opportunity cost of writing this book. My wife, Afaf, did not only bear most of the opportunity cost of writing the book, but proved once again to be my best research assistant by producing the diagrams shown in various chapters. This book was written over a period in which I was affiliated with three universities: Gulf University for Science and Technology,

Kuwait; La Trobe University, Melbourne; and Monash University, Melbourne, which is my present affiliation. Therefore, I would like to thank Razzaque Bhatti, Dan Packey, Hussain Al-Sharoufi, Sulaiman Al-Abduljader, Masoud Al-Kandrai, Nayef Al-Hajraf, Salah Al-Sharhan (of GUST), Greg Jamieson, Robert Waschik, Liam Lenten, Larry Li, and Colleen Harte (of La Trobe), Michael Dempsey, Kim Langfield-Smith, Petko Kalev, Param Silvapulle, and Mervyn Silvapulle (of Monash).

In preparing the manuscript, I benefited from discussion with members of Table 14 at the John Scott Meeting House, and for this reason I would like to thank Bob Parsons, Greg O'Brein, Bill Horrigan, Bill Breen, Donald MacPhee, Rodney Adams, and Greg Bailey. A special thank you must go to James Guest who, by helping me with a problem that was distracting me from writing, facilitated the writing of this book (and the same goes for Greg O'Brien). Muhareem Karamujic provided a lot of information that helped me write the book, and for this reason I am grateful to him.

My thanks go to friends and former colleagues who live far away but provide help via means of telecommunication, including Kevin Dowd, Ron Ripple, Bob Sedgwick, Sean Holly, Dave Chappell, Dan Hemmings, Ian Baxter, Nabeel Al-Loughani, Khalid Al-Saad, and Talla Al-Deehani. Kevin, whom I owe a great intellectual debt, has provided a lot of input in one of his areas of expertise, banking regulation. I am also grateful to Kevin for introducing me to Victor Dowd, who is cited frequently in this book, not having realized that Kevin and Victor are actually brothers. Last, but not least, I would like to thank Alexandra Dawe, Steven Kennedy, and Stephen Rutt, of Palgrave, for encouragement, support, and positive feedback.

Naturally, I am the only one responsible for any errors and omissions in this book. It is dedicated to my beloved children, Nisreen and Danny, who are always exposed to the operational risk of eating junk food.

Imad A. Moosa
Melbourne

CHAPTER 1

The Science of Risk Management

1.1 DEFINITION OF RISK

In its broadest sense, risk means exposure to adversity. The *Concise Oxford Dictionary* defines risk to imply something bad, "the chance of bad consequence, loss, etc." *Webster's* defines risk in a similar manner to imply bad outcomes, "a measure of the possibility of loss, injury, disadvantage or destruction". Following the *Concise Oxford Dictionary*, Vaughan (1997) defines risk as "a condition of the real world in which there is an exposure to adversity".

Kedar (1970) believes that the origin of the word "risk" is either the Arabic word *risq* or the Latin word *risicum*. The Arabic *risq* has a positive connotation, signifying anything that has been given to a person (by God) and from which this person can draw profit or satisfaction. The Latin *risicum*, on the other hand, implies an unfavorable event, as it originally referred to the challenge that a barrier reef presents to a sailor. The Greek derivative of the Arabic *risq*, which was used in the twelfth century, relates to chance outcome in general. It may not be clear that what is given by God (according to the Arabic *risq*, which is always good) relates to risk, a situation that is typically understood to imply the potential of something bad (or something good) happening. However, what *risq* and risk have in common is uncertainty of the outcome. There is no guarantee that *risq* would come, and if it does, there is no guarantee how much it will be. Likewise, risk situations are characterized by the uncertainty of outcome (the word "uncertainty" is not used here in the formal sense it is used in the risk literature, as we are going to see later).

In his *General Theory*, Keynes (1936, p. 144) defined an entrepreneur's risk as the risk arising "out of doubts in his own mind as to the probability of him actually earning the prospective yield for which he hopes". The implication of this definition is that the word "risk" must imply the possibility of both favorable and unfavorable outcomes. This is in contrast with the definition of the *Concise Oxford Dictionary*, *Webster's*, and Vaughan (1997), in which reference is made to bad outcomes only. But the uncertainty of outcome must imply the potential of favorable and unfavorable outcomes, which means that risk is not one-sided. Indeed, no one would bear risk if only unfavorable outcomes are expected. The emphasis on the unfavorable outcome in some of the definitions of risk is a reflection of the fact that people facing risk are more concerned about the unfavorable than the favorable outcome (the utility lost when an unfavorable outcome materializes is greater than the utility gained from an equivalent unfavorable outcome).

To explain the idea of favorable and unfavorable outcomes, consider the following example in which one is offered to choose among the following alternatives: (i) a certain payment of $100, (ii) a payment of either $80 or $120 with equal probabilities, (iii) a payment of either $40 or $160 with equal probabilities, and (iv) a payment of either $20 or $180 with equal probabilities. In all cases, the expected value of what will be received is $100, but risk is highest in option (iv). There is no risk in option (i), since there is no probability distribution to govern the outcome (actually, there is a probability distribution showing one outcome that materializes with a probability of 1). Hence, a person who is risk averse would choose (i), but a person who is very much into bearing risk would choose the most risky option (iv), because this person would hope that the favorable outcome of getting $180, not the unfavorable outcome of getting $20, would materialize.

When both the favorable and the unfavorable outcomes are considered, risk can be defined as the uncertainty surrounding (or lack of knowledge about) the distribution of outcomes. This is why Vaughan (1997) considers another definition of risk as "a condition in which there is a possibility of an adverse deviation from a desired outcome that is expected or hoped for". Likewise, the definition of risk in the *Wikipedia* (http://en.wikipedia. org) is that it is the potential impact (positive or negative) on an asset or some characteristic of the value that may arise from some present process or from some event. Indeed, the *Wikipedia* recommends that reference to negative risk should be read as applying to positive impacts or opportunity (for example, reading "loss or gain" for "loss").

The degree of risk is related to the likelihood of occurrence. Events with a high probability of loss are more risky than those with low probability. To use Vaughan's definition, the degree of risk is measured by the possibility of an adverse deviation from a desired outcome that is expected or hoped for. If the probability of loss is 1, there is no chance of a favorable result.

If the probability of loss is 0, there is no possibility of loss and therefore no risk. Sometimes the terms "more risk" and "less risk" are used to indicate the possible size of loss.

There is no general agreement on the most suitable definition of risk for economists, statisticians, decision theorists, and insurance theorists. The definition of risk differs from one discipline to another. In the insurance business, for example, risk may mean either a peril insured against or a person or property protected by insurance (a young driver is not a good risk). This, however, may sound like an issue of semantics rather than a conceptual issue. Other definitions of risk that are typically found in the literature are as follows: (i) the chance of loss; (ii) the possibility of loss; (iii) the dispersion of actual from expected results; (iv) the probability of any outcome being different from the one expected; and (v) the significance of the hazard in terms of the likelihood and severity of any possible adversity. All definitions share two common elements: indeterminacy (at least two possible outcomes) and loss (at least one of the possible outcomes is undesirable). In general, risk may be viewed as the mean outcome (which is the actuarial view of risk), as the variance of the outcome, as a catastrophic downside outcome (focusing on the worst-case scenario), and as upside opportunity (focusing on the favorable outcome).

Two terms that are associated with the concept of risk are sometimes (wrongly) used interchangeably with risk. These are the concepts of uncertainty and exposure, both of which appear in the definitions of risk mentioned above. The distinction between risk and uncertainty, which is due to Knight (1921), is straightforward. Risk means that we do not know what outcome will materialize but we have a probability distribution for the possible outcomes. The probability distribution is typically based on historical experience and/or judgment about what is likely and less likely to happen in the future, given the *status quo* and possible changes to the *status quo*. Under uncertainty, by contrast, probability distributions are unavailable. In other words, risk implies that the randomness facing a decision maker can be expressed in terms of specific numerical probabilities, whereas uncertainty means that no probabilities are assigned to possible occurrences or that there is lack of knowledge about what will or will not happen in the future.

As for exposure, it may mean one of two things, the first of which is that it is a measure of what is at risk. For example, the risk of being mugged is indicated by the probability of being mugged, but exposure is what you have in your wallet. Sometimes, particularly in finance, exposure is defined as a measure of sensitivity, the sensitivity of the outcome to changes in the source of risk. For example, exposure to foreign exchange risk may be defined as the sensitivity of the base currency value of foreign currency assets, liabilities, and cash flows to changes in the exchange rate (for a detailed account of the difference between risk and exposure, see Moosa, 2003).

The *Wikipedia* also distinguishes between risk and threat in scenario analysis. A threat is defined as a "very low probability but serious event", implying that it may not be possible to assign a probability to such an event because it has never occurred. Thus, risk may be defined as a function of three variables: (i) the probability that there is a threat, (ii) the probability that there are vulnerabilities, and (iii) the potential impact. If any of the three variables approaches 0, the overall risk approaches 0. Finally, Vaughan (1997) distinguishes risk from "peril" and "hazard", which are often used interchangeably with each other and with risk. Peril is a cause of a loss (for example, we speak of the peril of mugging or fire). Hazard, on the other hand, is a "condition that may create or increase the chance of a loss arising from a given peril". It is a rather fine line that separates the concept of risk from those of hazard and peril, but it is a fine line that should be recognized. This is not merely an issue of semantics.

1.2   RISK MEASUREMENT

The various definitions of risk outlined in the previous section indicate that risk can be measured in different ways, which may depend on the kind of risk under consideration (for example, financial versus nonfinancial risk). If, for example, we take the first two definitions (those of the *Concise Oxford Dictionary* and *Webster's*), then risk should be measured by the probability of making loss. If we define risk in terms of the deviation from a desired outcome, then risk should be measured in terms of the variance or the standard deviation of the underlying probability distribution. And if we define risk as the potential impact of an event, then we are more or less talking about the probabilistic loss amount.

As an example of measuring risk in terms of the probability of loss, Stulz (1996) argues that measuring risk in terms of the probability that the firm will become financially troubled or will reach a financial situation that is worse than the one that would allow the firm to pursue its overall strategy. More prevalent, however, is the definition of risk as the deviation from a desired outcome, which is consistent with the definition of risk in finance.

1.2.1   Measures of dispersion

Assume that the underlying variable (for example, the rate of return on an investment) is believed to take n possible values, X_i, each of which materializes with probability, p_i, such that $i = 1, 2, \dots n$ and $\sum p_i = 1$. In this case, the expected value of X is calculated as

$$E(X) = \sum_{i=1}^{n} p_i(X_i)$$

(1.1)

whereas the variance and standard deviation are calculated, respectively, as

$$\sigma^2(X) = \sum_{i=1}^{n} p_i [X_i - E(X)]^2 \qquad (1.2)$$

$$\sigma(X) = \sqrt{\sum_{i=1}^{n} p_i [X_i - E(X)]^2} \qquad (1.3)$$

For a given expected value, a higher variance or standard deviation implies a higher degree of risk.

The numerical example of the previous section can be used to illustrate these concepts. Assume that a decision maker is faced with the problem of choosing among four options with various degrees of risk. These four options are represented in Figure 1.1, which effectively shows four different probability distributions representing the four options. Option 1, represented by the middle column, involves no risk because there is no dispersion around the expected value of $100 (the standard deviation is 0). Option 2 shows less dispersion than Option 3, which in turn shows less dispersion than Option 4, meaning that Option 2 is less risky than Option 3, which is less risky than Option 4. The standard deviations associated with Options 2, 3, and 4 are 20, 60, and 80, respectively.

Now, consider Figure 1.2, which shows one probability distribution representing six possible outcomes (as opposed to two in Options 2, 3,

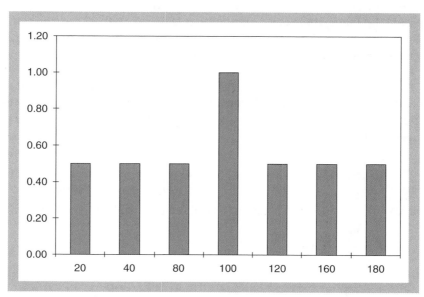

Figure 1.1 The probability distributions of four options with an expected value of $100

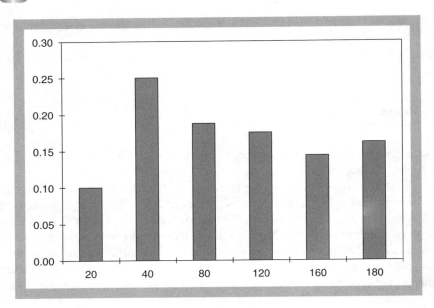

Figure 1.2 The probability distribution of six outcomes with an expected value of $100

and 4 in the previous example). The six possible outcomes in this example produce an expected value of $100 but the dispersion around the expected value is different from that in any of the four distributions represented by Figure 1.1. Hence, there is a different degree of risk in this case (the standard deviation is 57). Table 1.1 summarizes the results presented in Figures 1.1 and 1.2, showing five different probability distributions with an expected value of $100 and various degrees of risk.

The standard deviation can be calculated on the basis of historical data, in which case the concept of the mean is used instead of the concept of the expected value. Let us assume that we have a sample of historical observations on X over points in time $t = 1,..., n$. The mean value is calculated as

$$\bar{X} = \frac{1}{n}\sum_{t=1}^{n} X_t \tag{1.4}$$

whereas the variance and standard deviation are calculated, respectively, as

$$\sigma^2(X) = \frac{1}{n-1}\sum_{t=1}^{n} (X_t - \bar{X})^2 \tag{1.5}$$

$$\sigma(X) = \sqrt{\frac{1}{n-1}\sum_{t=1}^{n} (X_t - \bar{X})^2} \tag{1.6}$$

Table 1.1 Expected values and standard deviations of five probability distributions

Distribution	Outcome	Probability	Exp. value	Std. dev.
1	100	1	100	0
2	80	0.5	100	20
	120	0.5		
3	40	0.5	100	60
	160	0.5		
4	20	0.5	100	80
	180	0.5		
5	20	0.10	100	57
	40	0.25		
	80	0.19		
	120	0.18		
	160	0.14		
	180	0.16		

The standard deviation as a measure of risk has been criticized for the arbitrary manner in which deviations from the mean are squared and for treating positive and negative deviations in a similar manner, although negative deviations are naturally more detrimental. This has led to the development of the downside risk measures, which are defined by Dhane, Goovaerts, and Kaas (2003) as "measures of the distance between a risky situation and the corresponding risk-free situation when only unfavorable discrepancies contribute to the risk". Danielsson, Jorgensen, and Sarma (2005) trace the downside risk measures back to the "safety first" rule of Roy (1952), which led to the development of partial moments and consequently to the definition of risk as "the probability weighted function of the deviation below a target return (Bawa, 1975; Fishburn, 1997). Danielsson et al. (2006) compare overall and downside risk measures with respect to the criteria of first and second order stochastic dominance.

Downside risk measures include, among others, the mean absolute deviation (MAD) and the downside semi-variance (DSV), which are, respectively, given by

$$MAD(X) = \frac{1}{n} \sum_{t=1}^{n} |X_t - \bar{X}| \tag{1.7}$$

$$DSV(X) = \frac{1}{n-1} \sum_{t=1}^{n} Y_t^2 \tag{1.8}$$

where $Y_t = X_t - \bar{X}$ if $X_t < \bar{X}$, and $Y_t = 0$ otherwise. The standard deviation, MAD, and DSV are not regarded as coherent measures of risk according to

Artzner et al. (1999) because they fail to satisfy at least one of the properties
of coherent risk measures: (i) sub-additivity, (ii) monotonicity, (iii) positive
homogeneity, and (iv) translation invariance. For example, the standard
deviation is not a coherent measure of risk because it does not satisfy the
property of monotonicity (that is, if one risk always leads to equal or
greater losses than another risk, the risk measure has the same or a higher
value for the first risk). The DSV (or downside semi-standard deviation) is
not coherent because it does not satisfy the property of sub-additivity (that
is, the value of the risk measure of the two risks combined will not be
greater than for the risks treated separately).

A more general measure of dispersion is given by

$$D = \int_{-\infty}^{\theta} (\theta - X)^\alpha f(X) dX \qquad (1.9)$$

where the parameter α describes the attitude toward risk and θ specifies the
cutoff between the downside and the upside that the decision maker is and
is not concerned about, respectively. Many risk measures (including the
DSV) are special cases of, or closely related to, this measure.

1.2.2 Value at risk

It is often claimed that risk quantification has gone through the stages of
(i) gap analysis, (ii) duration analysis, (iii) scenario analysis (what-if analysis), and (iv) value at risk, (VAR; for a simple description of gap analysis,
duration analysis, and scenario analysis, see Dowd, 2002, Chapter 1). Here,
we concentrate on VAR, which is a downside measure of risk that gives
an indication of the amount that can be lost, because it is essentially
what is used to measure operational risk. It is different from the standard
deviation as a measure of risk because the latter assumes symmetry of
profits and losses, that a $1 million loss is as likely as a $1 million gain
(which is not true for option positions). VAR captures this asymmetry by
focusing only on potential large losses. The 1996 market risk amendment
to the Basel I Accord allowed the use of VAR models to determine regulatory capital (the capital charge) against market risk. Currently, banks and
most large financial institutions use such models to measure and manage
their market risk (see Chapter 2). For more details on and extensions
of the VAR methodology, the reader is referred to KPMG-Risk (1997) and
Dowd (1998, 2002).

Essentially, the VAR approach is used to answer the question, "over a
given period of time with a given probability, how much money might be
lost?" The money lost pertains to the decline in the value of a portfolio,
which may consist of a single asset or a number of assets. The measurement of VAR requires the choice of: (i) a measurement unit, normally the
base currency; (ii) a time horizon, which could be a day, a week, or longer,

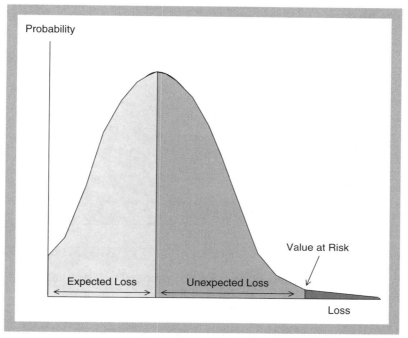

Figure 1.3 Expected loss, unexpected loss and value at risk

provided that the composition of the portfolio does not change during this period; and (iii) a probability, which normally ranges between 1 and 5 percent. Hence, VAR is the maximum expected loss over a given holding period at a given level of confidence (that is, with a given probability). In terms of Figure 1.3, which shows the probability distribution of the loss, VAR can be related to the terms "expected loss" and "unexpected loss". While the expected loss is the mean value of loss distribution, the unexpected loss is the difference between the VAR and the expected loss. VAR can also be looked upon by considering the probability distribution of profits and losses as shown on Figure 1.4.

VAR has become a widely used method for measuring financial risk, and justifiably so. The attractiveness of the concept lies in its simplicity, as it represents the market risk of the entire portfolio by one number that is easy to comprehend by anyone. It thus conveys a simple message on the risk borne by a firm or an individual. The concept is also suitable for setting risk limits and for measuring performance based on the return earned and the risk assumed. Moreover, it can take account of complex movements, such as a nonparallel yield curve shifts. In general, VAR has two important characteristics: (i) it provides a common consistent measure of risk across different positions and risk factors; and (ii) it takes into account correlation among various factors (for example, different currencies).

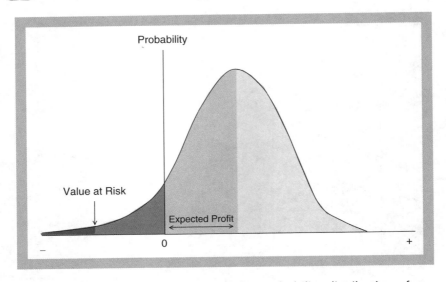

Figure 1.4 VAR as it appears on the probability distribution of profits and losses

There are, however, several shortcomings associated with the VAR methodology. First, it can be misleading to the extent of giving rise to unwarranted complacency. Moreover, VAR is highly sensitive to the assumptions used to calculate it. Jorion (1996) argues that VAR is a number that itself is measured with some error or estimation risk. Thus, the VAR results must be interpreted with reference to the underlying statistical methodology. Moreover, this approach to risk measurement cannot cope with sudden and sharp changes in market conditions. It neglects the possibility of discrete, large jumps in financial prices (such as exchange rates), which occur quite often. Losses resulting from catastrophic occurrences are overlooked due to dependence on symmetric statistical measures that treat upside and downside risk in a similar manner. Finally, Stulz (1996) argues that the information provided by VAR (with a given probability, one could have a loss of at least X on a given day or month) is not useful when the firm is concerned about the possibility of its value falling below some critical level. Numerous studies have been conducted to evaluate the empirical performance of VAR models (for example, Hendricks, 1996; Pritsker, 1997; Moosa and Bollen, 2002). However, research on how well these models perform in practice has been limited by the proprietary nature of both the model and the underlying data. Berkowitz and O'Brien (2002) were able to obtain VAR forecasts employed by commercial banks, but concluded that VAR models were not particularly accurate measures of risk.

A related measure of risk is the expected tail loss (ETL), which is also known as the expected shortfall, conditional VAR, tail conditional expectation,

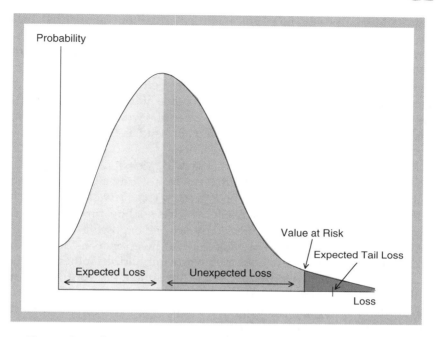

Figure 1.5 The positions of VAR and ETL on the loss distribution

and worst conditional expectation. The concept is very simple: ETL is the expected value of a loss that is in excess of VAR. It is defined formally as

$$ETL = E(L \mid L > VAR) \tag{1.10}$$

While the VAR is the most that can be expected to be lost if a bad event occurs, the ETL is what is expected to be lost if a bad event occurs. While the VAR is the threshold value for which in c percent of instances (where c is the confidence level), the loss is smaller than the VAR, the ETL is an estimate of the average loss when the loss exceeds VAR. With reference to the loss distribution, Figure 1.5 shows the ETL in relation to the VAR. One reason why the ETL may be preferred to VAR is that it is a coherent risk measure, as it satisfies the properties of sub-additivity, monotonicity, positive homogeneity, and translation invariance (see Artzner et al., 1999).

1.2.3   The probability, frequency, and severity of loss

In general, risk is measured in terms of two parameters: the probability of making loss and the potential amount lost if a loss event occurs. Thus, total risk may be measured as the product of the loss amount and the probability that the loss will occur. Sometimes, particularly in operational risk measurement, the terms severity (amount) and frequency (probability) are used to measure risk. Both of these terms are described by using separate probability distributions, which are combined to arrive at a probability distribution of total loss. Prouty (1960) distinguishes between the concepts of the maximum possible loss (MPL) and the probable maximum loss (PML). The MPL is the worst loss that could occur, given the worst possible combination of circumstances. The PML, on the other hand, is the likely loss, given the most likely combination of circumstances.

Kritzman and Rich (2002) argue that viewing risk in terms of the probability of a given loss or the amount that can be lost with a given probability at the end of the investment horizon is wrong. This view of risk, according to them, considers only the final result, which is not how investors (should) perceive risk because they are affected by risk and exposed to loss throughout the investment period. They suggest that investors consider risk and the possibility of loss throughout the investment horizon (otherwise, their wealth may not survive to the end of the investment horizon). As a result of this line of thinking, Kritzman and Rich suggest two new measures of risk: within-horizon probability of loss and continuous VAR. These risk measures are then used to demonstrate that the possibility of making loss is substantially greater than what investors normally assume.

1.3   THE TAXONOMY OF RISK

Fischer (2002) lists the following kinds of risk that banks are exposed to: credit risk, interest rate risk, liquidity risk, price risk, foreign exchange risk, transaction risk, compliance risk, strategic risk, reputational risk, and operational risk. For internationally active banks, we need to add country risk. This set of risks is an impressive reminder of the complexity of risk management, but the list is not exhaustive in the sense that it does not include all kinds of risk faced by banks, while excluding other kinds of risk faced by other firms and individuals. Other kinds of risk not explicitly mentioned by Fischer include, among others, political risk, sovereign risk, settlement risk, Herstatt risk, purchasing power risk, equity price risk, commodity price risk, legal risk, and macroeconomic risk. One advantage of risk classification is that it allows us to identify the factors driving a particular kind of risk.

Risks can be arranged along a spectrum, depending on how quantifiable they are. At one extreme lie the market risks arising from changes in the values of liquid assets. In this case, data on past history are available, which makes risk, however defined, fully quantifiable. At the other extreme lie the risks arising from infrequent events (such as a contagious financial crisis) with potentially massive consequences for the banks. In this case, risk is very difficult to quantify. There are other schemes of risk classification. These include endogenous versus exogenous risk, financial versus nonfinancial risk, static versus dynamic risk, pure versus speculative risk, fundamental versus particular risk, systematic versus unsystematic risk, and others. Table 1.2 provides the definitions of these concepts.

These kinds of risk differ in the degree of seriousness and importance for banks. In its "Banana Skins" survey of 70 bankers worldwide, the

Table 1.2 The concepts of risk

Concept	Definition
Market risk	The risk arising from changes in market prices.
Interest rate risk	The type of market risk arising from changes in interest rates.
Foreign exchange risk	The type of market risk arising from changes in exchange rates.
Transaction risk	The type of foreign exchange risk arising from the effect of changes in exchange rates on the base currency value of contractual cash flows.
Economic risk	The type of foreign exchange risk arising from the effect of changes in exchange rates on the base currency value of noncontractual cash flows and market share.
Translation risk	The type of foreign exchange risk arising from the effect of changes in exchange rates on the base currency consolidated financial statements.
Equity price risk	The type of market risk arising from changes in equity prices.
Commodity price risk	The type of market risk arising from changes in commodity prices.
Energy price risk	The type of market risk arising from changes in energy prices.
Real estate risk	The type of market risk arising from changes in real estate prices.
Asset-liability management risk	The type of market risk arising from changes in the prices of assets and liabilities.
Credit risk	The risk arising from the possibility of the failure of a borrower to meet the terms of a contractual agreement by defaulting on the payment of interest or the principal.
Operational risk	The risk of loss resulting from the failure of processes, people, systems, or from external events.
Settlement risk (counterparty risk)	The operational risk arising from the possibility of the failure of a counterparty to settle a transaction that has been agreed upon.
Liquidity risk	The type of settlement risk that results from the inability of a counterparty to settle a transaction because of the lack of liquidity.

(Continued)

Table 1.2 (*Continued*)

Concept	Definition
Herstatt risk	The type of settlement risk that results from the insolvency of a counterparty. It is named after Bankhaus Herstatt, a German bank that in 1974 failed to settle foreign exchange transactions because of liquidation.
Compliance risk	The operational risk of regulatory sanctions or financial losses resulting from failure to comply with laws, regulations and internal policies, processes, and controls.
Behavioral compliance risk	The compliance risk arising from failure to comply with internal risk management practices.
Regulatory compliance risk	The compliance risk arising from failure to comply with external regulatory and legal obligations.
Processing risk	A kind of operational risk, it is the risk of financial losses from failed processing due to mistakes, negligence, accidents, or fraud by directors and employees.
System risk	A kind of operational risk, it is the risk of losses due to system and telecommunication failures.
Tangible asset risk	A kind of operational risk, it is the risk of damage to tangible assets from disasters or accidents.
Human resources risk	A kind of operational risk, it is the risk of loss of key personnel or failure to maintain staff morale.
Regulatory risk	The operational risk of losses due to changes in the regulatory environment, including the tax system and accounting system.
Crime risk	The operational risk of losses arising from crime, such as theft, fraud, hacking, and money laundering.
Disaster risk	The operational risk of losses arising from disasters, such as fire, flood, etc.
Information technology risk	The operational risk of losses arising from the failure of IT systems.
Reporting risk	The operational risk of losses arising from errors in reporting the amounts of risk in quantitative terms.
Accounting risk	The operational risk of losses arising from the use of estimates in preparing financial statements.
Fiduciary risk	The operational risk of losses arising from the possibility of the product implementation differing from how it was presented to the client.
Model risk	The operational risk of losses incurred by making a wrong decision on the basis of a faulty or inadequate model.
Legal risk	The risk that a transaction proves unenforceable in law or that it has been inadequately documented.
Reputational risk	The risk of incurring losses because of the loss or downgrading of the reputation of firms and individuals.
Macroeconomic risk	The risk of incurring losses because of adverse macroeconomic developments (for example, a sharp rise in the inflation rate).

(*Continued*)

Table 1.2 (*Continued*)

Concept	Definition
Business cycle risk	The macroeconomic risk arising from fluctuations in economic activity.
Business risk (strategic risk)	The risk of financial loss resulting from inappropriate strategic business decisions (for example, plant location and product mix).
Lapse risk	The type of business risk arising from the possibility that clients may choose to terminate contracts at any time.
Efficiency risk	The type of business risk that is triggered by the internal organization of the firm (for example, inability to manage costs effectively).
Expense risk	The type of business risk arising from the possibility that actual expenses could deviate from expected expenses.
Performance risk	The business risk of underperforming the competitors.
Country risk	The risk arising from unanticipated changes in the economic or political environment in a particular country.
Transfer risk	The type of country risk arising from the possibility that foreign currency funds cannot be transferred out of the host country.
Convertibility risk	The type of country risk arising from inability to convert foreign currency proceeds into the domestic currency.
Political risk	The type of country risk arising from the possibility of incurring losses due to changes in rules and regulations or adverse political developments in a particular country.
Sovereign risk	The type of country risk arising from the possibility of incurring losses on claims on foreign governments and government agencies.
Purchasing power risk	The risk arising from the adverse effect of inflation on the real value of the rate of return on investment.
Systemic risk	The risk of breakdown in an entire system as opposed to breakdown in individual parts or components.
Inherent risk versus residual risk	Inherent risk is the risk arising from the absence of any action the management might take (the absence of risk management) to alter either the likelihood or the impact of risk. Residual risk (also known as net risk or composite risk) is the remaining risk after the management has taken action to alter the likelihood or impact of the risk.
Financial versus nonfinancial risk	Financial risk is the risk arising from changes in financial prices, such as interest rates and equity prices. Nonfinancial risk includes everything else, such as the risk of fire.
Static versus dynamic risk	Dynamic risk results from changes in the economy (changes in taste, output, and technology). Static risk involves losses that would result even if no changes in the economy occurred (perils of nature and dishonesty of individuals). This distinction was first introduced by Willett (1951).

(*Continued*)

Table 1.2 (*Continued*)

Concept	Definition
Pure versus speculative risk	Speculative risk describes a situation in which there is a possibility of either loss or gain (for example, gambling). Pure risk involves situations of loss or no loss. This distinction was introduced by Mowbray and Blanchard (1961). Pure risks can be classified into personal risks, property risks, liability risks (unintentional injury of other persons or damage to their property through negligence or carelessness), and risks arising from the failure of others (for example, the risk of default on a loan). It appears that the distinction between pure and speculative risks is disappearing, as a loss or no loss situation represents the bad side of risk, which is invariably two-sided.
Fundamental versus particular risk	Fundamental risk involves losses that are impersonal in origin and consequence, group risks that are caused by economic, social, and political developments. Particular risk involve losses that arise out of individual events and felt by individuals rather than entire groups. This distinction was introduced by Kulp (1956).
Systemic versus idiosyncratic risk	Systemic risk implies that the effect of a loss event endured by one firm spreads to the whole industry. Idiosyncratic risk affects one firm without spreading to other firms in the industry. The distinction between systemic and idiosyncratic risk may sound similar to the distinction between fundamental and particular risk, but this is not the case. Unlike fundamental risk, systemic risk may result from a firm-specific event if, for example, this firm is unable to meet its obligations to other firms.
Endogenous versus exogenous risk	This distinction is due to Danielsson and Shin (2003). Endogenous risk refers to the risk from shocks that are generated and amplified within the system. Exogenous risk refers to shocks that arise from outside the system.
Systematic versus unsystematic risk	Systematic risk is market risk that cannot be diversified away. Unsystematic risk is nondiversifiable.
Expected, unexpected, and catastrophic risk	Expected risk is the risk of incurring losses affecting the firm's day-to-day operations. Unexpected risk is the risk of incurring more significant losses with lower frequency of occurrence and higher size, but still under the firm's control. Catastrophic risk, which is extreme risk that threatens the firm's activity, is due to external factors or deliberate actions (such as the risk of fraud).
Nominal, ordinary, and exceptional risk	Nominal risk is the risk of repetitive losses associated with day-to-day activities. Ordinary risk is the risk of larger, less-frequent, but not life-threatening, losses. Exceptional risk is the risk of rare but life-threatening losses.

Center for the Study of Financial Innovation (2002) identified the following kinds of risk facing banks:

- Credit risk: Most respondents are concerned about the quality of loan portfolios.

- Macroeconomic risk: Most respondents believe that the state of the economy could hurt the industry.

- Complex financial instruments: Many respondents are concerned about the complexity of derivatives.

- Domestic regulation: There is rising concern about domestic regulatory cost and pressure.

- Equity risk: Equity risk is still seen as relevant to the banking industry although the consensus view is that this kind of risk is more relevant to pension funds and insurance companies.

- Banking overcapacity: Bankers are concerned about excess lending capacity.

- Money laundering: Many respondents are concerned, not about money laundering itself but about the overregulation of money laundering, as it dilutes traditional bank secrecy.

- High dependence on technology: This is a major kind of operational risk.

- International regulation: Bankers are concerned about the failure of international regulators to establish effective cross-border regulation. This is some sort of compliance risk.

In a more recent survey, Servaes and Tufano (2006) asked the chief financial officers (CFOs) of major companies to rank the ten most important risks facing their companies. The results of the survey revealed that of the top ten risks, four were financial risks and six were broader business risks. The financial risks and their rankings are: foreign exchange risk (1), financing risk (3), commodity-price risk (8), and interest rate risk (10). The top rank of foreign exchange risk is attributed to the global operations of the participating companies, whereas the low rank of interest rate risk is due to the exclusion of financial institutions from the survey.

Lam (2003a) points out that there is overlapping and interdependence among different kinds of risk. The following are some examples:

- Inadequate loan documentation (operational risk) would intensify the severity of losses in the event of loan default (credit risk).

■ An unexpected decline in real estate prices (market risk) would lead to a higher default rate on real estate loans and securities (credit risk).

■ A general decline in stock prices (market risk) would reduce asset management, mergers and acquisitions, and investment banking fees (business risk).

■ A sharp increase in energy prices (market risk) would impact the credit exposure of energy traders (counterparty risk) as well as the credit conditions of energy-dependent borrowers (credit risk).

■ A natural disaster would affect not only the facilities of a bank (operational risk) but also the loss experience of the impacted real estate loans and securities (credit risk).

Furthermore, the risk profile facing any firm evolves over time. Some of the risks facing business these days were not known a generation ago: potential liability for environmental damage, discrimination in employment, and sexual harassment and violence in the workplace. Other risks are linked directly to information technology, interruptions of business resulting from computer failure, privacy issues, and computer fraud. The bandits and pirates that threatened early traders have been replaced by computer hackers.

Finally, the classification of risk has implications for risk measurement. For example, while market risk can be measured by using VAR and scenario analysis, credit risk is measured by the probability of default, loss given default, and exposure at default. Table 1.3 shows the risk measures

Table 1.3 Risk measures for major risk types

Risk type	Measures
Market risk (trading)	• VAR • Scenario analysis
Market risk (asset–liability management risk)	• Duration mismatch • Scenario analysis • Liquidity gaps
Credit risk	• Probability of default • Loss given default • Exposure at default • Capital at risk
Operational risk	• Scorecards • Expected and unexpected loss • VAR • Extreme value theory
Business risk	• Historical earnings • Volatility • Peer comparison

used in conjunction with major risk types as identified by Knot et al. (2006). However, it remains the case that VAR can be used to measure market risk, credit risk, and operational risk. For example, the probability of default, loss given default, and exposure at default are used to estimate the underlying credit loss distribution, with the ultimate objective of measuring VAR (or capital at risk). Likewise, scorecards, extreme value theory, and the concepts of expected and unexpected losses can be used to construct an operational loss distribution for the purpose of measuring VAR.

1.4   WHAT IS RISK MANAGEMENT?

Vaughan (1997) makes the interesting remark that the entire history of the human species is a chronology of exposure to risk and adversity and of efforts to deal with it. He concedes that it is perhaps an exaggeration to claim that the earliest profession was risk management, but he points out that from the dawn of their existence, humans have faced the problem of survival, dealing with the issue of security and avoidance of risk that threatens extinction in the face of adversities arising from predators and mother nature (among other things). McLorrain (2000) makes the interesting remark that "the original risk management expert is Mother Nature" because natural systems (such as species and ecosystems) have been able to survive and prosper by dealing with challenges ranging from hostile predators to climate change.

In the rest of this section, risk management is dealt with as a business activity. We start with the techniques of dealing with risk, then we define risk management and describe the development and structure of the risk management process. Afterwards, we examine the concept of enterprise-wide risk management (ERM).

1.4.1   The techniques of dealing with risk

Before describing the risk management process, it may be useful to consider in general the techniques of dealing with risk, which include the following:

- Risk avoidance: Risk is avoided when the individual or firm refuses to accept it, which is accomplished by merely not engaging in the action that gives rise to risk (for example, choosing not to fly to avoid the risk of hijacking). This is a negative technique of dealing with risk, because avoiding risk means losing out on the potential gain that accepting the risk may allow. Remember that risk is two-sided, involving favorable and unfavorable outcomes.

■ Risk reduction (mitigation): Risk may be reduced by (i) loss prevention and control and (ii) combining a large number of exposure units (the law of large numbers). Risk reduction effectively means reducing the severity of potential loss.

■ Risk retention (assumption): When no positive action is taken to avoid, transfer, or reduce risk, the possibility of loss resulting from that risk is retained, which means that the risk is assumed (or taken or borne). This course of action may be followed consciously or unconsciously. Risk retention is a viable strategy for small risks where the cost of insuring against the risk would be greater over time than the total losses sustained.

■ Risk transfer: The process of hedging is viewed as the best example of risk transfer, as it can be used to deal with speculative and pure risks. Insurance is considered as another means of risk transfer that is based on contracts. However, it is arguable that hedging and insurance provide risk financing, not risk transfer. For example, one cannot transfer the risk of being killed in a car accident to the insurance company by taking motor insurance. The same goes for the idea of transferring the risk of hijacking by taking flight insurance (this point will be discussed further in Chapters 4 and 8).

■ Risk sharing: This is a special case of risk transfer and also a form of (partial) retention. When risk is shared, the possibility of loss is (partially) transferred from the individual to the group (the best example is the shareholding company).

These techniques of dealing with risk in general will be described again in Chapter 8 but only in reference to operational risk.

1.4.2 Definition of risk management

The definition of risk management takes many shapes and forms. Vaughan (1997) defines risk management as a scientific approach to dealing with pure risks by anticipating possible accidental losses and designing and implementing procedures that minimize the occurrence of loss or the financial impact of the losses that do occur. The problem with this definition is the concept of pure risk, as risk management may also be used with speculative risk, assuming for the time being that the distinction between pure risk and speculative risk is valid. Take, for example, a holder of a foreign equity portfolio, who is exposed to two kinds of risk: equity price risk and foreign exchange risk. The holder of the portfolio may decide to hedge the foreign exchange risk (for example, via forward contracts) while remaining exposed to the equity price risk. Here, risk management (hedging) is directed at speculative risk, which is ruled out by Vaughan's definition.

The *Wikipedia* defines risk management as "the process of measuring or assessing risk, then developing strategies to manage the risk". In general, the strategies employed include transferring the risk to another party, avoiding the risk, reducing the negative effect of the risk, and accepting some or all of the consequences of a particular risk. For this purpose, distinction is made between risk control and risk financing. Risk control encompasses techniques designed to minimize (at the least possible costs) those risks to which the firm is exposed, including risk avoidance and the various approaches to risk reduction through loss prevention and control efforts. Risk financing, on the other hand, focuses on guaranteeing the availability of funds to meet the losses that do occur, fundamentally taking the form of retention or transfer. Hence, risk transfer through insurance does not involve the transfer of risk to the insurance company but rather it is financing the risk through the insurance company, as an alternative to financing it through reserves and capital.

Pezier (2003a) argues that in an uncertain world, good decisions no longer equate to good outcomes and good management becomes synonymous with good risk management, describing as a "tragedy" the possibility of viewing risk management as a discipline that is divorced from that of general management when it should be an integral part of it. However, risk management differs from general management in that it is concerned with pure risks only, whereas general management is concerned with all kinds of risk facing the firm. Although risk management has evolved out of insurance management, risk management is concerned with both insurable and uninsurable risks. Moreover, while insurance management sees insurance as the norm, risk management requires that insurance be justified. Again, there is a problem here with the concept of "pure risk".

1.4.3 The development and structure of risk management

The general trend in the current usage of the term "risk management" began in the early 1950s. Gallagher (1956) was the first to suggest the "revolutionary" idea that someone within the firm should be responsible for managing the firm's pure risks". The function of risk management, however, had been recognized earlier. Writing in 1916, Fayol (1949), for example, divided industrial activities into six broad functions, including what he called security, which sounds surprisingly like risk management. He defined this function as activities involving the protection of the property and persons of the enterprise. Dowd (2002) argues that the theory and practice of financial risk management have developed enormously since the pioneering work of Harry Markowitz in the 1950s. He suggests that the rapid development of risk management has resulted from at least three contributory factors: (i) increased market volatility, (ii) growth in trading activity, and (iii) advances in information technology.

Mengle (2003) argues that the risk management process exists to carry out the following general functions: (i) designating responsibility and establishing accountability for risk management; (ii) collecting, analyzing, and reporting (to management) quantitative information on the risk taken by businesses; (iii) developing and enforcing standards, limits and controls; and (iv) identifying and resolving the problems associated with the risks taken by business units. The form of the processes used by firms to perform these functions may vary greatly across firms according to corporate culture, management philosophy, regulatory environment, and other factors. Some firms might make business units responsible for carrying out many elements of risk management while others assign authority and responsibility to a centralized risk management unit. Despite differences, it is possible to identify some general characteristics of current risk management processes:

- Internal controls and independence of functions: While monitoring, internal controls and independence are not recent inventions, a risk management function that is independent from the risk-taking functions is a recent innovation.

- Quantification of risk: Risk quantification makes risk management more precise.

- Management of risks rather than products: Derivatives contracts have made it possible to break down contracts into component risks and then to manage these risks separately.

- Diversification: The financial benefits of diversification are well known.

- Marking to market: Widespread acceptance of the principle that firms should mark their portfolios to market on a daily basis for risk management purposes.

- The efficient use of economic capital: The risk management function plays a role in the capital optimization process because it is the source of measurement of the amount of capital used by the firm's risk-taking activities.

The risk management process consists of the following steps:

- Determining objectives: For example, maintaining the firm's survival and minimizing the costs associated with risk. The objectives are typically formalized in a corporate risk management policy.

- Identifying risks: Some risks are obvious whereas many can be over-looked. The tools used for this purpose include internal records of the firm, insurance policy checklists, risk analysis questionnaires, analysis of financial statements, inspection of the firm's operations, and interviews. The preferred approach is to utilize is a combination of these tools.

- Risk evaluation: Measuring the potential size of the loss and the probability that the loss is likely to occur, then preparing some ranking in order of priorities. For example, we could have (i) critical risks, where losses are of magnitude that will result in bankruptcy; (ii) important risks, which do not lead to bankruptcy but require borrowing in order to remain in operation; and (iii) unimportant risks, in which case losses can be met out of the firm's existing assets or current income.

- Considering alternatives and selecting the risk treatment device: The choice among avoidance, reduction, retention, and transfer.

- Implementing the decision, including the means of implementation requirements. For example, the decision to take insurance must be accompanied by the selection of an insurer.

- Evaluating and reviewing the process, which is important because of the changing environment, and because mistakes are made sometimes.

A point that is noteworthy here is that raised by Stulz (1996) concerning the apparent divide between the academic research into risk management and actual corporate practice. While the findings of academic research into risk management lead to the conclusion that risk management reduces the variability of the value or the cash flows of a firm, the practice of risk management is rather limited in relation to the recommendations of academics. In an attempt to resolve this inconsistency, Stulz argues that it is not correct to view modern risk management theory as implying that firms should minimize risk, but rather that what a firm should do depends on the underlying situation. He expresses the view that management should exploit market inefficiencies to boost shareholders' wealth while paying attention to the probability of the firm becoming close to or in financial distress. It is this probability that matters, not the variability of the firm value or cash flows.

1.4.4 Enterprise-wide risk management

A concept that often appears in the risk management literature is that of the ERM, which is also known as integrated risk management. It is based on the proposition that a firm can benefit from the management of all risks together. The idea here is that the management of risks individually, rather than collectively, can lead to inefficient risk management decisions.

For example, banks may overstate their risk exposure (and hence spend too much on risk management) because the management of risks individually does not take into account risk correlation. Doherty (2000) and Consiglio and Zenios (2003) suggest that one advantage of ERM is that it provides a natural hedge against risk: the pooling of risks ensures that the firm-wide exposure is less than the sum of individual exposures.

Lam (2003a) argues that ERM is widely recognized as the best-practice approach to measuring and managing risk. Firms that are successful at ERM have reported dramatic improvements in shareholder value, early risk detection, loss experience, and regulatory capital relief. He identifies the following key forces behind the growth in and acceptance of ERM:

- Corporate disasters (such as Enron, WorldCom, Long-Term Capital Management, and Barings Bank) resulting from corporate governance failures, management incompetence, corruption, and other kinds of risk (predominantly operational risk).

- Regulatory actions, both domestic and international.

- Industry initiatives for establishing frameworks and standards for corporate governance and risk management.

- Corporate programs, as firms have reported significant benefits from their risk management programs.

The process of measuring and managing enterprise-wide risk is too complex to do without a systematic framework, which should address seven key components of internal control and risk management:

- Corporate governance: To ensure that the board and management have established the appropriate organizational processes and corporate controls to measure and manage risk across the firm.

- Line management: To integrate risk management into the revenue-generating activities.

- Portfolio management: To aggregate risk exposures, incorporate diversification effects, and monitor concentrations against established risk limits.

- Risk transfer: To mitigate risk exposures that are deemed too high to transfer to a third party or to hold in the firm's own risk portfolio.

- Risk analytics: To provide the risk measurement, analysis, and reporting tools to quantify the firm's risk exposures and track external variables.

- Data and technology resources: To provide the data management and processing capabilities.

■ Shareholder management: To communicate and report the firm's risk information to its shareholders as well as rating agencies and regulators.

ERM may be based upon an integrated measure of risk that is derived from an integrated risk management model. If market risk, credit risk, and operational risk are measured (and managed) separately, the total risk facing a firm would be the sum of market VAR, credit VAR, and operational VAR. But this would produce an overstated measure of risk because the simple summation of VARs ignores correlations among the three kinds of risk, which are less than perfect. By taking into account risk dependence through integrated risk measurement, a more accurate estimate of the risk facing a firm will be obtained.

1.5   WHAT IS NEXT?

This chapter presents a general introduction to the concepts of risk and risk management. The idea behind starting with a chapter like this in a book that deals primarily with the concepts of operational risk and operational risk management is to put things into perspective. And, as we are going to see later, different kinds of risk overlap and interact with each other. The concept of ERM, introduced in this chapter, is relevant to the subject matter of the next two chapters, as the Basel II Accord is designed to deal not only with operational risk but also with market risk and credit risk.

The following two chapters deal with the Basel I and Basel II Accords. The Basel II Accord is introduced briefly in Chapter 2, as a successor to Basel I. Chapter 3, however, examines the Basel II Accord in detail, undertaking a critical evaluation of the Accord.

The Basel Committee, Basel I and Basel II

2.1 THE BASEL COMMITTEE

In 1974, the German authorities ordered the immediate liquidation of Bankhaus Herstatt, a German commercial bank that, as a result of its closure, failed to deliver U.S. dollars to counterparties with whom it had previously struck foreign exchange deals. This event gave rise to the concept of "Herstatt risk", which is a kind of operational risk associated with the settlement of foreign exchange transactions. Losses can result from Herstatt risk because currency trading requires the settlement of commitments in two independent national payment systems. The process typically involves the delivery of the currency sold before the receipt of the currency bought. Thus, the bank delivering the currency sold would lose if the bank buying this currency does not deliver the other currency (because of insolvency or liquidation, which is what happened in the Herstatt case). In this case, the selling bank effectively extends unsecured loan to the buying bank. How much of the loan will be recovered depends on the estate in the bankruptcy's treatment of the bank's dividend demand. For details of the Herstatt case, see BCBS (2004b, pp. 4–6).

In response to the Herstatt event, which had significant adverse implications for the foreign exchange market and banks in other countries, the Basel Committee on Banking Supervision (BCBS or the Committee) was established by the central bank governors of the Group of Ten (G10) countries to maintain an open and constructive dialogue among banking supervisors. As Herring and Litan (1995) put it, the Committee focuses on facilitating and enhancing information sharing and co-operation among bank regulators in major countries and developing principles for the supervision of internationally active large banks. The BCSB seeks to improve the quality of banking supervision by (i) exchanging information on national supervisory arrangements; (ii) improving the effectiveness of the techniques used for supervising international banking business; and (iii) setting minimum supervisory standards where they are considered desirable. The Committee does not have any supranational authority with respect to banking supervision, and this is why its recommendations and set standards do not have legal force, in the sense that it is up to the national authorities to implement them. The BCBS has no jurisdiction over the issues of "how" and "when" to implement its recommendations and standards.

As the losses incurred by some large international banks from Third World loans mounted in the late 1970s, the Committee became increasingly concerned that the potential failures of one or more of these banks could have serious adverse effects, not only on banks in their own countries but also on banks from other countries. Fear of cross-border contagion mounted and so did concern about insufficiency of the capital held by large banks in relation to the risks they were assuming, as indicated by the deteriorating capital ratios. This gave rise to the concept of capital adequacy (or inadequacy), reflecting the reluctance of national governments to require higher capital ratios for fear of putting their national banks at a competitive disadvantage relative to banks in other countries.

In the 1980s, concern about capital inadequacy was particularly directed at Japanese banks, which were expanding at a rapid pace, buoyed by valuations of capital that included large amounts of unrealized capital gains from Japanese stock holdings. These gains were not permitted as part of capital valuation in most other countries, where equity ownership by banks was more restricted. As a result, the BCBS began to focus on the development of international regulation with the objective of establishing and implementing higher and more uniform capital standards for banks across countries. These capital standards were introduced in 1988 as the Basel I Accord.

Under the Basel I Accord, banks were required to hold capital based on what Nash (2003) described as a "crude assessment" of credit risk exposure, including a buffer for other risks. For many reasons that will be outlined later, and in response to the criticism directed at Basel I by academics and practitioners, the BCBS decided to shift to the Basel II Accord. The remaining parts of this chapter deal with Basel I and introduces Basel II. But before that, it may be worthwhile to have a brief account of the activities of the BCBS since inception.

The BCBS met for the first time in February 1975, and since then it has been meeting regularly, three or four times a year. The Committee has 12 member countries (the G10 countries and two others: Belgium, Canada, Germany, Italy, Japan, Luxembourg, the Netherlands, Spain, Sweden, Switzerland, the United Kingdom, and the United States) represented by their central banks as well as other banking supervision authorities (such as the Financial Services Authority of the U.K.). The name "Basel Committee" comes from the fact that the Committee's secretariat is provided by the Bank for International Settlements (BIS), which is based in Basel, Switzerland, where the meetings of the Committee take place. The Committee maintains links with national supervisors from other countries by developing and disseminating papers on supervisory matters, the pursuit of supervisory co-operation and the provision of supervisory training. This work is carried out by the constituent components of the Committee: Accord Implementation Group, Accounting Task Force, Capital Group, Capital Task Force, Core Principle Liaison Group, Cross-Border Banking Group, Joint Forum, Risk Management Group, Securitization Group, Transparency Group, and the Basel Core Principles Reference Group.

Table 2.1 provides a chronological account of the activities and products of the BCBS. Although these activities fall mainly in the areas of supervising banks' foreign establishments and capital standards, the BCBS has addressed other banking issues, including the supervision of banks' foreign exchange positions, the management of international lending, the management of off-balance sheet exposures, customer due diligence, the supervision of large exposures, risk management guidelines for derivatives, loan accounting and disclosure, corporate governance, credit risk management, and electronic banking.

Table 2.1 A chronology of the activities of the BCBS

Date	Activity/Product
February 1975	First meeting was held.
1975	The Concordat was published. This is a document on the supervision of banks' foreign establishments.
1978	The Concordat was extended and reformulated to take account of changes in the market and to incorporate the consolidated supervision of international banking groups.
May 1983	A revised version of the Concordat was published.
December 1987	The Basel I Accord was approved by the G10 central bank governors.
July 1988	The Basel I Accord was released to banks (BCBS, 1988).
April 1990	A supplement to the 1983 Concordat was issued to improve the flow of information between banking supervisors across countries.
November 1991	The Basel I Accord was amended to present a more precise definition of the loan-loss reserves that can be included in capital for the purpose of calculating capital adequacy.

(Continued)

Table 2.1 (*Continued*)

Date	Activity/Product
June 1992	Some of the principles of the Concordat were reformulated as minimum standards.
September 1993	Confirmation that all banks in the G10 countries with international business were meeting the minimum requirements stipulated by the 1988 Accord.
April 1995	The BCSB issued an amendment to the Basel I Accord to recognize the effects of the bilateral netting of credit exposures in derivative products.
January 1996	Amendment to the Basel I Accord designed to incorporate the market risks arising from open positions in foreign exchange, traded debt securities, equities, commodities, and options.
April 1996	A document was issued to explain the recognition of the effects of multilateral netting.
October 1996	The BCSB presented proposals for overcoming the impediments to effective consolidated supervision of the operations of international banks.
November 1999	First-round proposals for a new accord to replace the 1988 Accord (Consultative Paper 1, BCBS, 1999).
January 2001	Additional (second-round) proposals for the Basel II Accord (Consultative Paper 2, BCBS, 2001b).
April 2001	The launch of QIS2.
May 2001	The launch of a second tranche of QIS2 focusing on operational risk.
September 2001	Publishing a working paper on the regulatory treatment of operational risk (BCBS, 2001a).
November 2001	Publishing the results of QIS2.
November 2001	The launch of QIS2.5.
January 2002	Publishing individual operational loss data gathered in QIS2.
June 2002	The launch of the operational loss data collection exercise.
July 2002	Publishing the results of QIS2.5.
October 2002	The launch of QIS3.
March 2003	Publishing the results of the 2002 operational loss data collection exercise (BCBS, 2003c).
April 2003	Additional (third round) proposals for the Basel II Accord (Consultative Paper 3, BCBS, 2003a).
May 2003	Publishing the results of QIS3.
June 2004	After refining the 1999 proposals over many years, the new Accord was issued (BCBS, 2004a).

(*Continued*)

Table 2.1 (*Continued*)

Date	Activity/Product
2004 (various dates)	The launch of QIS4 (national QISs).
October 2005	The launch of QIS5.
November 2005	Publishing a revised Basel II document (BCBS, 2005b).
June 2006	Publishing the results of QIS5.
June 2006	Publishing a comprehensive version of the revised Basel II document (BCBS, 2006a).
June 2006	Publishing a document on home-host information sharing for effective Basel II implementation (BCBS, 2006b).
October 2006	Publishing a document on the observed range of practices in key elements of the advanced measurement approach to the measurement of operational risk (BCBS, 2006c).

2.2 SOME PRELIMINARIES

To be in a position to understand the discussion in this chapter and the following chapters, basic knowledge of some issues and concepts is required. In this section we consider the issue of why banks are particularly important and present an insight into the concept of capital in the sense used in this book.

The Basel Accords are designed primarily to minimize the possibility of bank failure. Thus, a question that must be asked is why it is that banks command more importance than other financial and non-financial firms. White (2004) puts forward the argument that banks are important for two reasons, the first of which is the difference between the degrees of liquidity of their assets and liabilities. In general, banks hold relatively illiquid assets (loans) and highly liquid liabilities (deposits). As a result, banks are highly vulnerable to depositor withdrawal or bank runs in extreme cases (for example, Diamond and Dybvic, 1983; Postlewaite and Vives, 1987; Chen, 1999). Banks are believed to be inherently unstable because they are structurally fragile, a characteristic resulting from the practice of holding low ratios of cash reserves to assets and capital to assets.

The second reason suggested by White is that banks are at the center of the payment system (they are the creators of money, the medium of exchange), which gives them constant creditor–borrower relationships among themselves and leaves them exposed to potential losses at each other's hands. Shirreff (2005) argues on similar lines by describing banks as being "too important to be left to themselves". Banks, he argues, are "too crucial to allow the possibility of a shock, such as a bank failure or a hiccup in the payment system".

One can also argue that banks are important because of their sheer size. One reason why credit risk and operational risk cannot be covered fully through insurance is that insurance companies are too small for banks. There is also the characteristic of banks that distinguishes them from other firms, which pertains to the reasons for holding capital. Rowe (2004b) argues that while capital matters to most firms, non-financial firms need capital mainly to support funding, to buy property and to build or acquire production facilities and equipment to pursue new risky areas of business. Banks, on the other hand, take risk on a daily basis as part of their core business processes. Finally, a big difference between banks (as financial firms) and non-financial firms is that they deal in a valuable commodity, money. The temptation for criminal activity (and hence exposure to operational risk) must be greater in the case of banks compared to, for example, brick factories).

On a related matter, the Basel Accords are designed to deal with the issue of banks' capital adequacy, which probably requires a definition or description of capital. White (2004) describes a bank's capital as the arithmetic difference between assets and liabilities, which is also known as net worth or shareholders' equity. He argues that a bank's capital "has no separate existence or measurement except as represented by this arithmetic difference". Thus, a bank is solvent if the difference is positive and vice versa.

Having introduced the concept of solvency (and therefore insolvency), it may be useful to introduce the concepts of economic capital and regulatory capital. Everts and Liersch (2006) argue that the concept of economic capital is not new, but the transition from the accounting measures of capital to economic capital has accelerated because of the reduction in computing costs, which made the calculation of economic capital cost-effective. Economic capital is the amount of capital that a firm (or a unit within the firm) must hold to protect itself with a chosen level of certainty (confidence level) against insolvency due to unexpected losses over a given period of time (for example, one year). The Economist (2003) defines economic capital as "the theoretically ideal cushion against unexpected losses".

Herring (2002) defines economic capital with reference to the risk of default as "the amount of capital a bank requires to achieve a given level of protection against default for its creditors". Gelderman, Klaassen, and Lelyveld (2006) describe the term "economic capital" as a number that "reflects the extent to which, at the company's desired level of comfort, in a given period results for (part of) an undertaking can be worse than originally expected, ie, it reflects unexpected losses". Knot et al. (2006) define economic capital as "the amount of capital that a transaction or business unit requires in order to support the economic risk it originates, as perceived by the institution itself". They also define it as "a buffer against all unexpected losses, including those not incurred on the balance sheet at the company's desired level of comfort". Everts and Liersch (2006) suggest the definition that it is "the capital that covers the potential value loss based on the inherent risks and desired level of comfort of an institution". But this is not all, as a survey conducted by the Societies of Actuaries (2004) revealed a variety of definitions, including the following:

■ Sufficient surplus to meet potential negative cash flows and reductions in the value of assets or increases in the value of liabilities at a given level of risk tolerance, over a specified time horizon.

■ The excess of the market value of the assets over the fair value of liabilities required to ensure that obligations can be satisfied at a given level of risk tolerance, over a specified time horizon.

■ Sufficient surplus to maintain solvency at a given level of risk tolerance, over a specified time horizon.

Economic capital may be assigned to a certain kind of risk or to individual business lines or activities. Thus, operational (credit) risk economic capital is set aside to protect the firm from insolvency due to unexpected operational (credit) losses. Knot et al. (2006) highlight two aspects of the determination of economic capital. The first is that the ownership of the economic capital process is not prescribed by an external party, such as a regulator. The second aspect is that one of the objectives of economic capital modeling is the ability to allocate economic capital to business lines or activities, which can be subsequently used to calculate risk-adjusted measures of performance, including the risk-adjusted return on capital (RAROC) and the return on risk-adjusted capital (RORAC).

While economic capital is calculated by the firm according to its internal models, regulatory capital (also called regulatory capital requirements or the capital charge) is determined by the regulators, for example, as a given percentage of the risk-weighted value of assets. Everts and Liersch (2006) distinguish between economic capital, on the one hand, and actual or regulatory capital, on the other, by describing economic capital as being "the amount of capital a ... firm itself deems necessary, given its risk profile and the state of controls". Likewise, Kalyvas et al. (2006) and Kalyvas and Sfetsos (2006) distinguish between the two concepts by stipulating that "economic capital is directed to cover probable unexpected losses arising from business activities" whereas regulatory capital is "required by regulatory and supervisory authorities to fulfill their expectations about the different sources of risk and to account for possible model errors risks of the internal models used to estimate economic capital". Economic capital and regulatory capital are bound to differ, perhaps significantly, unless the regulator agrees to make the regulatory capital equal to the economic capital as determined by internal models. As we are going to see later, one of the proclaimed advantages of the Basel II Accord is that it allows the use of internal models to calculate regulatory capital under stringent conditions that the underlying bank must meet.

For regulatory purposes, capital consists of equity and retained earnings (tier 1 capital) and supplementary capital (tier 2 capital). Short-term subordinated debt may be used as tier 3 capital, provided that (i) tier 1 capital is limited to 250 percent of tier 1 capital, (ii) the tier 2 capital elements may be substituted for tier 3 capital up to 250 percent, and (iii) tier 3 capital is only appropriate to meet market risk. Capital adequacy implies that a sufficient amount of capital should be held to protect depositors from losses and support asset growth. The capital ratio, which is a measure of capital adequacy, is the required capital as a percentage of the risk-weighted assets. These concepts crop up very frequently in the BCBS's publications, and they are critical for understanding the Basel Accords.

2.3   THE BASEL I ACCORD

In 1988, the BCBS established a global standard for measuring capital adequacy for banks that has become to be known as the Basel I Accord (also known as the 1988 Accord). One motive for establishing this framework, which is described in detail in BCBS (1988), was to bring consistency to the way banks were regulated in different countries. The Accord made it possible to pursue better capital allocation and regulatory decision-making, helping to make the financial system more sound and stable. According to Fischer (2002), Basel I had two basic objectives: (i) to establish a more level playing field for international competition among banks, and (ii) to reduce the probability that such competition would lead to bidding down of capital ratios to excessively low levels.

Starting in 1991, Basel I was implemented by an increasing number of countries, becoming worldwide capital standards for banks. Given that this standard does not carry the force of law directly, its success has been impressive, making banks around the world use a common framework to allocate capital according to their mix of assets.

2.3.1   Features of the Basel I Accord

The most important feature of Basel I is relating the capital a bank must hold to the perceived credit risk of the bank's portfolio. Before that, regulators focused on simple leverage ratios that used only total assets as the base. Basel I incorporates off-balance sheet items in the base as well as on-balance sheet items, and weighted individual assets by a risk factor. Individual assets are divided into four basic credit risk categories according to the identity of the counterparty and assigned weights ranging from 0 to 100 percent. The weighted values of on- and off-balance sheet items are then summed and classified as "risk-weighted assets". Banks are required to hold as capital an amount of no less than 8 percent of their risk-weighted assets. This capital ratio is referred to as risk-based capital (RBC).

Following the introduction of the Basel I Accord, several revisions were introduced. In November 1991, the Accord was amended by revising the definition of the general provisions or general loan–loss reserves that can be included in capital for the purpose of calculating capital ratios to determine capital adequacy. Another amendment was introduced in April 1995 to recognize the effects of bilateral netting of credit exposures in derivative products. Recognizing the effects of multilateral netting was dealt with in a document that was published in April 1996.

While the Basel I Accord was primarily concerned with credit risk, the BCBS amended the Accord in 1996 to incorporate the market risk arising from open foreign exchange positions, traded debt securities, equities, commodities and options. That was in effect the introduction of regulatory capital against market risk. One important implication of this amendment was that banks were allowed to use internal value at risk models to measure the required capital as an alternative to a standardized measurement method. However, this was possible only for banks meeting strict quantitative and qualitative standards as judged by the supervisor.

Fischer (2002) argues that the Basel I Accord made important progress toward achieving its objectives, establishing in the process a more equitable basis for competition and greatly strengthening capital standards, both within and beyond the G10 countries. He also argues that relative to what was available before, it was a major breakthrough, not least because of the general acceptance and implementation of its capital requirements well beyond the member countries of the Basel Committee. One reason for the effectiveness of the Basel I Accord is its simplicity. It makes it possible to compare banks of different sizes and complexity of operations, by using similar calculations to determine if they have sufficient capital to protect themselves against certain risks.

2.3.2   A critique of the Basel I Accord

Fischer (2002), whose comments in the previous subsection give the impression that he is fully supportive of the Accord, argues that Basel I has significant shortcomings, the most important of which is its very limited sensitivity to risk. While categorizing debtors into a few risk "buckets" was certainly an innovation in 1988, it also gave rise to a significant gap between the regulatory measurement of risk of a given transaction and its actual economic risk. The most troubling side effect of the gap between regulatory and economic risk is the distortion of financial decision making, including large amounts of regulatory arbitrage, or investments made on the basis of regulatory constraints rather than genuine economic opportunities. He suggests that this implies a significant deadweight cost of regulation relative to an efficient market. Likewise, it is argued that differences started to emerge between regulatory capital as assigned by the regulators and economic capital as required by market forces.

The following are specific points of criticism that have been directed at the Basel I Accord (the list is certainly not exhaustive):

1. The problem, according to Kaufman (2003), is that the formula that is used to calculate regulatory capital against credit risk is relatively simple, treating all banks in the same manner, "one size fits all", as he put it. This is what Dowd (2003) calls "the crude bucketing of risk asset classes", which is "far from generating risk sensitive capital requirements". Inadequate differentiation among credit risks resulted in banks lending more to low-rated borrowers.

2. The arbitrary way whereby risk classes and weights are determined means that the resulting RBC requirements are neither realistic nor useful.

3. Adding up the credit risks of individual assets ignores the gains from diversification across less-than-perfectly correlated assets.

4. Capital adequacy is strictly a financial calculation. Capital is measured as if it were reserved for protection primarily against financial risk (credit and market).

5. The Accord's focus is on credit risk as the most prominent risk category. However, the Accord explicitly acknowledges the proposition that "other risks need to be taken into account by supervisors in assessing overall capital adequacy" (BCBS, 1988, p. 1).

6. The Accord gives very limited attention to credit risk mitigation despite the remarkable growth in credit derivatives as a risk management tool.

7. The accord focuses on a minimum capital requirement without due emphasis on the risk management process (unlike Basel II, it has one pillar only).

8. High regulatory costs pushed banks toward securitization, leading to the elimination of better quality loans from the balance sheets and leaving banks with low-quality loans on their books.

For these reasons and others, it was felt, toward the end of last century, that it was time to do something about Basel I. Upgrading Basel I was perceived to be a necessity.

2.3.3 Upgrading Basel I

Apart from the criticisms directed at Basel I, the principal motivation for the desire to upgrade the Accord was that it had become outdated because the banking system had, since its invention, become more complex with the emergence of new risks and opportunities. This view was put in a cover story of the *Structured Finance International* (2004) about Basel II, stipulating that "although Basel 1 served the global banking industry and the economies which depend on it reasonably well over the last decade, it was clearly flawed and failed to present numerous bank failures". The problem is that it is rather difficult to answer the question whether or not the creation of Basel II in 1990 would have helped Barings survive in the aftermath of that catastrophic event (if it had held adequate capital to cover losses) or prevented Leeson from doing what he did. The idea behind Basel II is that preventative measures as well as capital adequacy are used in combination to protect banks from operational loss events.

Furthermore, some banks have learned how to "play" the system, particularly in international banking (see, for example, Matten, 2003). Changes in the banking environment have been the driving force behind the need for new capital measures that incorporate broader risk management models. In this respect, the following points have been raised:

1. If not properly controlled, the greater use of automated technology has the potential to transform risk from manual processing errors to system failure risk.

2. E-commerce brings with it the risks of internal and external fraud, authentication problems, and system security issues.

3. When banks act as large-volume service provides, the need arises for the maintenance of internal controls and back-up systems.

4. Market and credit risk mitigation techniques (for example, credit derivatives) may produce other kinds of risk (for example, legal risk).

5. Outsourcing arrangements and participation in clearing and settlement systems can mitigate some kinds of risk while creating other kinds.

6. During the ten years ending early in the 21st Century, there were over 100 operational loss events exceeding $100 million each (de Fountnouvelle, 2003).

Having exposed all of the weaknesses of Basel I, a last word in favor of the Accord is warranted. In defense of Basel I, Fischer (2002) argues that any strictly rule-based approach to regulation is bound to run the risk of distorting activity in unexpected ways and encouraging regulatory arbitrage.

This view constitutes negative defense of Basel I, in the sense that it is not the only accord that will fail. Is this an omen for Basel II?

2.4   THE BASEL II ACCORD: AN INTRODUCTION

"The Accord is dead – long live the Accord". This is how Howard Davis, Chairman of the Financial Services Authority (the UK regulator) commented on the launch of the first set of proposals to revise the Basel I Accord in 1999. In response to the criticism of the Basel I Accord, to address changes in the banking environment that the 1988 Accord could not deal with effectively, and in response to the view that the Basel I Accord was becoming outdated, the BCBS decided to create a new capital accord, Basel II. In its introduction of the first set of proposals that gave birth to Basel II, the BCBS proclaimed a critical need to redesign the 1988 Accord in the light of market innovations and a fundamental shift toward more complexity in the banking industry. Furthermore, one of the main objectives behind the introduction of the Basel II Accord is to narrow the gap between regulatory capital requirements and the economic capital produced by the banks' own internal models.

2.4.1   Objectives of Basel II

The main objective behind the revision of the Basel I Accord is the development of a framework that boosts the soundness and stability of the international banking system without introducing competitive inequality among international banks. While retaining the key elements of the Basel I Accord, including the general requirement that banks ought to hold total capital equivalent to at least 8 percent of their risk-weighted assets, the revised framework provides a range of options for determining the capital requirements for credit risk and operational risk, allowing banks to use approaches that are most appropriate for their operations. The framework also allows for a limited degree of national discretion in the way they apply the options. Foot (2002) expresses the view that the objective of Basel II is "to move to risk-sensitive capital requirements that mirror banks' own methods of measuring risk and allocating capital".

As under Basel I, national authorities will be free to adopt arrangements that set higher levels of capital. The Basel Committee has stated that the Basel II Accord does not aim at changing the global level of capital in the banking industry but rather at creating an incentive to encourage banks to adopt what they consider "best practices" for risk management (BCBS, 2003b). Fischer (2002) argues that the Basel II Accord has been designed to encourage more effective and comprehensive global risk management practices, and to provide supervisors and the market with more accurate measures of capital adequacy and risk. In practice, this has led to emphasis on increasing risk-sensitivity, particularly for sovereign and corporate credit risk, and on using banks' own internal credit risk ratings. By far, the most distinctive elements of Basel II are the approach to credit risk and the inclusion of new capital requirements for operational risk.

2.4.2 Development of Basel II

Following the publication of the first round of proposals for revising the capital adequacy framework in November 1999 (BCBS, 1999), the BCBS subsequently released additional proposals in January 2001 and April 2003 (Consultative Papers 2 and 3; BCBS, 2001b, 2003a) and conducted quantitative impact studies (QISs) pertaining to these proposals. This consultation process has resulted in the revised framework that was published in June 2004 (BCBS, 2004a), whereas other revised frameworks appeared in November 2005 and June 2006 (BCBS, 2005b; 2006a). The framework has been endorsed by the central bank governors and heads of banking supervision of the G10 countries.

The 2004 document (BCBS, 2004a) has several significant changes relative to the proposal of April 2003 (BCBS, 2003a). These include changes in the treatment of expected losses and unexpected losses and to the treatment of securitization exposure. In addition, there are changes to the treatment of credit risk mitigation and qualifying revolving retail exposure. The 2005 document (BCBS, 2005b) aims at enhancing home/host supervisory information-sharing guidelines and to aid the effective cross-border implementation of Basel II, with the ultimate objective of reducing the regulatory burden on banks and conserving supervisory resources. It is basically an updated version of the 2004 document that incorporates additional guidelines. The 2006 document (BCBS, 2006a) is described as a comprehensive version of the revised framework of capital adequacy.

Central to the development of the Basel II Accord have been the five QISs conducted over the period 2001–6 to facilitate the revision of the Accord. In 2001, the BCBS conducted QIS2 and QIS2.5, which amounted to major data collection exercises. The QIS1 (launched in April 2001) was aimed at collecting the data necessary to allow the BCBS to gauge the impact of the second Consultative Paper across a wide range of banks in the G10 countries and beyond. A second tranche of QIS2, which focused on operational risk (in particular, the collection of information on individual loss events) was launched in May 2001, and its results were released in January 2002. The QIS2.5, launched in November 2001, was an updated version of QIS2, designed primarily to collect information on the effect that revisions to the proposals in Consultative Paper 2 would have on banks.

In general, QIS2 and QIS2.5 were intended to collect information to find out whether or not the BCBS had met its objectives with respect to the revised capital framework.

In October 2002, the QIS3, which comprised all aspects of pillar 1 of the Basel II Accord, was launched and its results were published in May 2003. More than 350 banks in 43 countries participated in the exercise. It was designed mainly to measure the impact of the Basel II proposals before the finalization of BCBS (2004a). A separate operational loss data collection exercise was launched in June 2002, the results of which were published on 14 March 2003.

QIS4 was not specifically a BCBS activity but rather a collection of national impact studies conducted by several member countries in 2004, effectively constituting tests based on the Basel II framework. The BCBS's contribution to this exercise was the development of templates for a workbook and accompanying instructions. Unlike, QIS4, QIS5 was a BCBS exclusive, designed to evaluate the effects of the Basel II Accord on capital levels in 356 banks across the world (except the US). The data collected between October and December 2005 was used to review the calibration of Basel II in 2006. The results of the QIS5 led the BCBS to maintain the current calibrations of the regulatory capital models (BCBS, 2006d).

2.4.3   Features of Basel II

The main features of Basel II and its differences from the Basel I Accord are the following:

1. The Basel II Accord includes a more sophisticated measurement framework for evaluating capital adequacy in banks.

2. Basel II is not only about capital adequacy, but it is about improving risk management in the finance industry by providing the correct incentives for better corporate governance and fostering transparency.

3. The main objective of the Basel II Accord is to improve the process of determining capital requirements, by modifying the structure of the credit risk weights and allowing their values to be determined by three alternative methods, depending on the size and sophistication of the bank.

4. Unlike Basel I, Basel II assigns explicit weights to operational risk. Indeed, it is arguable that the main focus of the Basel II Accord is operational risk rather than market risk or credit risk, which can be justified on the basis of the observation that operational losses have intensified in terms of severity and frequency. The Basel I weights for market risk were maintained.

5. The Accord provides a more flexible and forward-looking capital adequacy framework (having the capacity to evolve over time), one that reflects in a better way the risks facing banks and encourages them to make ongoing improvements in risk assessment capabilities.

6. The Accord is designed to accommodate future changes in the way banks measure and manage their risks by giving them a range of options for calculating capital charges and incentives for using best practices.

7. The Basel II Accord is more risk-sensitive than Basel I. The BCBS (2005b) notes that it has sought "to arrive at a significantly more risk-sensitive capital requirements that are conceptually sound and at the same time pay due regard to particular features of the present supervisory and accounting systems in individual member countries".

8. Countries where risk is relatively high need to consider if banks should be required to hold additional capital over and above the Basel minimum. National authorities are also free to implement supplementary measures of capital adequacy.

9. The Accord is designed to be applied on a consolidated basis to internationally active banks (banks with subsidiaries).

10. A significant innovation of the Basel II Accord is the greater use of internal models for risk assessment and the calculation of regulatory capital. The accord provides a range of options for determining the capital requirements for credit risk and operational risk with the objective of allowing banks and supervisors to select approaches that are most appropriate for their operations.

Perhaps an indication of the importance of Basel II is that Berens (2004) cites a risk management expert (Colin Lawrence) as warning banks to "follow Basel II or else". He is cited to have said that "banks around the world are likely to implode if they fail to take the risk management guidelines in the proposed Basel II regulations seriously". It is easy to respond to this claim by saying that, notwithstanding fiascos like the collapse of Barings and Long-term Capital Management, banks seem to have survived without Basel II and even without Basel I. Likewise, Foot (2002) puts forward the view that "Basel 2 is probably the most ambitious regulatory reform program any group of regulators has ever attempted".

In various publications, the BCBS lists the following explicit benefits of the Basel II Accord:

1. Important public policy benefits can be obtained by improving the capital adequacy framework because it encompasses three pillars and because it produces substantially higher risk-sensitivity of minimum capital requirements.

2. It is intended to foster strong emphasis on risk management and encourage ongoing improvements in banks' risk assessment capabilities.

3. Improvements in the risk sensitivity of the minimum capital requirements will provide benefits through a stronger and more accurate incentive structure.

4. Risk-sensitive capital requirements provide more meaningful and informative measures of capital adequacy.

5. Basel II calls on banks to conduct their own internal assessment of capital relative to risk and for supervisors to review and respond to the assessment.

6. Basel II calls for greater disclosure of key risk elements and capital, which provides important information to investors and stakeholders to form a view on the bank's risk profile.

Despite all of these proclaimed benefits of Basel II, the Accord has been subject to a barrage of criticism from academics, practitioners, and even regulators, some of whom have said that the Accord might blow up two European banking systems (The Economist, 2006), whereas some bankers think that it is complex and dangerous (Centre for the Study of Financial Innovation, 2002). Chapter 3 presents a thorough critical evaluation of Basel II by surveying what academics and practitioners have to say about it.

The Pillars of the Basel II Accord

3.1 INTRODUCTION

Unlike the Basel I Accord, which had one pillar (minimum capital requirements or capital adequacy), the Basel II Accord has three pillars: (i) minimum regulatory capital requirements, (ii) the supervisory review process, and (iii) market discipline through disclosure requirements. Fischer (2002) argues that the three pillars should be mutually supporting. The effectiveness of the first pillar depends on the supervisor's ability to regulate and monitor the application of the three approaches to the determination of the minimum regulatory capital, whereas wider public disclosure and market discipline will reinforce the incentives for sound risk management practices. The BCBS (2005b) notes that banks and other interested parties have welcomed the concept and rationale of the three pillars approach on which the Basel II Accord is based. The Committee also notes that it is critical for the minimum capital requirements of the first pillar to be accompanied by a robust implementation of the second and third pillars.

The three pillars of the Basel II Accord will be discussed in turn. We start with pillar 1, which pertains to the calculation of minimum capital requirements for credit, market and operational risk. The following three sections describe how regulatory capital is determined for credit risk, market risk and operational risk.

3.2 PILLAR 1: CREDIT RISK

Credit risk is the risk to a bank's earnings or capital base arising from a borrower's failure to meet the terms of any contractual or other agreement it has with the bank (Hills, 2004). Calculating capital requirements for credit risk can be based on the standardized approach (STA) and the internal-ratings-based (IRB) approach. The latter may be one of two versions: the foundation IRB approach and the advanced IRB approach. The STA is to be applied to the smallest, least sophisticated banks, the foundation IRB approach to larger banks, and the advanced IRB approach to the largest and most sophisticated banks.

The STA is structurally similar to what is found in the 1988 Accord. Banks are required to classify their exposures into broad categories, such as the loans they have extended to corporate and sovereign borrowers and other banks. An improvement over the 1988 Accord is aligning risk weights with a borrower's creditworthiness as indicated by external rating, provided that rating is determined by an institution (a rating agency) that, according to the supervisors, meets the criteria of objectivity, independence, international access, transparency, disclosure, resources and credibility. Moreover, the STA is intended to be a more risk-sensitive version of the 1988 Accord.

The IRB approach goes further than the STA, and it is one of the most innovative features of the Basel II Accord according to McDonough (2003). Banks using the IRB approach will be permitted to quantify key measures of creditworthiness in determining regulatory capital, including the estimation of the likelihood that the borrower will default. Many banks will also be able to provide estimates of other key variables (such as the recovery rate if a borrower were to default) and the likelihood of a credit line being drawn upon.

Subject to certain minimum conditions and disclosure requirements, banks that have received supervisory approval to use the IRB approach may rely on their own internal estimates of credit risk to determine the capital requirement for a given exposure. The risk components include measures of the probability of default (PD), the loss given default (LGD), and exposure at default (EAD). The PD, which is also known as expected default frequency, is the default probability for a borrower over a one-year period, which is often a function of the risk rating of the borrower. The LGD, also known as loss severity, is the expected amount lost on a credit facility. Recovery given default is the mirror image of LGD, as they should sum to the amount owed by the borrower. EAD, also known as usage given default, is the amount the borrower owes to the bank at the time of default. While significant attention has been devoted by the credit risk literature to the estimation of PD, much less attention has been dedicated to the estimation of LGD or to the relation between PD and LGD (Resti and Sironi, 2004). Notice that the product of PD, LGD, and EAD is the expected loss (EL). Since all of these parameters are based on a default event, it is essential to come up with a definition of default. For this purpose, default arises when the borrower fails to make the payment of principal or interest.

When payment is past due 90 days, banks no longer accrue interest on the loan, placing it on "non-accrual" or describing it as "non-performing".

The IRB approach is based on measures of unexpected losses (UL) and EL. The risk-weighted functions produce capital requirements for the UL portion, whereas the EL portion is treated separately. Under the IRB approach, banks must classify banking book exposures into broad classes of assets with different underlying characteristics: (i) corporate, (ii) sovereign, (iii) bank, (iv) retail, and (v) equity. For each of these classes, the IRB has three key elements:

1. Risk components: Estimates of risk parameters.

2. Risk-weighted functions: The means whereby risk components are transformed into risk-weighted assets and therefore capital requirements.

3. Minimum requirements: The minimum standards that must be met so that the IRB approach can be used for a given asset class.

The difference between the foundation IRB approach and the advanced IRB approach is straightforward. In the foundation approach, banks compute their own PD for individual loans but use the values for LGD provided by regulators. In the advanced IRB approach, on the other hand, banks are permitted to determine own values for both PD and LGD. In all cases, the models used by the banks to obtain their values need to be evaluated and approved by the regulators. Before a bank is allowed to use its internal estimates of PD and/or LGD, it must satisfy strict regulatory criteria. They must demonstrate that their internal models are conceptually sound and historically consistent with their past experience.

3.3   PILLAR 1: MARKET RISK

Market risk is defined as the risk of losses in on- and off-balance sheet positions arising from movements in market prices. The underlying risks in this case are the risks pertaining to interest-related instruments and equities in the trading book, as well as foreign exchange and commodity price risk throughout the bank. The capital charges for interest rate-related instruments and equities would apply to the current market value of the items in banks' trading books, which include the following positions: (i) the bank's proprietary positions in financial instruments held for short-term resale; (ii) positions taken by the bank to benefit from short-term variation in interest rates; (iii) financial positions arising from matching and brokerage activities; and (iv) positions in financial assets used as hedging instruments.

Two approaches are used to measure market risk: the STA and the internal models approach. To be eligible for the use of internal models, a bank must satisfy the following conditions: (i) criteria concerning the adequacy of the risk management system; (ii) qualitative standards for internal oversight of the use of models; (iii) guidelines for specifying an appropriate set of risk factors; (iv) quantitative standards; (v) guidelines for stress testing; (vi) validation procedures for external oversight of the use of models; and (vii) rules for banks that use a mixture of models and the STA. As a rule, banks that adopt an internal model will not be permitted to revert to the STA, while a combination of two methods will not be permitted within the same risk category (interest rate, equity, foreign exchange, and commodity price).

The STA is to add a fixed percentage of the value of a position, depending on certain rules for the classification and calculation of gross and net positions. The following are the specific procedures used with each kind of market risk:

- For interest rate risk, capital requirement is expressed in terms of two separately calculated charges, one pertaining to the specific risk of each security and general market risk. Either the maturity method or the duration method can be used.

- For equity positions, specific risk pertains to gross equity positions (the sum of long and short positions), whereas the general market risk is the difference between long and short positions. The capital charge for specific risk is 8 percent unless the portfolio is both liquid and well diversified, in which case it would be 4 percent. For general market risk, it is 8 percent.

- For foreign exchange risk, net positions in each foreign currency and gold are converted at the spot exchange rate into the reporting currency. The capital charge is 8 percent of the net open position.

- For commodity price risk, all commodity derivatives and off-balance-sheet positions that are affected by changes in commodity prices are included. The capital charge is 15 percent of the net position.

The incentive for banks to use the internal models approach, which relies on the models developed by the banks themselves, is that it produces lower capital charges. The internal models are invariably VAR models. A bank can only use internal models after the supervisory authority has approved it. Certain minimum standards have to be kept in mind for calculating the capital charge: (i) VAR must be calculated on a daily basis, using a 99th percentile one-tailed confidence interval; (ii) to calculate VAR, the minimum holding period is 10 days; (iii) the sample period is constrained to a minimum length of the year; and (iv) banks should update their data sets at least once in three months. The risk models must also contain a sufficient number of risk factors, and they must be assessed by both back testing and stress testing. Back testing involves a comparison of daily VAR measures calibrated to a one-day movement in market prices and a 99 percent (one-tailed) confidence level against the actual net trading profit/loss for each of the last 250 business days. Stress testing aims at identifying and managing situations that could cause extraordinary losses.

3.4   PILLAR 1: OPERATIONAL RISK

The measurement and management of operational risk has become the most topical issue in the current debate on risk management. Dowd (2003) points out that the work of the BCBS to devise a regulatory regime for operational risk has contributed to the width and depth of the debate. The BCBS (2004a, p. 137) defines operational risk as the risk of loss resulting from inadequate or failed internal processes, people and systems or from external events. The definition includes legal risk (such the risk of fines, penalties, supervisory actions, and private settlements), but excludes strategic and reputational risk.

The Basel II Accord suggests three methods for calculating operational risk capital charges: (i) the basic indicators approach (BIA), (ii) the STA, and (iii) the advanced measurement approach (AMA). As banks become more sophisticated, they are encouraged to move along the spectrum of available approaches. The underlying hypothesis here is that the use of sophisticated approaches to the calculation of regulatory capital by a bank that has an appropriate risk management framework should result in lower operational risk minimum regulatory capital. This means that the prospects of lower regulatory capital induces firms to use sophisticated risk management practices and modeling approaches. There are certain criteria as to what to use:

1. Internationally active banks and those exposed to significant operational risk (for example, specialized processing banks) are expected to use a more sophisticated approach than the BIA.

2. Once a bank has been approved to use a more advanced approach, it will not be allowed to move back to a simpler approach without supervisory approval.

3. If, on the other hand, a bank using a more advanced approach is no longer meeting the criteria, the bank may be required to revert to a simple approach for some or all of its operations until it meets the conditions required to do that by the supervisors.

4. Swenson (2003) refers to what he calls the "Basel paradox" that puts supervisors and the financial industry in a dilemma. The dilemma is that "internationally active" and/or "significant operational risk" firms may be expected to use more sophisticated approaches while the eligibility requirements to use such approaches may not be met.

3.4.1 The basic indicators approach

There are no eligibility criteria to use the BIA, because this approach represents the "default position". It is presumably designed for small domestic banks. According to Basel II, banks must hold capital for operational risk that is equal to the average of the previous three years of a fixed percentage (α) of positive annual gross income, which means that negative gross income figures must be excluded. Hence

$$K = \frac{\alpha \sum_{i=1}^{n} Y_i}{n} \tag{3.1}$$

where K is the capital charge, Y positive gross income over the previous three years, and n the number of the previous three years for which gross income is positive. Averaging is used in the formula as a smoothing mechanism. The fraction α is fixed by the Basel Committee at 15 percent. For the purpose of estimating K, the Committee defines gross income as net interest income plus net non-interest income as defined by the national supervisors and/or national accounting standards. The Committee suggests that the recognition of Y requires the satisfaction of the following criteria: (i) being gross of any provisions, (ii) being gross of operating expenses, (iii) excluding realized profits/losses from the sale of securities, and (iv) excluding extraordinary and irregular items as well as income from insurance claims. Pezier (2003b) suggests that the definition of gross income proposed by the Committee is not a standard accounting definition.

Dowd (2003) raises the question of why the BIA is included in the Basel II Accord, given that the Accord is specifically designed for sophisticated, large, and internationally active banks. The answer, according to Dowd, is that Basel has developed a spectrum of increasingly sophisticated approaches, with the BIA being the staring point in this "evolutionary framework". It is not obvious that the answer is appropriate for the question, because the answer means that Basel II is designed for not only sophisticated banks, but also for less sophisticated banks and this is why the BIA is included. Allowing the least sophisticated banks to use the BIA is actually indicative that Basel II is not specifically designed for sophisticated banks, as Dowd (2003) claims.

3.4.2 The standardized approach

Accepting that some financial activities are more exposed than others to operational risk (at least in relation to gross income), the BCBS divides banks' activities into eight business lines. Within each business line, gross income is taken to be a proxy for the scale of the business operation and hence a likely measure of the extent of operational risk (as in the BIA). The capital charge for each business line is calculated by multiplying gross income by a factor (β) that is assigned to each business line. β is essentially the loss rate for a particular business line with an average business and control environments. The total capital charge is calculated as a three-year average of the simple sum of capital charges of individual business lines in each year. Hence

$$K = \frac{\alpha \sum_{t=1}^{3} \max\left[\sum_{j=1}^{8} \beta_j Y_j, 0\right]}{3} \tag{3.2}$$

where β_j is set by the Basel Committee to relate the level of required capital to the level of gross income for business line j. Figure 3.1 displays the betas assigned to the eight business lines, whereas Figure 3.2 shows the subcategories of each business line. For example, the business line of retail banking also covers the activities of private banking and card services.

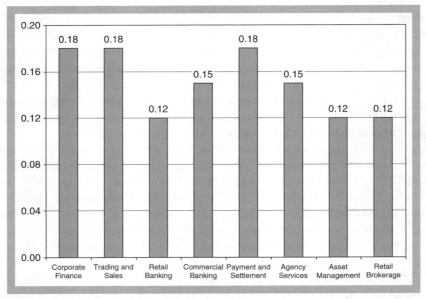

Figure 3.1 The betas assigned to business lines

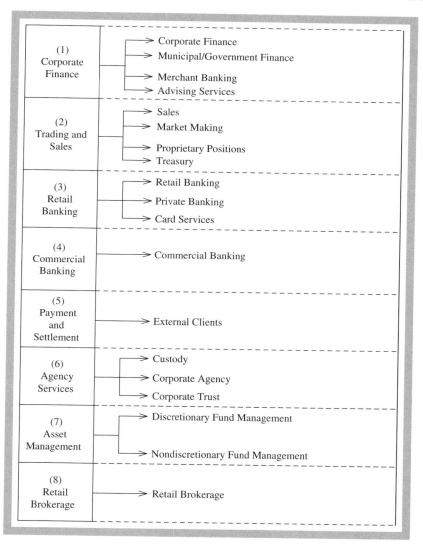

Figure 3.2 The BCBS's business lines

Table 3.1 displays some examples of the activities falling under each business line. For example, mergers and acquisitions fall under corporate finance. Dowd (2003) lists the principles of business line mapping (that is, relating activities to business lines) as follows:

1. All activities must be mapped into the eight business lines in a "mutually exclusive and jointly exhaustive manner".

Table 3.1 Examples of activities falling under business lines

Business line	Example of activities
Corporate finance (CF)	• Mergers and acquisitions • Underwriting • Privatization • Securitization • Research • Syndication • IPOs • Secondary private placements
Trading and sales (TS)	• Fixed income • Equity • Foreign exchange • Commodities • Credit • Funding • Own position securities • Lending and repos • Brokerage • Debt • Prime brokerage
Retail banking (RB)	• Retail lending and deposits • Private lending and deposits • Banking services • Trust and estates • Investment advice • Merchant/commercial/corporate cards • Private labels and retail
Commercial banking (CB)	• Project finance • Real estate • Trade finance • Factoring • Leasing • Lending • Guarantees • Bills of exchange
Payment and settlement (PS)	• Payments and collections • Funds transfer • Clearing and settlement
Agency services (AS)	• Depository receipts • Securities lending • Corporate actions • Issuer and paying agents

(Continued)

Table 3.1 (*Continued*)

Business line	Example of activities
Asset management (AM)	• Pooled • Segregated • Retail • Institutional • Closed • Open • Private equity
Retail brokerage (RB)	• Execution • Full services

Source: BCBS (2004a)

2. Activities representing an ancillary function to an activity included in business lines that cannot be readily mapped into the business lines must be allocated to the business line it supports.

3. If an activity cannot be mapped into a particular business line, the business line yielding the highest charge must be used.

4. The mapping of activities into business lines for operational risk capital purposes must be consistent with the definition of the business lines used for regulatory capital calculations in other risk categories.

5. The mapping process must be clearly documented.

6. A process must be in place to define the mapping of any new activities or products.

7. Subject to the approval of the board, senior management is responsible for the mapping process.

8. The mapping process must be subject to independent review.

A slight modification of the STA produces what is known as the alternative STA, which is similar to the STA except that the capital charges for retail banking and commercial banking are calculated in a different way. Instead of using gross income as the exposure indicator, the value of loans and advances is used for this purpose. Thus, gross income is replaced by a figure that amounts to 0.035 times the value of loans and advances, which gives

$$K_{RB} = 0.035 \, \beta_{RB} \, L_{RB} \tag{3.3}$$

where K_{RB} is the capital charge against retail banking, β_{RB} the beta assigned to retail banking (0.12), and L_{RB} the total outstanding loans and advances (retail banking, non-risk weighted, and gross of provisions) averaged over the previous three years. Likewise, the capital charge for commercial banking is calculated as

$$K_{CB} = 0.035\, \beta_{CB}\, L_{CB} \tag{3.4}$$

where the subscript CB refers to commercial banking. Supervisors may allow the use of the alternative STA if it provides an improved basis for the calculation of the capital charge.

For a bank to be qualified for the use of the standardized approach, the supervisor must be satisfied that: (i) the board of directors and senior management are actively involved in operational risk management; (ii) the bank has an operational risk management system that is conceptually sound and implemented with integrity; and (iii) it has sufficient resources in the use of the approach in the major business lines and the audit areas. An internationally active bank must, for this purpose, satisfy the following additional criteria: (i) it must have an operational risk management system with clear responsibilities assigned to an operational risk management function; (ii) it must track, in a systematic way, relevant operational risk data (including material losses) by business lines; (iii) there must be regular reporting of operational risk exposures to business unit management, senior management, and the board of directors; (iv) the risk management system must be well documented; (v) the operational risk management processes must be subject to validation and regular independent review; and (vi) the operational risk assessment system must be subject to regular review by external auditors and/or supervisors.

A question may arise here as to the differences between the BIA and STA, given that both are based on gross income. Unlike the BIA, Dowd (2003) argues, the STA presupposes that operational risk is explicitly recognized and managed as a distinct and separate risk category. A second difference is, of course, the use of the business lines. The BIA treats the bank as a single entity, whereas the STA subdivides it into smaller units, the eight business lines.

3.4.3   The advanced measurement approach

The BCBS (2004a) suggests that if banks move from the BIA along a continuum toward the AMA, they will be rewarded with a lower capital charge. The BCBS makes it clear that the use of the AMA by a certain bank is subject to the approval of the supervisors. The regulatory capital requirement is calculated by using the bank's internal operational risk measurement system. The Committee considers insurance as a mitigator of operational risk only under the AMA. Under this approach, banks must quantify operational risk capital requirements for seven types of risk and eight business lines, a total of 56 separate estimates. These estimates are aggregated to a total operational risk capital requirement for the bank as a whole.

The AMA is more reflective of the actual operational risk taken by the bank. Unlike the other two approaches whereby regulatory capital increases as the business grows, the AMA recognizes the proposition that a business that keeps the level of controls consistent with its growth keeps its risk constant (which implies no automatic increase in regulatory capital against operational risk). The AMA also encompasses the expectation of regulators that a well-managed firm will be able to (i) identify its operational risk exposure and assess its potential impact; (ii) monitor and report its operational risk on an ongoing basis; and (iii) create proper incentives by factoring operational risk into its overall business strategy.

The Basel II accord allows three alternative approaches under the AMA: (i) the loss distribution approach (LDA); (ii) the scenario-based approach (SBA); and (iii) the scorecard approach (SCA), which is also called the risk drivers and controls approach (RDCA). An alternative version of the LDA is the internal measurement approach (IMA). The three approaches differ only in the emphasis on the information used to calculate regulatory capital. While the LDA depends on historical data, the SBA uses forward-looking "what-if" scenarios, but both of them utilize Monte Carlo simulations to estimate the capital charge. The SCA is based on a series of weighted questions whose answers yield scores for the allocation of the overall capital charge to individual business units. Unlike the other two approaches, the SCA reflects improvement in the control environment that reduces both the frequency and severity of operational losses

In order to qualify for the use of the AMA, a bank must demonstrate to the supervisor that as a minimum (i) the board of directors and senior management are actively involved in operational risk management; (ii) the availability and integrity of a sound operational risk management system; and (iii) the bank has sufficient resources in the use of the AMA in the major business lines as well as the control and audit areas.

Moreover, the BCSB (2004a) lists some qualitative and quantitative standards that a bank wishing to use the AMA must meet. The qualitative standards are the following:

1. The availability of an independent operational risk management function in charge of the design and implementation of the operational risk management framework.

2. The operational risk measurement system must be closely integrated into the day-to-day risk management process.

3. Regular reporting of operational risk exposures and losses to the management and the board.

4. The operational risk management system must be well documented.

5. Internal and external auditors must perform regular reviews of the operational risk measurement and management functions.

6. Supervisors and external auditors must verify that (i) the internal validation process is satisfactory, and (ii) operational risk data flows are transparent and accessible.

On the other hand, the quantitative standards are:

1. The operational risk measurement system must be consistent with the definition proposed by the Basel Committee.

2. Regulatory capital must be calculated as the sum of EL and UL, unless it can be demonstrated that the EL is adequately captured in the internal business practices (see Chapter 6 for some elaboration on this point).

3. The operational risk management system must be able to capture the major factors shaping the tail of the distribution of losses.

4. Regulatory capital must be calculated by adding up individual risk estimates (measures from various sources) unless it can be demonstrated that correlations are soundly determined and implemented with integrity.

5. The operational risk measurement system must have, as sound elements, the use of internal data, relevant external data, scenario analysis, as well as business environment and internal control factors.

6. The approach to weighting the elements of the operational risk management system must be credible, transparent, well documented, and verifiable.

The Basel II Accord identifies explicitly the properties of internal and external loss data that can be used to calculate regulatory capital against operational risk. Internal data must possess the following properties:

1. Internal loss data is most relevant when it is obviously linked to current business activities, technological processes, and risk management procedures.

2. A minimum five-year of internal loss data must be used to estimate operational risk for the purpose of calculating regulatory capital.

3. A sound internal data collection process must satisfy the following requirements: (i) documented objective criteria for allocating losses to the specified business line and event types; (ii) loss data must be comprehensive; (iii) information must pertain to more than gross loss amounts; (iv) criteria must be used for assigning loss data arising from

an event in a centralized function; and (v) operational risk losses related to credit risk are treated as credit risk, but operational risk losses that are related to market risk are treated as operational risk losses.

Presumably, the cause of the loss is the criterion used to distinguish between operational losses related to credit risk and those related to market risk. Thus, a loss resulting from default caused by the failure of a loan officer to follow the guidelines is an operational loss related to credit risk. On the other hand, a loss incurred because of a market downturn when a dealer has taken a position that is not allowed by the guidelines is an operational loss related to market risk. If there is no breach of guidelines (deliberate or otherwise), the losses are considered as resulting purely from credit risk and market risk. We will come back to this issue in Chapter 4.

The properties of external data as specified by the Accord are:

1. External data includes public data and pooled industry data (see Chapter 5 for a description of these two modes of external databases).

2. Used only when there is a reason to believe that the bank is exposed to infrequent yet potentially severe losses.

3. External data should be on (i) actual loss amounts, (ii) the scale of business operations where the event occurred, (iii) information on the causes and circumstances of the loss events, (iv) other information that can be used to assess the relevance of the loss event.

4. There must be a systematic process for determining the situations for which it can be used.

A bank adopting the AMA must use scenario analysis in conjunction with external data to evaluate its exposure to high-severity events (see Chapter 6 for more elaboration on scenario analysis). Moreover, scenario analysis should be used to assess the impact of deviations from the correlation assumptions embedded in the bank's operational risk measurement framework. In addition to using loss data, a bank's firm-wide risk assessment methodology must capture key business environment and internal control factors that can change its risk profile. This sounds as if using the AMA amounts to a combination of the LDA, SCA, and SBA rather than choosing one of them.

The Basel II Accord makes provisions for risk mitigation in conjunction with, and the partial use of, the AMA. As far as risk mitigation is concerned, a bank will be allowed to recognize the risk mitigating impact of insurance in the measures of operational risk used for regulatory minimum capital requirements. This will be limited to 20 percent of the total operational risk capital charge calculated under the AMA. The Basel II Accord also makes provisions for the partial use of the AMA, which refers

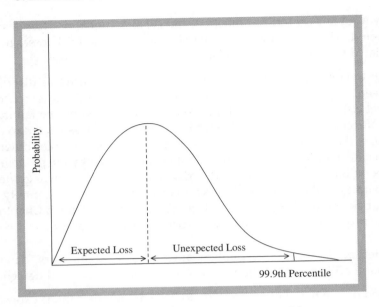

Figure 3.3 Expected and unexpected loss

to a situation when a bank is permitted to use the AMA for some parts of its operations and the BIA or STA for the remaining operations. It is allowed if: (i) all operational risks of the entire bank's operations are captured; and (ii) operations that are covered by the AMA meet the qualitative criteria for this approach, while those operations using a simpler approach meet its criteria.

Operational risk capital requirement under the AMA is the UL in the total loss distribution corresponding to a confidence level of 99.9 percent and a risk horizon of one year. Figure 3.3 shows the UL as the difference between the 99.9th percentile and the EL (which is the mean of the loss distribution). The 99.9th percentile is the loss that is greater than 99.9 percent and smaller than 0.1 percent of all potential losses, whereas the EL is the mean of the loss distribution. Losses below the EL should be covered by the general provisions, and losses above the 99.9th percentile could make a firm bankrupt. Capital charges (that is, regulatory capital) are to cover UL.

3.5 PILLAR 2

Pillar 2 of the Basel II Accord, which pertains to the supervisory review process, is designed to ensure that an operational risk framework has been developed within the firm and that the process is adequately audited and supervised. The BCBS (2004a) discusses the importance and principles of the supervisory review, pointing out the following:

1. The review process is designed to ensure that banks have adequate capital to support all the risks and to encourage them to develop better risk management techniques to monitor and mitigate risk.

2. Bank management continues to bear the responsibility for ensuring that banks have adequate capital to support its risks beyond the core minimum requirements.

3. Supervisors are expected to evaluate the banks' assessment of their capital needs relative to the risk they bear.

4. There is a relation between the amount of capital held against risk and the effectiveness of the risk management process.

5. There must be an assessment of compliance with the minimum standards and disclosure requirements of the more advanced methods in pillar 1.

6. Banks should have a process for assessing their overall capital adequacy in relation to their risk profile, as well as a strategy for maintaining their capital levels.

7. Supervisors should review and evaluate banks' internal capital adequacy assessment and strategies.

8. Supervisors should expect banks to operate above the minimum regulatory capital ratios and should have the ability to require banks to hold capital in excess of the minimum.

9. Supervisors should seek to intervene at an early stage to prevent capital from falling below the minimum levels required to support the risk characteristics of a particular bank. Rapid remedial action should be required if capital is not maintained or restored.

3.6   PILLAR 3

Pillar 3 is about market discipline, which may be defined as actions by shareholders to monitor and influence the behavior of entities to improve their performance (Bliss and Flannery, 2002). Pillar 3 is designed to complement the minimum capital requirements (pillar 1) and the supervisory review process (pillar 2). The Committee notes that the disclosure provided under pillar 3 is essential to ensure that market discipline is an effective complement to the other two pillars. The objective is to encourage market discipline by developing a set of disclosure requirements that allow market participants to assess key pieces of information on the scope of capital, risk exposure, risk assessment processes, and the capital adequacy of the institution. It is believed that such disclosures are particularly relevant because reliance on the internal methodologies gives banks more discretion in assessing capital requirements. The Committee has made a considerable effort to see that the narrower focus of pillar 3, which is aimed at disclosure of capital adequacy, does not conflict with the broader accounting requirements.

A bank should decide which disclosures are relevant to its operations on the basis of the materiality concept. Information would be regarded as "material" if its omission or misstatement could change or influence the assessment or decision of a user relying on that information for the purpose of making economic decisions. The disclosures set out in pillar 3 should be made on a semi-annual basis, subject to certain exceptions. Table 3.2 provides a summary of selected disclosure requirements as envisaged by the BCBS, which include qualitative and quantitative aspects of the disclosure.

Table 3.2 Selected disclosure requirements

Aspect of disclosure	Disclosure requirements
Scope of application: Qualitative	• Name of top corporate entity • Outline of differences in the basis of consolidation for accounting and regulatory purposes • Restrictions and impediments on the transfer of funds within the group
Scope of application: Quantitative	• Amount of surplus capital of insurance subsidiaries included in consolidated capital • Amount of capital deficiencies in all subsidiaries not included in the consolidation • Aggregate amounts of the firm's total interests in insurance entities
Capital: Qualitative	• Information on the terms and conditions of the main features of all capital instruments
Capital: Quantitative	• Paid up share capital/common stock • Reserves • Minority interest in the equity of subsidiaries • Innovative instruments • Other capital instruments • Surplus capital from insurance companies • Regulatory calculation differences deducted from capital • Other amounts deducted from capital, including goodwill and investments
Capital adequacy: Qualitative	• Discussion of the approach to assessing capital adequacy

(Continued)

Table 3.2 (*Continued*)

Aspect of disclosure	Disclosure requirements
Capital adequacy: Quantitative	• Capital requirements for credit risk • Capital requirements for market risk • Capital requirements for operational risk • Total and capital ratio (for significant subsidiaries)
Credit risk: Qualitative	• Definitions of past due • Description of approaches followed for specific and general allowances and statistical methods • Discussion of credit risk management policy • The nature of exposures within each portfolio that are subject to the standardized, foundation and the advanced IRB approaches
Credit risk: Quantitative	• Total gross credit risk exposures • Geographical distribution of credit exposures • Industry or counterparty type of exposures • Contractual maturity breakdown of portfolio • Amount of impaired loans • Reconciliation of changes in the allowances for loan impairment • The amount of exposures subject to the standardized, foundation and advanced IRB approaches
Market risk: Qualitative	• General qualitative disclosure requirement for market risk • For each portfolio covered by the IMA: (i) characteristics of the models used, (ii) stress testing, (iii) backtesting/validation • The scope of acceptance by the supervisor
Market risk: Quantitative	• Capital requirements for (i) interest rate risk, (ii) equity position, (iii) foreign exchange risk, (iv) commodity risk • For trading portfolios under the IMA: (i) high, mean, and low VAR values over the reporting period; (ii) a comparison of VAR estimates with actual gains/losses experienced by the bank
Operational risk: Qualitative	• The approaches for operational risk capital assessment • Description of the AMA • For banks using the AMA, a description of the use of insurance for risk mitigation

Source: BCBS (2004a)

3.7   A CRITICAL EVALUATION OF BASEL II

The Basel II Accord has attracted a lot of commentary from academics and practitioners. Between the time of the release of the first set of proposals in 1999 and the release of the 2004 document, several changes and revisions were introduced as a result of the comments received by the Committee and others appearing in the published literature and the media. In this section, selective views that collectively represent a critical evaluation of the Basel II Accord are presented. It must be emphasized here that the comments have been made on different versions of the Accord. Therefore, some of the comments pertain to a particular version of the Accord, but not to a subsequent one if the latter was amended as a result to deal with the point or points raised by the comment. However, most of the comments are valid for the general principles that are still embodied in the Accord.

To start with, one has to confront the basic question of why we need a capital accord, and why not rely on pure market forces to manage the banking system. The answer to this question must lie in the objective of consumer and systemic protection. A run on a bank causing private depositors to be out of pocket is politically unacceptable because it could destroy the public's confidence in the financial system upon which, according to Leddy (2003), the last 250 years of capitalist growth has been based. Banks, as we saw in Chapter 2, have special importance that distinguishes them from other firms (for more on banking regulation, see Chapter 9). In the following subsections, a critique of the Basel II Accord is presented as put forward by several authors.

3.7.1   The Danielsson et al. (2001) critique

Danielsson et al. (2001) concede that the Basel II Accord goes a long way toward addressing some of the main defects of the Basel I Accord by, for example, suggesting more risk-sensitive capital ratios, taking into account the increased importance of risk mitigation techniques, and emphasizing supervision and market discipline. However, they believe that the Accord fails to address many of the key deficiencies of the global financial regulatory system and even creates the potential for new sources of stability. Specifically, they put forward the following arguments:

■ The Accord fails to consider the fact that risk is endogenous (that is, the risk from shocks generated and amplified within the system as defined by Danielsson and Shin, 2003). Market volatility, they argue, is (at least in part) the outcome of interaction between market players, which makes it endogenous. This endogeneity may matter enormously in crises (see also Danielsson, 2001; Danielsson et al., 2002).

■ The VAR methodology, which is used extensively to calculate regulatory capital, can destabilize the economy, perhaps inducing crashes that could not happen in the absence of VAR-based regulation. VAR has been described as a misleading measure of risk when the returns are not normally distributed, which is typically the case with market risk, credit risk, and (particularly) operational risk. Furthermore, it does not mea-sure the distribution or the extent of risk in the tail, but only provides an estimate of a particular point in the distribution (see Chapter 1 for other defects of VAR).

■ The Basel Committee has chosen poor-quality measures of risk when better measures are available. Clearly, this criticism also refers to VAR.

■ Heavy reliance of the standardized approach to credit risk on credit rat-ing agencies is misguided because these agencies do not provide con-sistent estimates of creditworthiness. Moreover, they are not regulated, which casts doubt on the quality of their risk estimates. Danielsson et al. (2001) put forward the proposition that credit risk is not entirely captured by credit ratings, a view that is supported by the Economist (2005), which casts doubt on the ability of the rating agencies to provide reliable estimates of the PD, arguing that they missed the crises of Enron, WorldCom, and Parmalat. According to the Economist (2005), some of the problems with rating agencies are the lack of competition and the absence of outside scrutiny.

■ Operational risk modeling is not possible in the absence of comprehen-sive databases, even if a meaningful and satisfactory definition of operational risk does exist (which, many argue, is not the case, as we are going to see in Chapter 4). Any estimation of operational risk is bound to be hampered by the absence of data and a proper definition. Even if we subscribe to the extremely optimistic view that databases on well-defined operational risk losses will be available in the near future, the nature of rare high-severity losses renders them very different from the loss data available on market risk and credit risk.

■ There is yet no convincing argument for the need to regulate activities with respect to operational risk. That is, they believe, it is not easy to justify the holding of capital against operational risk. In contrast to market and credit risk, operational risk is predominantly idiosyncratic, which means that there is no need to regulate it in order to prevent contagion. Any losses created by operational events accrue directly to a particular firm and do not spread to other firms. This point boils down to the proposition that if capital adequacy requirements exist to rule out systemic failures through contagious bank failures (as what could happen through credit risk) then there is no point imposing capital requirements against operational risk. However, the claim that operational risk is idiosyncratic and not contagious is questionable, as we are going to see in Chapter 4. Actually, it sounds rather strange that a credit loss event could affect other banks but an operational loss event (resulting, for example, from the overindulgence of a rogue trader) would be benign as far as other banks are concerned.

This is indeed a strange argument and gross misrepresentation of operational risk (see Moosa, 2007).

■ Given the belief that financial regulation is inherently procyclical, the Basel II Accord will exacerbate the procyclical tendencies significantly, making the financial system more susceptible to crises. This point is also made by Goodhart, Hofmann, and Segoviano (2004) who argue that the regulation of bank capital in the form of capital adequacy requirements is procyclical and may therefore amplify business cycle fluctuations and that the Basel II Accord may considerably accentuate the procyclicality of the regulatory system.

Furthermore, Danielsson and Zigrand (2003) argue that although risk-sensitive regulation can reduce systemic risk, this is accomplished at the expense of poor risk sharing, an increase in risk premia, higher asset price volatility, lower liquidity, more comovements in prices and the chance that markets may not clear. By analyzing VAR-based regulatory regimes within a multi-asset general equilibrium model, they also show that systemic risk may become more severe as a result of regulation if too many firms are left outside the regime (which would be the case under Basel II). Danielsson (2003) argues that the implementation of Basel II carries with it "a host of potentially perverse side effects".

3.7.2 The Kaufman (2003) critique

In his evaluation of the Basel II Accord, Kaufman (2003) focuses on pillars 2 and 3, which have received far less attention than pillar 1. He concludes that pillars 2 and 3 have major design flaws that make the achievement of the capital requirements determined by pillar 1 questionable. These flaws, the argument goes, help explain why US regulators decided to limit the mandatory application of Basel II to only the ten or so largest internationally active US banks and why these requirements may be ineffective even for these banks. Kaufman (p. 2) puts forward the strong statement that "although Basel II roared loudly when proposed, it is likely to have only a relatively minor lasting effect on the capital of at least most U.S. banks".

Furthermore, Kaufman (2003) finds it rather strange that the credit risk exposure of banks (which are widely assumed to be the beneficiaries of private information on their loan customers) is measured by the ratings assigned to their public debt traded on the capital market, which has little (if any) private information. He also questions the validity of the IRB approach, although he admits that it overcomes some of the criticism of Basel I. In particular, he believes that the loss rates determined by the regulators are subject to large errors, whereas the internal models are likely to be too complex for supervisors to understand. Hence, he concludes that the resulting regulatory capital will be difficult to evaluate for adequacy and compliance with the requirements.

Kaufman also raises several questions about the definition and measurement of capital. For example, he wonders what capital is for the purpose of implementing the Basel II Accord and whether or not dividing capital into tiers is appropriate. He also raises a question about the relation between capital and loan loss reserves and another on how loss reserves are to be determined over the business cycle. In Kaufman's view, these questions are of critical importance because failure to consider the underlying issues weakens significantly the usefulness of the recommendations. Similar arguments can be found in Shadow Financial Regulatory Committee (2000); Laeven and Majnoni (2003); and Borio, Furfine, and Lowe (2001).

A particular criticism is directed at pillar 3, which is intended to complement pillars 1 and 2. Lopez (2003) argues that the requirements for effective market discipline are not discussed in as much detail as what information on a bank's financial and risk positions need to be disclosed to the public. But Kaufman (2003) argues that disclosure and transparency constitute a necessary but not sufficient condition for effective market discipline. Shareholders not at risk, Kaufman argues, would have little or no incentive to monitor and influence their banks, and thus have little if any use for the information disclosed about the financial performance of banks. He concludes that while market discipline is likely to encourage it, disclosure on its own is less likely to produce market discipline in the absence of a significant number of at-risk shareholders.

3.7.3 The Fischer (2002) critique

Fischer (2002) argues that Basel II has the potential to improve significantly risk management practices in banking systems around the world and that in doing so it should also boost the efficiency of the financial system. But Fischer also makes a point about correlations, by saying that risk should not be measured by the variability of the return on a particular asset but rather by the covariance of the return with the market portfolio. This simple point bears on one of the key concerns that internationally active banks have about Basel II. He also argues that certain elements of Basel II will pose difficulties for banks and supervisors in emerging market economies, which the Basel Committee needs to take into account for the purpose of encouraging countries to make the move to the new regime. He predicts that the Accord will likely affect the banks operating in emerging markets (local banks and internationally active banks) differently.

Fischer (2002) discusses in detail the potential implications of Basel II in emerging countries. In particular, he seems to be concerned about the ability of supervisory authorities in many emerging and developing countries to meet the standards set by Basel II. The greatest concern, he argues, pertains to the reliance on external rating agencies in the standardized approach to the calculation of regulatory capital. Because domestic credit rating agencies are not well developed in many non-OECD countries, most domestic credit risks will be in the unrated 100 percent category, which could reduce the risk-sensitivity of Basel II relative to Basel I. Another consequence of putting most domestic credit risks in the unrated category would be that better-rated borrowers in those countries could borrow at lower cost from international than from local banks, which leaves domestic banks at a competitive disadvantage (with respect to lending to high-quality borrowers) in their own countries. This issue has led to calls for an interim standard between Basel I and Basel II (perhaps Basel 1.5?) that would afford domestic banks in emerging countries some of the benefits, but less of the costs, of Basel II.

Another issue that Fischer (2002) discusses is the impact of the Basel II Accord on internationally active banks. Under Basel II, the largest internationally active banks in developed countries will adopt one of the IRB approaches to credit risk, most likely the advanced option. This means that in their operations in emerging countries, these banks will operate under a different system than the domestic banks, which leads to concerns about competitive equity. In lending to lower-grade local borrowers, local banks will have less stringent capital requirements than their more sophisticated international competitors. Fischer also raises the related question of how emerging market operations of banks will be supervised under Basel II. In an ideal scenario, he argues, home and host supervisors will work well together, such that their respective regimes will rarely come into conflict. In reality, he believes, it is difficult to foresee things running quite so smoothly. Basel II, therefore, is unlikely to create a "level playing field", but rather an uneven one, which is the inevitable result of allowing different regulatory standards to be applied to different banks.

3.7.4 The Herring (2002) critique

One aspect of the evaluation of Basel II pertains to the use of internal models, which, according to Herring (2002), is expected to deliver the following benefits: (i) it would reduce or eliminate incentives for regulatory arbitrage since the capital charge would reflect the bank's own estimate of risk; (ii) it would deal in a more flexible manner with financial innovations, incorporating them in the regulatory framework as soon as they are embodied in the bank's own risk management models; (iii) it would provide banks with an incentive to improve their risk management processes and procedures in order to qualify for the internal models approach; and

(iv) compliance cost would be reduced to the extent that the business is regulated in the same way that it is managed. Indeed, it is the success of the internal models approach to market risk that led to the extension of the methodology to credit risk. The problem is that the internal models are insufficiently reliable to replicate the approach to operational risk. This point has been raised by the Shadow Financial Regulatory Committee (2001), Altman and Saunders (2001), and Llewellyn (2001).

Herring (2002) believes that the attempt to set capital charges for operational risk is "fundamentally misguided". The Basel Committee hopes that, by imposing a risk-sensitive capital requirement for operational risk, firms will be compelled to enhance the measurement and management of operational risk and discouraged from substituting operational risk for credit or market risk. The objective has been to set capital charges for operational risk in conjunction with an anticipated reduction in the capital charge for credit risk, so that overall capital charges will remain the same on average. However, Herring argues that in contrast to credit risk and market risk, there is no compelling rationale for setting a capital charge for operational risk. This is, he argues, because institutions can increase the option value of deposit insurance by taking bigger market or credit risks, since higher risks may yield higher returns. Risk-sensitive capital requirements, therefore, have a direct impact on incentives to take greater risks. But, the argument goes, operational risk is downside risk only, which means that more operational risk does not enhance the option value of deposit insurance. Again, the proposition that operational risk is one-sided is not really valid, as we are going to see in Chapter 4.

Herring (2002) further argues that it is by no means clear that capital regulation is the most efficient means of achieving reduction in exposure to operational risk, and that there is no systemic risk rationale for imposing capital requirements because losses due to operational risk tend to be to a particular institution (which is the point raised by Danielsson et al., 2001 that we tend to dispute). Since the sort of destructive operational risk losses that have occurred (often due to the actions of a rogue trader) are usually due to failure of internal controls rather than inadequate capital, it makes a lot of sense to think that no reasonable amount of capital would be sufficient to cover extreme events of this sort. According to Herring, the most effective means of reducing operational risk are sound policies, practices and procedures, as well as insurance (see Calomiris and Herring [2002] for an extension of the argument to the case of investment management companies).

A particular problem with the last argument pertains to the use of insurance as a substitute for capital, as we are going to see in Chapter 8. Another problem is that risk mitigation and risk financing are not mutually exclusive. Rather, they are complementary: what is wrong with imposing controls and at the same time set aside capital just in case someone is clever enough to evade these controls and inflict serious damage on the firm. In the aftermath of Barings, banks worldwide started to impose sizeable controls on traders' activities. This, however, did not stop John Rusnak inflicting serious damage on the bank he worked for, seven years after the collapse of Barings. Herring's argument is flawed because (i) it is based on the improper characterization of operational risk as being one-sided and idiosyncratic, and (ii) it confuses prevention with cure. Yes, setting aside capital against operational risk will not prevent another Nick Leeson from surfacing somewhere, but it might make the difference between survival and otherwise, should a Nick Leeson-type trader inflict serious damage on a bank.

Like others, Herring (2002) casts doubt on the usefulness of the BIA to calculate the capital charge as a percentage of gross income (defined to include net interest income and net noninterest income, but exclude extraordinary or irregular items). Herring argues that it is doubtful if this indicator captures even the scale of an institution's operations adequately. He believes that it has no tenuous link to the risk of an EL due to internal or external events. While these points are valid, Dowd (2003) argues that gross income is "the least worst [bad] option available", because (i) it is a reasonably reliable indicator of the size of activities; (ii) it is readily available; (iii) it is verifiable; (iv) it is reasonably consistent and comparable across jurisdictions; and (v) it has the advantage of being countercyclical. This is, therefore, an issue of pragmatism versus misrepresentation.

As far as the standardized approach is concerned, Herring argues that the losses revealed by the quantitative impact study of the Basel Committee (referring to QIS2) do not necessarily reflect differences in risk. This is because (i) frequent small losses tend to be expensed, which means that they do not contribute to the risk for which capital is held; and (ii) the loss data does not reflect recoveries and indemnification from insurance.

Herring's criticism of the AMA is based on the argument that the approach "requires multiple pages of preconditions that most institutions could not be expected to meet for years". He also argues that neither the BIA nor the standardized approach provides a persuasive way of relating capital charges to actual differences in operational risk across firms, whereas the AMA remains to be fully specified.

What is more fundamental, as far as Herring is concerned, is that it is not clear why the Basel Committee insists on dealing with operational risk under pillar 1, which means that it is an issue of capital adequacy. In Herreing's view, this is rather strange given that interest rate risk in the banking book, which is easier to quantify than operational risk, is dealt with only under pillar 2, as a supervisory issue. He insists that pillar 2 is the most efficient way of dealing with internal events, and that insurance is the most effective way of dealing with external events. He believes that dealing with operational risk under pillar 1 may end up distorting competition further. This view is also presented in an article in Regulation (2001), citing the critics as saying that "the committee's reliance on capital charges to mitigate unexpected operational losses undermines the other two pillars of supervision". These critics, according to the article, argue that "a combination of well-designed systems and controls, and insurance that satisfies minimum requirements, is a reasonable substitute to regulatory capital for mitigating operational risk". Finally, Herring believes that supervisors will be able only to impose an additional capital charge if they find policies, processes and procedures to be inadequate. However, they will not reduce the capital charge for firms that have exemplary controls.

3.7.5 The Pezier (2003b) critique

Pezier (2003b) presents a rather comprehensive review of the Basel II Accord, particularly, the operational risk proposals. To start with, he believes that the documents published by the BCBS give the impression that the Basel Committee strives to reconcile multiple conflicting objectives and constrains. In this respect, he makes the following points:

- The Committee wants to leave the overall level of capital requirements more or less unchanged while introducing more comprehensive and risk-sensitive methods for calculating these requirements.

- The need to remedy accounting inadequacies, meaning that some EL are not recognized under the current accounting standards.

- An overwhelming desire to rely on objective inputs and methods to facilitate the role of the supervisors, which may be over-ambitious when dealing with rare events.

- The need to provide a menu of methodologies that are accessible to a wide range of financial institutions with different types of activities, sizes, and degrees of sophistication.

- The desire to provide incentives for better risk management, which translates into reduced capital charges for insinuations that qualify for the use of more advanced risk assessment methodologies.

Pezier further raises the question whether the advanced approaches assist better operational risk management, which means that all banks should put into place an advanced methodology. He also wonders if the imposition of capital charges is largely irrelevant to the task of managing operational risk. Further points raised by Pezier are as follows:

- The connection between gross income and operational risk is loose: gross income is about the past whereas operational risk is about the future. Instead, he advocates the use of operating expenses because it is more related to operational risk than to credit or market risk. He also questions the linearity assumption when larger firms should be expected to have better operational risk management and thus subject to less operational risk.

■ Although the STA is subject to eligibility criteria, it does not appear to be significantly more risk-sensitive than the BIA. It offers neither any hope of a reduction in capital charges compared to the BIA, nor any incentive for better risk management.

■ The two simple approaches may have the consequence that banks may retain more operational risk than before the imposition of capital charges. The new capital buffer may lead to complacency that takes the form of refraining from covering risk with traditional insurance products.

■ The Basel II Accord seems to allow "cherry picking" of the methodologies according to business lines. This means that a bank could select the BIA for some marginal business line, the STA for other lines, and the AMA for some core activities. However, Pezier provides no explanation, of why this "cherry picking" represents a problem.

■ There is no point in trying to assess operational risk separately from other risks. All major costs and revenues attached to a particular activity and their variability should be assessed, otherwise there cannot be any sensible risk management. This argument is for an integrated risk management approach, but it is not obvious how the three kinds of risk can be assessed collectively.

■ Business and reputational risks, which are not recognized by Basel II (as they are excluded from the BCBS's definition of operational risk), may be more significant than the direct operational losses that the banking industry has been asked to monitor. Those risks are left out not because they are small but because they are difficult to assess. This is definitely a valid point, which we shall return to when we discuss the concept of operational risk in Chapter 4.

■ The data that banks are asked to collect is defined in an arbitrary manner, one-sided and incomplete and therefore incapable of being assessable into a meaningful whole. In a survey, Raft International (2002) has shown that only a minority of banks collect internal loss data in a systematic way. Subscription to external databases seems to be motivated solely by the desire to appear compliant with the Basel quantitative standards for using the AMA.

■ It is doubtful if Basel II is going to be feasible in terms of costs and benefits. As is the case with any regulatory exercise, this point makes a lot of sense.

Pezier argues that banks have natural incentives to improve the quality of their risk management and that there are many institutions (such as universities and professional bodies) that strive to carry out research and promote knowledge. Therefore, he wonders, why is the BCBS in a privileged position to carry out this role? This view seems to be skeptical of the viability of the BCBS itself, which cannot be discarded altogether. It sounds familiar for some one who is aware of the views of the International Monetary Fund (IMF) skeptics. The problem here is that there are more reasons to criticize the IMF than the Basel Committee on the grounds of their contribution to "human welfare".

3.7.6   The practitioners' view

The issue of disclosure and market discipline (pillar 3) has sparked significant debate and responses from practitioners. Atkins (2003) of Wells Fargo stated that "disclosures will create an uneven playing field between banks and their nonbank competitors, who will be free to pursue their business activities unencumbered by supervisory capital rules and the excessive compliance costs that they will engender". Thomson (2003) of Citigroup made the point that "requiring disclosures related to operational risk could harm banks when attempting to negotiate insurance policies that could be used as a risk mitigation strategy." And Edelson (2003) of JPMorganChase argued that "the disclosure requirement will create a situation where the data they disclose could be subject to misinterpretation that could only be addressed by disclosing more information, and the resulting burden will be costly".

The practitioners are not only skeptical about pillar 3, but rather they subscribe to most of the views surveyed earlier, including those pertaining to pillars 1 and 2. It has been said that Basel II could, at worst, blow up one or two European banking systems (The Economist, 2003). In a survey of 70 bankers worldwide conducted by the Centre for the Study of Financial Innovation (2002), the participants expressed the view that Basel II is "dangerous and complex". But it is not only the provisions of the Basel II Accord that raise concern in the financial community. The implementation of the Accord seems to be rather controversial, and this is what we will examine in the final section of this chapter.

3.8   IMPLEMENTATION OF THE BASEL II ACCORD

The original objective was to make the Accord available for implementation at the end of 2006. Although the 2005 document (BCBS, 2005b) emphasized what it called "the effective cross-border implementation" of the accord, a lot of flexibility has been shown with respect to the implementation date. For example, in November 2005, the Committee declared that "one further year of impact studies or parallel calculations will be needed for the most advanced approaches, and these will be available for implementation as of year-end 2007". The Committee also declared that "the document is being circulated to supervisory authorities worldwide with a view to encouraging them to consider adopting this revised framework at such time as they believe is consistent with their broader supervisory priorities". Similar statements are made in BCBS (2006a).

3.8.1   The US decision on implementation

Perhaps an important reason for the delay in the implementation of the Accord was the September 2005 announcement of the U.S. (represented by the four federal agencies responsible for regulating bank: the Federal Reserve, the Federal Deposit Insurance Corporation (FDIC), the Office of the Comptroller of the Currency, and the Office of Thrift Supervision) that implementation would be postponed by a year to January 2008. According to Ho (2006), the decision to delay the implementation of the Accord came in the aftermath of the fourth quantitative impact study early in 2005, showing a larger than expected drop in regulatory capital for the banks implementing the advanced IRB approach, which prompted smaller banks to complain that they would be at a competitive disadvantage.

Ho further argues that the Federal Reserve never had the intention of delaying implementation and that the decision was taken only after disagreement with the FDIC, which tends to represent the interest of small banks. Rowe (2005) makes this explicit by saying that it was largely in defense of the power of the small bank lobby that the U.S. chose to diverge from the EU's across-the board application of Basel II. He further explains that "the small banks are well connected with the local politicians and thereby exercise significant influence in Washington, especially in the House of Representatives". The primary concern of smaller banks seems to be that larger rivals would be able to reduce their minimum required capital for credit risk through the sophisticated IRB models, which are beyond the reach of smaller banks. Moreover, smaller banks seem to believe that using the standardized approach would result in a higher capital requirement against operational risk, leaving them at a competitive disadvantage vis-à-vis larger banks.

It is reported that the delay of implementation has created uncertainty among US banks and overseas regulators. Furthermore, it is believed that the delay raises questions about how supervisors will approach the home/host regulators issue and how they will validate the models of the internationally active banks that apply the advanced IRB approach. This delay has also created fears about the so-called "staggered implementation", which refers to implementation at different dates by the U.S. and the EU. In November 2005, the Institute of International Finance (IIF) released a report in which it warned that "any further delays in implementing the Basel II capital accord would cause serious problems". At around the same time, the chairman of the IIF's Regulatory Capital Committee described (the problem of) staggered implementation as "the most important issue", stating that "any more delay would be a mistake". Moreover, Imeson (2006b) cites John Hawke, the US Comptroller of the Currency until 2004, as saying that "because the US has delayed its Basel programme by a year, and made some other changes to its US rules, the entire project should be delayed worldwide". He further warns that "a chaotic situation will arise if implementation goes ahead in other countries a year before the US" because "US banks with operations abroad and foreign banks with operations in the US will potentially be caught in crossfire between their host and home country regulators".

3.8.2 Effective cross-border implementation

The November 2005 document (BCBS, 2005b) outlines a framework for effective cross-border implementation of Basel II. It is anticipated that the home regulator should take the lead in the validation of models, and any question from the host regulator should be directed to the home supervisor rather than to the bank. The Basel Committee recognizes the important role that home country supervisors play in leading the enhanced co-operation between home and host country supervisors, which will be required for effective implementation. While bankers and regulators agree with the general principles of Basel II, none seems to be confident how it will work, given differences in the implementation timing between Europe/Asia and the U.S. For example, it would be problematical for a British bank with a US subsidiary to implement the advanced IRB approach from January 2008 across its international operations, either because t he bank itself wants to avoid duplication of work on the implementation or because the home regulator wants to eliminate the potential for regulatory arbitrage by making sure that the switch by a bank to the advanced IRB approach across its businesses happens all at once.

In general, six principles govern practical co-operation between supervisors:

1. Basel II will not change the legal responsibilities of national supervisors for the regulation of domestic firms or the existing arrangements for consolidated supervision.

2. The home country supervisor is responsible for the oversight of the implementation of Basel II for a banking group on a consolidated basis.

3. Host country supervisors, particularly where banks operate as subsidi-aries, have requirements that need to be understood or recognised.

4. Of high importance is enhanced and pragmatic co-operation among supervisors with legitimate interests. The home country supervisor should lead the co-ordination exercise.

5. To reduce the implementation burden on banks and conserve supervi-sory resources, supervisors should (whenever possible) avoid the per-formance of redundant and unco-ordinated approval and validation work.

6. In implementing Basel II, supervisors should communicate the roles of home country and host country supervisors as clearly as possible to banking groups with significant cross-border operations.

In its strive to achieve a consistent implementation of the Basel II across borders through enhanced supervisory co-operation, the Committee has created the Accord Implementation Group (AIG), which serves as a forum on implementation matters. The AIG discusses issues of mutual concern with supervisors from non-member countries through contacts with regional associates as well as the Core Principles Liaison Group. This is felt to be necessary because a consequence of Basel II is to approve the use of approaches and models in multiple jurisdictions.

3.8.3   Geographical differences in implementation

Some observers argue that the BCBS gives so much latitude to individual countries that the implementation of the Accord will differ from one coun-try to another. We have already seen the differences between the United States and the European Union. This, with other examples, have led Imeson (2006b) to conclude that "it looks as though it will become another example of disunity among nations and a monument to discord".

The problem is that without flexibility, the agreement would not have been signed, but this flexibility means it will be applied around the world inconsistently, which means that there is the danger of the Accord becom-ing a "sad case of banking discord", as Imeson (2006b) puts it. Further-more, Imeson identifies five areas of inconsistencies: (i) each country can implement a different version of Basel II; (ii) each country has a different time table for implementation; (iii) each country is likely to have different home-host methods of banking supervision; (iv) emerging countries are not bound by any time table and might not implement Basel II; and (v) in the EU, which has transposed Basel II into law through the Capital Require-ments Directive (CRD), each country can implement a different version of the directive. Imeson (2006b) discusses these issues by citing the views of some important international figures, reaching the following conclusions:

- The adoption of inconsistent versions of Basel II could ultimately disrupt its successful implementation, undermine its basic fabric and create serious level playing field issues.

- The only solution is for the Basel Committee is to delay implementation worldwide to fit in with the U.S.

- Different approaches to the implementation of Basel II will prove costly to banks that are active in more than one market.

- Although emerging countries are encouraged to adopt Basel II eventually, the time table does not apply to them and, in practice, most will use the less sophisticated Basel II approaches or stay on Basel I indefinitely.

- By allowing a number of national discretions, the CRD will have a disruptive effect on the implementation of Basel II.

Geographical differences are not limited to the U.S. and the EU. Take, for example, the implementation process in Australia and Asia at large. In Australia, the Australian Prudential Regulatory Authority (APRA) announced in September 2004 that Basel II would apply eventually to all Australian deposit-taking institutions, including banks, building societies, credit unions, and specialist credit-card issuers. These institutions will be required to meet the capital requirements of Basel II from 1 January 2008, whereas their prudential reporting for the quarter ending 31 March 2008 will be based on the requirements of the framework. On the other hand, a study of the Asian approach to Basel II shows that the "widespread non-risk culture at the majority of banks in Asia over the years has meant that progress towards Basel II compliance is inevitably slow and patchy" (Crooke, 2006). The study talks about evidence for marked differences across Asia in the progress of both individual banks and whole jurisdictions in preparing for and implementing Basel II.

3.9   WHAT IS NEXT?

This book is about operational risk management, not about Basel II as such. But it is impossible to talk about operational risk without talking about Basel II, because it sets the rules for the calculation of the capital charge against operational risk. Furthermore, operational risk is related to, and overlaps with, credit risk and market risk, and this is why the brief discussion of how Basel II deals with credit risk and market risk presented in this chapter is warranted.

From Chapter 4 onward, it is all about operational risk. The starting point is the concept of operational risk and how it differs from, and relates to, market risk and credit risk. This will be the subject matter of Chapter 4. Chapter 5 deals with what constitutes operational risk and operational loss events.

The Concept of Operational Risk

4.1 AN ANECDOTAL DESCRIPTION OF OPERATIONAL RISK

What is common between Nick Leeson and John Rusnak? Do they in any way have anything in common with Saddam Hussein? What is common among rogue trading, fraud, theft, computer hacking, industrial espionage, the onslaught of computer viruses, threats to personal privacy, loss of reputation, loss of key staff members, and the loss of information technology infrastructure? What is common among what happened to the Bank for Credit and Commerce International (BCCI) in 1993, Barings Bank in 1995, Diawa Securities in 1995, Bank of America in 2001, the Allied Irish Bank in 2002, the Central Bank of Iraq in 2003, and the Central Bank of Brazil in 2005? And what is common among Enron, Arthur Andersen, WorldCom, and HealthSouth? The general answer is simple: the names, (mal)practices, and events pertain to operational losses resulting from exposure to operational risk. To see the connections, let us examine these questions in turn.

What is common between Nick Leeson and John Rusnak, who have become notorious celebrities, is that they were rogue traders, whose activities destroyed or severely damaged the health of the banks they worked for. Nick Leeson was indulged in unauthorized and undeclared trading activities that proved fatal to the long-run survival of Barings Bank that (thanks mainly to Mr Lesson's "dubious" trading) incurred losses totaling $1.6 billion in 1995. By indulging in similar activities (though in different markets), John Rusnak incurred losses amounting to $640 million for the Allied Irish Bank in 2002. The second question about what is common between these rogue traders and Saddam Hussein will be answered later.

While the Leeson and Rusnak cases of rogue trading have been widely publicized, operational risk pertains to more than rogue trading, which brings about the third and fourth questions. The risk of fraud, and other misdeeds are kinds of operational risk that could give rise to operational losses. What happened to those financial institutions in those years was that they incurred huge operational losses due to rogue trading, involvement in illegal activities (drugs, etc.), and management incompetence. It is all about incurring operational losses due to an event triggered by malpractices and other forms of operational failure.

Before answering the question about the Saddam Hussein connection, we will examine fraud as a major source of operational losses. It is fraud in particular that put an end to the spectacular success of Enron, Arthur Andersen, WorldCom, and HealthSouth. Once upon a time, Enron was a high flying energy company, Arthur Andersen was one of the leading accounting firms, WorldCom was famous for its boldness in telecommunication, and HealthSouth was a growing firm in the health service industry. Because of fraud, Enron and Arthur Andersen have gone the way of the dinosaurs, WorldCom has made it to the *Guinness Book of Records* as the largest accounting fraud ever, and HealthSouth would make people raise eyebrows and drop jaws because of the number of senior officers who actively participated in fraud. It is not greed on its own that leads to corruption but, as Schofield (2003) puts it, "greed coupled with a weak or completely absent sense of moral compass in the leaders in these organizations".

Things, it seems, change over time, as the demise of Arthur Andersen came after glorious history that started with a 1914 event involving Andersen, the founder of the firm. What happened then was that a railroad executive demanded the approval of his books by the auditors. Andersen refused to comply, having discovered that the railroad firm was inflating its profits. Noncompliance with the railroad executive's demand cost Andersen an important client but gained him a reputation for integrity that made his firm one of the top accounting firms. It was also fraud and involvement in criminal activity that brought about the end of the BCCI, which as a result lost the name "Bank for Credit and Commerce International" to the name "Bank for Crooks and Criminals International" (Gup, 2000).

So where does Saddam Hussein fit in? Unlike many others, Nick and John did not receive bribes or kickbacks from the UN–Saddam food-for-oil program, neither did they do any nuclear physics or microbiology work for him. The two rogue traders are (or were) certainly not similar to Saddam in that they did not commit genocide, neither did they launch wars against neighboring countries (they were not in a position to do that, anyway). But it is true that the trio have something in common: Nick, John, and Saddam appear on the operational loss databases in three high-profile operational loss events. Yes, Saddam was no rogue trader, but he was reported to have been responsible for the biggest operational loss the

Central Bank of Iraq (or any bank for that matter, central or otherwise) has suffered by initiating the biggest bank "robbery" ever. In March 2003, on the eve of the US invasion of Iraq, Saddam sent his son to the Central Bank of Iraq with a letter ordering the governor to surrender an amount of cash reported to have been $1 billion. Actually, the exact amount demanded by Saddam was $980 million and $100 million according to Saddam's letter (Ellis, 2006). It was, therefore, not a bank robbery in the same sense as the gang that dug a tunnel leading to the vaults of the Central Bank of Brazil and managed to snatch the equivalent of $80 million, but both of the episodes represent operational loss events resulting from external fraud. The answer to the second question, therefore, is that the three initiated operational loss events, and this is what is common among them. There is one difference, however: unlike Saddam Hussein, Nick Leeson and John Rusnak were involved in internal fraud.

4.2   THE INCREASING IMPORTANCE OF OPERATIONAL RISK

Operational risk has been receiving increasingly significant media attention, as financial scandals have appeared regularly. The trend toward greater dependence on technology, greater competition among banks, and globalization have left the banking industry more exposed to operational risk than ever before. Buchelt and Unteregger (2004) argue that the risk of fraud and external events (such as natural disasters) have been around ever since the beginning of banking but it is technological progress that has boosted the potential of operational risk. Likewise, Halperin (2001) argues that "operational risk has traditionally occupied a netherworld below market and credit risk" but "headline-grabbing financial fiascos, decentralized control, the surge in e-commerce and the emergence of new products and business lines have raised its profile".

Apart from the examples of operational losses presented in the previous section, other notable examples (which are not related to rogue trading) include the $484 million settlement due to misleading sales practices at Household Finance and the estimated $140 million loss stemming from the 9/11 attack at the Bank of New York. While losses like the $1.6 billion suffered by Barings in 1995 capture most of the attention, operational losses are more widespread than what is commonly believed, and these events are by no means a recent phenomenon. Recently, Lynn (2006) reported the results of two surveys: the February 2006 payment risk survey of more than 350 companies and the US Federal Bank and Regulatory 2004 loss collection exercise. The first survey showed that 68 percent of the respondents experienced payments fraud and that 54 percent of the companies made significant changes to their payments controls. The second survey showed that the 23 participating banks reported 10,000 loss events worth almost

$15 billion. About 74 percent of these losses were attributed to external fraud or execution, process or product management. Beales (2006) reports the results of a survey of 67 financial institutions conducted by International Swaps and Derivatives Association (ISDA), which showed that one in every five credit derivatives trades made by the big dealers initially contained mistakes. Improper documentation seems to be a major hazard in this business. Finally, Groenfeldt (2006) reports the results of a 2005 survey of 76 large pension funds and non-profit organizations worldwide. The results of this survey showed that although market risk remained a chief concern, 80 percent of the participants planned to spend more time to "grasp and tame operational risk".

Strongly supported by the Barings Bank fiasco, Blunden (2003) argues that operational risk is as likely to bring a company to its knees as a market collapse, and in many cases it is clearly within management control (definitely so in the Barings case), but it is not fully understood or exploited. While market risk has traditionally caught the attention of financial institutions, operational risk is increasingly considered more seriously, perhaps even regarded as being more detrimental than market risk. Furthermore, a study of large operational loss events in the US by Cummins, Lewis, and Wei (2006) and Wei (2006) show that a bank (or a financial institution in general) can suffer a market value decline in the days surrounding the announcement of a large loss that is significantly larger than the loss itself.

Financial institutions (and firms in general) take on operational risk in running their daily business. The following are examples of common ways of taking operational risk:

- The use of sophisticated techniques for mitigating credit risk and market risk such as collateralization.

- The use of netting, credit derivatives, and asset securitization.

- Trading activities in increasingly complex products or those based upon complex arbitrage strategies lead to significant exposure to operational risk.

- Any form of disintermediation implies that those acting in the capacity of agents take operational risk instead of the mediated credit or market risks.

Dowd (2003) attributes the increasing significance of operational risk to some developments that appear to have boosted the likelihood of operational loss events. These developments include:

- The growth of e-commerce, which brings with it operational risk resulting from exposure to external fraud and system security risks.

■ Large-scale mergers, demergers, and consolidations.

■ The use of automated technology, which creates high-impact system failure risk.

■ The growing use of outsourcing arrangements and participation in clearing and settlement systems.

■ The growing trend for banks to act as large-volume service providers, insourcing back and middle office functions.

Likewise, Mestchian (2003) attributes the growing level of interest in operational risk management to the following factors:

1. Increasing complexity of financial assets and trading procedures, particularly the rapid growth of financial engineering and the resulting derivative products.

2. Introduction of regulatory capital requirement by regulators.

3. General acceptance by business leaders of the proposition that operational risk management procedures are still inadequate.

4. The development of sophisticated statistical techniques that can be applied to the measurement of operational risk.

Mestchian's second point about the role of the regulators has also been raised by Hubner, Laycock, and Peemoller (2003) who attribute the greater interest of the regulators in operational risk to the changing risk profile of the financial services sector for many reasons including the growth in e-business activity and reliance on technology. The BCBS (1999) expressed the view that operational risk is "sufficiently important for banks to devote the necessary resources to quantify". As we have seen from the history of the Basel Committee and its work, emphasis was initially placed on market risk, then it shifted to credit risk, but most of the emphasis in the Basel II Accord seems to be placed on operational risk. In the UK, the BCCI and Barings cases generated the political impetus for the transfer of banking supervision from the Bank of England to the newly created regulator, the Financial Services Authority. Operational risk has struck a fundamental part of doing business, and as such it cannot be eliminated completely. For this reason, financial institutions and supervisors have a common interest in identifying, measuring, monitoring, and controlling operational risk.

It is perhaps appropriate to close this section with some light-hearted remarks about the reasons for interest in operational risk. Ong's (2002) top three of the updated list of the "top 10 reasons why so many people are interested in operational risk" are: (i) it is sexy, hot, and completely nebulous; (ii) people think they have already conquered both market risk and credit risk; and (iii) operational risk is a convenient catch-all "garbage dump" for all kinds of possible risks".

4.3   THE DISTINGUISHING FEATURES OF OPERATIONAL RISK

In this section we discuss the characteristics of operational risk that distinguish it from other kinds of risk. These characteristics are that it is diverse, one-sided, idiosyncratic, as well as other characteristics.

4.3.1   The diversity of operational risk

The diversity of the scope of operational risk is one feature that distinguishes it from the relatively narrowly defined market risk and credit risk, which are more widely understood and appreciated (by firms and regulators) as risk types. The diversity of operational risk (ranging from legal concerns to technological issues to behavioral matters to acts of God) makes it difficult to limit the number of dimensions required to describe it. Operational risk encompasses the types of risk emanating from all areas of the firm: front office to the back office and support areas. Hence, identifying operational risk is more difficult than identifying market risk and credit risk. Buchelt and Untregger (2004) describe operational risk as "a highly varied and interrelated set of risks with different origins". Milligan (2004) describes operational risk as the risk that "includes everything from slip-and-fall to the spectacular collapse of Barings Bank". Likewise, the Economist (2003) describes operational risk as "the risk of all manner of mishaps and foul-ups, from a lost document to a bomb blast".

This feature of diversity, as compared with market risk and credit risk, gives rise to differences in determining what level of operational risk is acceptable (the so-called risk appetite). In the case of market risk and credit risk, a wide range of methods can be used to determine the risk appetite, including risk concentrations and VAR-type calculations. At present, it is not possible to set up a formal structure of limits across operational risk because the calculation methodologies are still at an early stage of development while the lack of data means that the results are not sufficiently detailed. The tools (procedures, methodologies, and data collection) needed to determine the appetite for operational risk are less well developed than for credit risk and market risk. Actually, it will be some time before operational risk limits similar to those used in conjunction with credit and market risk can be derived and discussed with the same level of clarity. Operational risk is so complex in its causes, sources, and manifestations that it is impossible to agree on any sort of common understanding as to its limits.

4.3.2 Is operational risk one-sided?

Some would argue that another distinguishing feature of operational risk is that it is "one-sided" in the sense that it is driven solely by its role as an undesired by-product of increasingly complex business operations. In this sense, the risk-return trade off associated with market risk has no equivalence in the case of operational risk, meaning that exposure to operational risk can cause losses without boosting the potential rate of return on capital and assets. In his critique of the Basel II Accord, Herring (2002) describes operational risk as being "downside risk". Crouchy et al (2003) suggest a similar idea by expressing the view that "by assuming more operational risk, a bank does not expect to yield more on average" and that "operational risk usually destroys value for all claimholders". This, they argue, is unlike market risk and credit risk because "by assuming more market or credit risk, a bank expects to yield a higher rate of return on its capital". Likewise, Lewis and Lantsman (2005) argue that operational risk is one-sided because "there is a one-sided probability of loss or no loss". Alexander (2003b) distinguishes between operational risk, one the one hand, and market risk and credit risk, on the other, by arguing that operational risk is mostly on the cost side, whereas the revenue side is associated with market risk and/or credit risk.

But it is wrong to believe that operational risk is one-sided in this sense, because it is becoming the kind of risk that banks and other financial institutions (and firms in general) are taking deliberately for the sake of realizing potential return. If it were one-sided, then the objective of any firm would be to eliminate it completely, and this can be best done by closing down the business. Would anyone in his or her right mind suggest a drastic course of action like this? By taking on operational risk, firms earn income while being exposed to the risk of incurring operational losses if and when a loss event materializes. If this is not risk–return tradeoff, then what is?

The fact of the matter is that operational risk can no longer be perceived as being solely associated with the cost of doing business. Instead, it has to be viewed as an integral part of the bundle of risks that are taken to generate profit. If this is the case, then the probability distribution of operational risk (as shown in Figure 4.1) should look more like the probability distributions B and C than distribution A, as the last represents the distribution of one-sided risk. As a matter of fact, the probability distribution of credit risk is closer to that of operational risk than to that of market risk, as shown in Figure 4.2. The distribution of market risk is more symmetrical than the distribution of credit risk and operational risk, and under normal condition it is approximately normal. The distribution of credit and operational risk is more skewed with fat tail because of the possibility of big losses. But it is widely believed that the distribution of losses from operational risk has

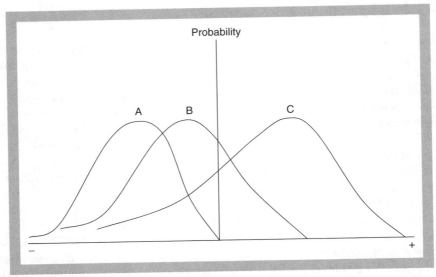

Figure 4.1 Possible distributions of operational risk

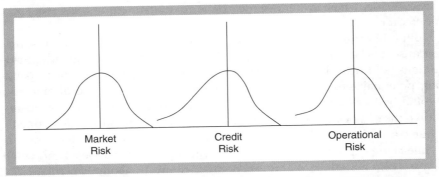

Figure 4.2 Distributions of market, credit, and operational risks

the thickest tail or, as Rowe (2004a) puts it, "operational risk exhibits the most extreme outliers".

The argument that operational risk is one-sided takes us back to the very definition of risk and whether it has bad connotation only or both good and bad connotations (Chapter 1). It may be plausible to talk about measures of downside risk, which emphasize the bad side of risk (as pointed out in Chapter 1), but this does not mean that the good side of risk (the probability of a favorable outcome) does not exist. It is the two-sidedness of risk that gives rise to the risk–return trade off, and this argument is as valid for operational risk as it is for market risk. Tripe (2000) makes this point, stipulating that operational risk is like other risks in the sense that it is subject to the risk–return trade off. He argues that "it is hard to believe that it

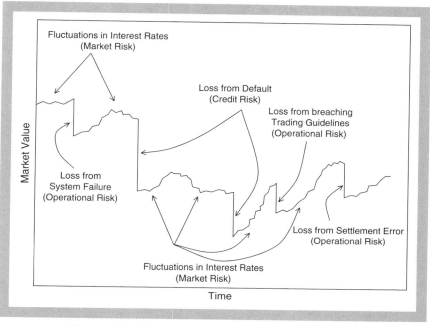

Figure 4.3 The market value of a bond portfolio
(credit and operational losses)

would be cost effective to eliminate all exposure to potential operating losses". Likewise, Simon Walker of Connley Walker Pty Ltd, views operational risk not simply as a hazard or threat, but as an opportunity to be embraced by firms that adopt a deliberate approach to risk taking (Risk Management, 2002).

The notion that operational risk is one-sided can be further examined with the aid of Figure 4.3, which shows the market value of a bond portfolio over time. The market value is affected by market risk (changes in interest rates), credit risk (default by the issuers), and operational risk (for example, system failure, breach of trading guidelines and settlement errors). By observing Figure 4.3, we may get the impression that the only kind of risk that is "two-sided" is market risk, as there are continuous gains and losses resulting from fluctuations in interest rates. Conversely, credit loss events (default) and operational loss events (system failure, breaching trading guidelines, and settlement errors) produce losses that are represented by big declines in the market value of the portfolio. Now, consider Figure 4.4, which shows (under favorable movements in interest rates) that the market value of the bond portfolio rises over time in the absence of operational loss and credit loss events. Fluctuations in the market value of the bond portfolio along an upward trend reflects market risk, but Figure 4.4 does not imply that the holder of this portfolio is not subject to credit risk and

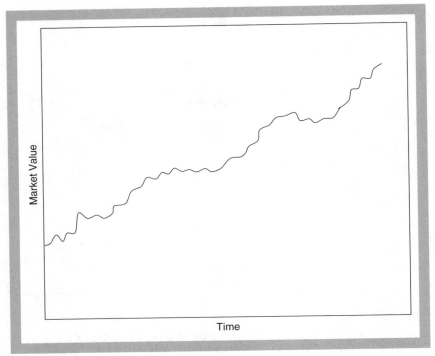

Figure 4.4 The market value of a bond portfolio
(no credit or operational losses)

operational risk. The fact that credit and operational loss events have not materialized does not mean that the position is not exposed to these risks. Note that risk is an ex ante concept (the possibility and/or amount of potential loss), whereas a loss event is an ex post concept. Loss events may or may not arise from exposure to risk. If the holder of the bond portfolio wants to eliminate completely credit risk and market risk, he will simply not hold the portfolio, in which case the gains realized from the portfolio represented in Figure 4.4 will be forgone. Hence, there is risk–return trade off in the case of operational risk.

4.3.3 Is operational risk idiosyncratic?

A view that has been put forward repeatedly is that, unlike market risk and credit risk, operational risk is idiosyncratic in the sense that when it hits one firm, it does not spread to other firms, implying the absence of contagion or the absence of system-wide effects (that is, it is firm-specific, not systemic). Lewis and Lantsman (2005) describe operational risk as being idiosyncratic because "the risk of loss tends to be uncorrelated with general market forces". This is not a characteristic of market risk and credit risk: a market downturn affects all firms, and a default by the customers of one firm affects its ability to meet its obligations to other firms. But, like the argument that operational risk is one-sided, this argument is questionable. Let us see why it is questionable.

If firm A suffers losses because of the activities of a rogue traders, this is not contagious only in the sense that firms B and C will not suffer direct losses from their own rogue traders. However, if firms B and C deal with firm A, then it is likely (depending on the size of loss) that firm A will fail to meet its obligations toward them. Hence, there is contagion and systemic effect here in the sense that firms B and C will incur (indirect) losses as a consequence of the rogue trading losses incurred by firm A. In general, if firm A is subject to the operational risk of rogue trading, firms B and C will be subject to at least two kinds of risk: credit risk, resulting from the possible default of firm A on its obligations to firms B and C and settlement (liquidity or Herstatt) risk, which is a type of operational risk. Indeed, it was the effect of the 1974 failure of Bankhaus Herstatt on other banks that led to the establishment of the BCBS, which has led to widespread interest in operational risk. Thus, operational loss events are not contagious only in a very limited sense. The liquidation of Bankhaus Herstatt did not lead to the liquidation of other banks, but it adversely affected them. Just like the counterargument that operational risk is not one-sided, the counterargument that it is not idiosyncratic seems to make some sense.

4.3.4   Other characteristics

Operational risk management is currently less well understood within firms and it is less sophisticated as a discipline compared with credit risk management and market risk management. But because both credit risk and market risk have operational risk embodied in them (for example, data quality), Pezier (2003b) argues that there is no point in trying to assess operational risk separately from other risks. Anders (2003) distinguishes operational risk from credit risk and market risk (what he calls external risks) on the grounds that it is the risk inherent in the firm (that is, within the operational processes and projects). This distinction was actually accepted for some time before the advent of the BCBS's definition of operational risk, which stipulates that operational risk can also result from external factors.

One major difference between operational risk, on the one hand, and market and credit risk, on the other, is the difficulty of defining a suitable "unit" of risk in the case of operational risk (McConnell, 2003). In the case of credit risk, the unit of risk is the entity or individual who could default. In the case of market risk, the unit of risk is an asset (bond, equity, currency, etc) whose adverse market price movements cause a loss. But in the case of operational risk, the unit of risk is an "operational process" whose failure causes a loss. The problem is that this unit varies across and within firms. Another difference pertains to definitions and measurement. Medova and Kyriacou (2001) argue that market or credit risk definitions come from specific businesses (trading, lending, investment, etc), which have consistent probabilistic definition of value at risk. On the other hand, they argue, operational risk definitions are based on an identification of causes whose consequences are often not measurable, which results in segregated capital allocation rules.

Yet another difference between operational risk, one the one hand, and credit risk and market risk, on the other, is that the concept of exposure is not clear in the case of operational risk. In the case of credit risk, for example, exposure is the amount lent to a customer. But in operational risk it is not straightforward, as can be seen from the following example that can be found in Hughes (2005). If a payment processing mechanism costing $10 million is used to process payments totaling $100 billion a day, what is the exposure if no wrong payments has been made in the last five years? Is it 0, $10 million, or $100 billion? Well, it can be anything between 0 and $100 billion, but no one is in a position to declare a figure with a reasonable level of confidence.

Buchelt and Unteregger (2004) distinguish operational risk from credit risk and market risk in the banking industry on the grounds that credit risk and market risk are business risks specific to the banking industry, whereas operational risk is a general business risk that has particular features in the banking industry. What is important to bear in mind is that operational risk is not limited to the operations function (the settling of transactions) because it is found across the entire firm. This is perhaps a reason for distinguishing between "operational risk" and "operations risk". Swenson (2003) makes this distinction by arguing that operations risk, which has traditionally been the concern of the internal audit function, is limited to back office reconciling, processing and the like, whereas operational risk permeates from the front via the middle to the back office platform.

4.3.5 Disentangling operational loss events

Despite the distinction between operational risk, on the one hand, and market risk and credit risk, on the other, it is sometimes difficult to distinguish among loss events attributed to the three kinds of risk. For example, trader X takes a long position on asset A, just before a market turndown, which leads to trading losses when the price of A declines. This is obviously a market risk loss event, or is it? It may be or it may be not. If the trader took the position by following the specified trading guidelines (or if there are no explicit guidelines but adequate supervision would have prevented him from doing that), then this is a market risk loss event. But if the trader takes this position when the guidelines stipulate that he cannot take a position on Asset A or that the position size is above the maximum allowable, then this is an operational risk loss event.

Breaching trading guidelines is actually the essence of rogue trading that put an end to the life of Barings Bank, among others. Grange (2000) describes the breach of guidelines as happening when "a trader knowingly commits a limit breach of authority, trades with unauthorised counterparties, or trades in unapproved products and then acts to conceal his/her actions from management or falsely record trades in the book of account". The risk of something like this happening is definitely operational risk, and not a combination of both market risk and operational risk as Kalyvas et al. (2006, Chapter 6) put it, arguing that "if Leeson was not taking improper or extreme positions (operational risk), he would not have faced extreme losses he faced (market risk)". Well, if Leeson had not breached the guidelines (by taking improper or extreme positions) that would have been market risk. If there had been no guidelines on the appropriateness and size of the positions, this would have been market risk. But if he had breached the guidelines, or if he did what he did because of the lack of supervision that would have curtailed his activities otherwise, then this makes it operational risk. It is either or, not a combination thereof. Their argument that the financial losses resulting from the 1995 Kobe earthquake was a combination of market and operational loss events is not convincing. It was pure operational loss resulting from external factors (specifically, the destruction of property and physical assets by the earthquake and the resulting fires). In this context, Buchelt and Unteregger (2004) argue that whether or not a loss event is to be classified as an operational loss event is determined by the cause(s) rather than the consequences of the event. In the Barings case, for example, it was market risk that generated the loss but the cause was operational risk (fraud and inadequate supervision).

Likewise, a loss resulting from a loan default is a credit risk loss if the loan officer follows the guidelines when she approves the loan, but it would be an operational loss event if the loan officer fails to follow the guidelines (for example, with respect to the credit rating of the borrower). But why would the trader and the loan officer in our examples not follow the guidelines? Well, it could be incompetence or it could be greed and corruption (loan officers are typically exposed to the temptation of accepting bribes in return for swift loan approvals). After all, King (2001) argues that people often do not do what they are supposed to do, either because they cannot or because they do not want to. Hence, he attributes operational risk to both stupidity and malice.

However, it may be possible to reconcile the two views (the "either or view" and the "and view") on the distinction between operational risk and other kinds of risk by referring to our example of the bond portfolio represented in Figure 4.3, where the value of the portfolio is subject to market risk, credit risk, and operational risk. With this in mind, consider the case of Nick Leeson who, by taking improper positions, lost $1.6 billion. If the limits allowed him to take positions that, under the same circumstances, produced a loss of $200 million only, then it is possible to say that market risk produced a loss of $200 million whereas operational risk produced a loss of $1.4 billion. But even if this is the case, we cannot attribute a big chunk of the loss to market risk. The reconciliation of the two views with respect to the Kobe disaster is not possible at all. It may be safer to use the cause to classify loss events.

4.4   THE DEFINITION OF OPERATIONAL RISK

Defining operational risk is very important because it sets it apart from other risk categories and, on the other hand, forms the basis for the treatment of operational risk ranging from raising awareness at the management level to the calculation of the regulatory capital (Buchelt and Unteregger, 2004). However, it must be obvious from the description of operational risk so far that defining it is not an easy task, again due to its diversity. Actually, Allen and Bali (2004) note that defining operational risk is easier said than done, and this is perhaps why it is dubbed "Risk X" by Metcalfe (2003). Likewise, Crouchy (2001) suggests that operational risk is a fuzzy concept because "it is hard to make a clear-cut distinction between operational risk and the normal uncertainties faced by the orgainsation in its daily operations".

The definitions of operational risk range from the very narrow (regulatory approach) to the extremely broad classifications. Few issues divide the risk management community so completely as operational risk, but this does not alter the fact that the measurement of operational risk must start with a clear understanding of what is to be measured. By the time of the launch of the review of the Basel I Accord around 1999, there was no acceptable definition of operational risk. Lynn (2006) takes this further by claiming that "up until 2001 no one really knew what operational risk meant". After a lengthy debate between regulators and the industry, views converged on the current BCBS definition, which will be examined in detail later.

4.4.1   The negative definition of operational risk

Cruz (2003a) argues that the term "operational risk" was first mentioned in the financial industry in 1995, the year when Barings Bank collapsed. This is not exactly true because the Group of Thirty came up with a definition in 1993. The push for a formal definition of operational risk came under the turmoil of large operational loss events, most notably the $1.6 billion loss incurred by Barings, as a definition is a prerequisite for risk measurement and management. This event led the financial industry to recognize rogue trading and the like as a separate risk category, comprising risks that could not be classified as either credit or market risk. Hence, it was rather tempting to define operational risk negatively as any risk that is not related to market risk and/or credit risk.

However, defining operational risk in this manner to imply any risk that cannot be classified as market or credit risk is difficult to work with and cannot be the basis of operational risk measurement. This is because defining operational risk as the difference between total risk and the sum of market risk and credit risk makes it impossible to identify activities that give rise to operational risk, which is a prerequisite for measuring and modeling this kind of risk. Buchelt and Unteregger (2004) argue along these lines, asserting that the "negative" definition of operational risk is hardly suitable for defining its scope precisely, although it indicates (to a certain extent) what might be meant. They also argue against definitions that focus on certain technical risks (such as those used in IT), which do not capture the full extent of the given risk potential because they ignore interdependence. However, Medova and Kyriacou (2001) are convinced that the view of operational risk as "everything not covered by exposure to credit and market risk" remains the one most often used by practitioners. This view is also held by Jameson (1998) who indicated that the definition most frequently given in telephone interviews was "every risk source that lies outside the areas covered by market risk and credit risk".

4.4.2   Early definitions of operational risk

Early definitions of operational risk appeared in the published literature of major international banks and other bodies in the 1990s before the Basel Committee adopted its official definition. The Group of Thirty (1993) defined operational risk as "uncertainty related to losses resulting from inadequate systems or controls, human error or management". Bankers Trust defined operational risk as encompassing "all dimensions of the decentralised resources-client relationship, personnel, the physical plant, property and assets for which Bankers Trust is responsible, as well as technology resources". Barclays Bank defined it more simply as "fraud, failures in controls and the like". Chase Manhattan defined operational risk as the risk arising from activities associated with their fiduciary dealings, execution, fraud, business interruption, settlement, legal/regulatory, and the composition of fixed costs. The Commonwealth Bank of Australia (1999) came up with the broad definition that operational risk is "all risks other than credit and market risk, which could cause volatility of revenues, expenses and the value of the Bank's business".

An early definition of operational risk came up in a seminar at the Federal Reserve Bank of New York when Shepheard-Walwyn and Litterman (1998) defined operational risk by saying that "operational risk can be seen as a general term that applies to all the risk failures that influence the volatility of the firm's cost structure as opposed to its revenue structure". The British Bankers' Association (1997) suggested an early and rather long definition, stipulating that operational risk encompasses "the risks associated with human error, inadequate procedures and control, fraudulent and criminal activities; the risks caused by technological shortcomings, system break-downs; all risks which are not 'banking' and arising from business decisions as competitive action, pricing, etc; legal risk and risk to business relation-ships, failure to meet regulatory requirements or an adverse impact on the bank's reputation; 'external factors' include: natural disasters, terrorist attacks and fraudulent activity, etc". It may be interesting to compare this definition with the definition found in Tripe (2000), which says that "opera-tional risk is the risk of operational loss". This last definition brings to mind an old Arabic proverb that says something like "it is not useful to describe water as water". And how about the early definition referred to by Lopez (2002) that operational risk is "every type of unquantifiable risk faced by a bank", and the definition of Crouchy (2001) that it is "the risk associated with operating a business"? More specific than Tripe, Lopez, and Crouchy is Halperin (2001) who defines operational risk as "loose-limbed concept that includes potential losses from business interruptions, technological failures, natural disasters, errors, lawsuits, trade fixing, faulty compliance, fraud and damage to reputation, often intangible fallout from these events".

The BCBS (1998) came up with some sort of an early definition (rather a description) of operational risk by stipulating that "the most important types of operational risk involve breakdown in internal controls and cor-porate governance" and that "such breakdowns can lead to financial losses through error, fraud, or failure to perform in a timely manner or cause the interests of the bank to be compromised in some other way, for example, by its dealers, lending officers or other staff exceeding their authority or conducting business in unethical or risky manner". Furthermore, the BCBS identified as other aspects of operational risk "major failure of information technology systems or events such as major fires or other disasters".

4.4.3   The current BCBS definition

The most common definition of operational risk first appeared in Robert Morris Associates et al. (1999), which is as follows: "operational risk is the direct or indirect loss resulting from inadequate or failed internal processes, people and systems, or from external events". The Basel Committee adopted this definition, as it was initially, but subsequently eliminated the reference to indirect losses (including those resulting from the loss of reputation) for the purpose of quantifying regulatory capital, since these losses are difficult to measure. More specifically, the BCBS (2004a) defines operational risk as "the risk arising from inadequate or failed internal processes, people and systems or from external events". This definition, which is based on the underlying causes of operational risk, includes legal risk but excludes business and reputational risk. Based on this definition, the concept of operational risk was subsequently developed to take into account the distinction between causes, events and the resulting operational losses (consequences or effects). Figure 4.5 shows some examples of causes, events, and effects. For example, internal fraud is an event that arises from the failure of internal processes, the effect of which would be a loss in the form of a write-down. We will come back to this point in Chapter 5, which deals with the classification of operational risk on the basis of these criteria.

The BCBS's definition of operational risk has been expressed differently by different people. For example, Marshall and Heffes (2003) cite

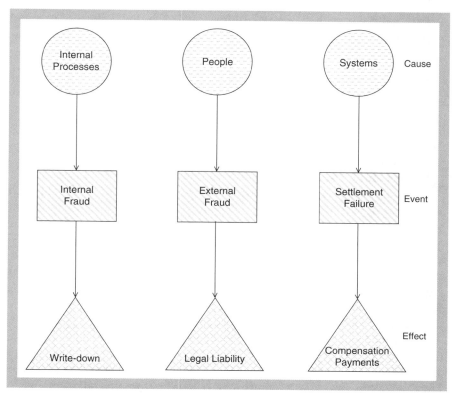

Figure 4.5 Examples of causes, events, and effects of operational risk

Peyman Mestchian, head of risk management as SAS UK, defining operational risk as "the threat coming from such factors as people, processes and internal systems, as well as external events unrelated to market and credit risk". This modification is some sort of a combination of elements of the BCBS definition and the negative definition of operational risk. Moreover, Mestchian (2003) suggests the decomposition of the definition of the BCBS into the following components:

1. Process risks, such as inefficiencies or ineffectiveness in the various business processes within the firm. These include value-driving processes, such as sales and marketing, product development and customer support, as well as value-supporting processes such as IT, HR, and operations.

2. People risks, such as employee error, employee misdeeds, employee unavailability, inadequate employee development, and recruitment.

3. Technology (or system) risks, such as the system failures caused by breakdown, data quality and integrity issues, inadequate capacity, and poor project management.

4. External risks, such as the risk of loss caused by the actions of external parties (for example, competitor behavior, external fraud, and regulatory changes) as well as macroeconomic and socioeconomic events.

Crouchy (2001) expresses the same idea to define operational risk but he excludes losses due to external factors. Specifically, he argues that firms use people, processes and technology to execute business plans, hence operational losses arise because of the failure of people, processes, or technology. Accordingly, he defines operational risk as "the risk that there will be a failure of people, processes, or technology within the business unit".

Buchelt and Unteregger (2004) use Mestchian's definition-based decomposition of operational risk to describe the sinking of the Titanic. The ship sank because of (i) the myth that it was unsinkable, which created careless complacency; (ii) the pressure put on the captain to get to New York as quickly as possible, thus traveling too far north and too quickly for safety; and (iii) inadequate safety measures, such as the small number of lifeboats, and poor emergency procedures. Thus, Buchelt and Unteregger (2004) argue, the ship sank because of the failure of people (the crew, passengers, and the boss), systems (the ship and its equipment), processes (emergency plans and procedures), and external factors (the iceberg).

The same can be said about the "mother of all operational failures", the US-led invasion and occupation of Iraq. One cannot imagine the enormity of this failure, as the US spent billions of dollars, lost thousands of lives and sustained a huge number of injuries, only to give Iraq on a silver-platter to sectarian militias backed by its bitter enemy, Iran. In the process, Iraq was made not the democracy they have been bragging about but rather the most lawless place on Planet Earth, and a secular country has been transformed into one run by a sixth-century style sectarian theocracy (albeit in disguise). The failure of people (for example, Rumsfeld, Bremmer and the two "elected" prime ministers Al-Jaffari and Al-Maliki) and external factors (the foreign terrorists who found in Iraq a front to fight America) are predominant in this case. But systems and processes also failed (for example, the failure of the US military to prevent the occurrence of the atrocities that took place at the notorious Abu Ghraib prison and the failure of democracy that put sectarian militias and their stooges in control of the country). It is probably more pleasant to talk about operational risk in the business world, so we will put an end to this unpleasant digression.

4.4.4   A critique of the BCBS definition

The BCBS's definition of operational risk has not been accepted without any challenge from academics and practitioners. To start with, Turing (2003) describes the definition as "so broad as to be totally unhelpful". Herring (2002) criticizes the definition on the grounds that it omits altogether basic business risk, which he defines as the risk of loss attributable to the firm's inability to reduce costs as quickly as revenues decline (implying that the definition is rather narrow). The underlying argument here is that most of the firms that attempt to allocate economic capital for operational risk find business risk to be the largest component (see, for example, Kuritzkes and Scott, 2002). Herring also criticizes the BCBS definition by arguing that it ignores the Committee's earlier attempt to include indirect costs and reputational risk.

Hadjiemmanuil (2003) describes the Committee's attempt to define operational risk as being "deeply flawed" because "it is not based on generally accepted understanding of operational risk since there is no consensus on this issue in the banking industry". He also describes the definition as being "opaque" and "open-ended", because it fails to specify the component factors of operational risk or its relation to other forms of risk. The definition, according to Hadjiemmanuil (2003), leaves unanswered many questions concerning the exact range of loss events that can be attributed to operational failures. Thirlwell (2002) argues that the BCBS's definition represents a "measurable view [of operational risk] if you are trying to come up with something which is quantifiable, but not good if you think about what causes banks to fail".

Three issues are disputed when it comes to what operational risk should include and exclude: (i) the exclusion of reputational risk, (ii) the exclusion of business risk, and (iii) the inclusion of legal risk. Starting with the first point, one may wonder how one can possibly accept the exclusion of reputational risk when a survey of 2000 private and public sector firms conducted by the Aon Corporation has shown that reputation was cited as the biggest business risk. Another survey of 100 leading European firms by the European Strategic Account Management Group reported similar results (Knowledge@Wharton and Aon Corporation, 2003). Thirlwell (2002) highlights the importance of reputational risk by arguing that "the main reason why banks have failed over the last couple of hundred years has generally been not that they made bad loans, but that people lost confidence in them and withdrew their investment in them or, in the earlier part of the twentieth century and before, simply withdrew their funds". It is all about the loss of reputation (on reputational risk, see Schofield, 2003).

Turning to the second point, Leddy (2003) justifies the exclusion of business risk from the definition of operational risk by redefining business risk as a risk that is undertaken lawfully by the firm to enhance its profitability. Although business risk is potentially huge, he argues, it falls outside the definition of operational risk, the reason being that banks as banks (as opposed to the employees of the bank) deliberately take business, credit, and market risks with a profit motivation. Operational risk, on the other hand, is driven by personal or collective greed, stupidity, or criminal tendencies, which is never or only rarely confused with a bank's own proper commercial objectives. This distinction between operational risk and business risk is in direct contrast with the view put forward by Evans (2004) who seems to believe that business risk is "operational risk at financial institutions". He actually defines business risk as involving a failure of people or business processes, or a set of external events outside of company control".

It is important to note that the arguments put forward by Herring (2002) and Leddy (2003) for (respectively) the exclusion and inclusion of business risk from the definition of operational risk is based on two different definitions of the former. Herring's definition is more supportive of the inclusion of business risk because it implies management incompetence. Leddy's definition, on the other hand, distinguishes between the bank as a business entity and the employees of the bank. Attributing operational risk to employees is more conducive to the exclusion of business risk.

On the third point, Hadjiemmanuil (2003) does not see why the BCBS takes it for granted that legal risk is part of operational risk, because it is "neither self-evident nor universally accepted". For example, the IFCI Financial Risk Institute (2000) sees the principal kinds of risk to be market, credit, settlement, and "other" risks, the latter including liquidity, legal, and operational risk. The distinction between operational risk and legal risk becomes clear if the former is defined as "the risk of unexpected losses arising from deficiencies in a firm's management information, support and control systems and procedures", while defining legal risk as "the risk that a transaction proves unenforeceable in law or has been inadequately documented".

Examples of legal risk include uncertainties surrounding the legal capacity of banks' contractual counterparties to enter into binding transactions, the legality of derivative transactions and/or the recognition and effectiveness of netting arrangements in particular jurisdictions. If this distinction is acceptable, then it is plausible to conclude that legal risk might potentially contribute to a more precise identification of the pathology of banking operations.

One reason why legal risk is associated with operational risk is that fraud is considered to be (i) the most significant category of operational loss events, and (ii) a legal issue. But Hadjiemmanuil argues that legal risk, in the sense of some uncertainty regarding the true legal position or the rights and duties of the parties involved, is rarely an active question in cases of fraud because what is important for the bank is its ability to recover the assets lost as a result. For this reason, the argument goes, legal risk and fraud should be analyzed separately, as independent sources of risk. The problem, however, is that legal risk can be defined in more than one way, and some of these definitions are more supportive of the inclusion of operational risk than others.

Apart from the definition we came across earlier, legal risk may be defined to include the loss attributed to (i) legally flawed actions of the firm or its employees and agents, (ii) uncertainties regarding the requirements and effects of the law itself, and (iii) the relative inefficiency of a country's legal system. Obviously, linking legal risk to the flawed actions of employees is more conducive to the inclusion of legal risk in operational risk. Turing (2003) defines legal risk as "the risk that one is unable to enforce rights against, or rely on obligations incurred by, counterparty in the event of a default or a dispute". He also mentions an old Basel/IOSCO definition, which is as follows: legal risk is the risk that contracts are not legally enforceable or documented correctly. This definition is based implicitly on the possibility of a human error in documentation, and so it fits into operational risk. Yet, Turing expresses the view that "fitting legal risk within the new Basel framework poses special challenges" because "legal risks may not parcel up readily into the business lines laid down by the Basel Committee".

4.4.5   Other definitions of operational risk

So, what is the alternative to the BCBS's definition of operational risk? By arguing that "operational risk is a collection of concepts that are not amenable to a single policy for management, or indeed reduction of regulatory capital", Turing (2003) suggests the following alternative definitions:

■ The risk that deficiencies in information systems or internal controls will result in unexpected loss.

- The risk that a firm will suffer loss as a result of human error or deficiencies in systems or controls.

- The risk run by a firm that its internal practices, policies, and systems are not rigorous or sophisticated enough to cope with untoward market conditions or human or technological errors.

- The risk of loss resulting from errors in the processing of transactions/breakdown in controls/errors or failures in system support.

Vinella and Jin (2005) come up with yet another definition of operational risk, claiming that the BCBS's definition is a special case of it. They define operational risk as "the risk that the operation will fail to meet one or more operational performance targets, where the operation can be people, technology, processes, information and the infrastructure supporting business activities". Based on this definition, they also define the "fundamental operational objective" as "operating within a targeted level of operational risk and in full compliance with regulatory and corporate guidelines, maximise operational performance while simultaneously minimising cost". They argue that the BCBS's definition is a special case of their "generalised" definition when the failure to meet an operational performance target results in a direct monetary loss. They further argue that while it is consistent with the definition of the BCBS, their definition has several advantages. First, it ties operational risk to distinct components of the operation via the operational performance targets. Second, it becomes possible, by using this definition, to measure operational risk in terms of operational performance metrics and target levels, as the probability that a component of the operation will fail to meet its target levels. Third, firms have substantial resources to define, capture, and report operational performance within the operation that can be used to estimate operational risk under their definition.

Cagan (2001) argues strongly for an alternative definition that can do a better job in guiding the data collection and risk management processes. She describes a desirable alternative definition as a definition that "encompasses qualitative concerns and can be used as a best practices signpost". The specific definition she recommends is that "operational risk is the risk of business disruption, control failures, errors, misdeeds or external events, and is measured by direct and indirect economic loss associated with business interruption and legal risk costs, and also by 'immeasurables' such as reputation risk costs". Ironically, Cagan was critical of the original BCBS's definition that encompassed direct and indirect losses (the Robert Morris Associates et al. [1999] definition) on the grounds that it was narrow. To her dismay, perhaps, the BCBS subsequently made the definition even narrower by deleting reference to (or rather excluding) indirect losses on the pragmatic grounds of easing measurement problems.

Yet another way of defining operational risk is not to look at causes or effects but rather at capital allocation against risk. King (1998) argues that many banks define operational risk as "the excess of allocation of capital in the firm after market and credit risk capital have been eliminated". The problem with this definition is the implication that the absence of excess capital means the absence of operational risk, which is unrealistic. This is why King utilized an idea put forward by Shewhart (1980) to define operational risk as "the uncertainty of loss in the book value of the firm due to failures in the manufacturing of the firm's goods and services". This definition includes both controllable and uncontrollable risks, but only to the extent that they are related to events (failures) in the manufacturing operations. For a bank, this definition pertains to losses resulting from transaction processing, thus excluding legal actions, natural disasters and competitive actions". It is unlikely that Cagan (2001) would agree with this definition, since it is even narrower than the narrower of the two BCBS's definitions.

4.5   THE LAST WORD

Is the definition of operational risk such a critical issue that triggers so much disagreement? One view is that to measure something, we must first define it. But Lam (2003b) seems to believe that being "fussy" about the definition of operational risk does not serve any purpose as far as operational risk management is concerned. This is why the first step in his "ten steps to operational risk management" is "define it and move on". Lam's underlying argument is that "many institutions do not get off the ground because too much time is spent trying to come up with the perfect definition of operational risk".

Defining operational risk is problematical because it is so diverse. To get a feel of how diverse it is, we need to examine the kinds of loss events that can be classified under operational risk. This is exactly what we are going to do in Chapter 5, which deals with the classification of operational risk. We will also have a look at some figures that will give us an idea of how serious operational risk is.

The Taxonomy of Operational Risk

5.1 THE CRITERIA OF CLASSIFICATION

The heterogeneity of operational risk makes it necessary to come up with a system for classifying it and identifying its components. Hubner, Laycock, and Peemoller (2003) argue that one important advance in the rapidly improving understanding of operational risk is that the disaggregation and classification of operational risk is being put on a more rational footing. All efforts to define, analyze, and interpret operational risk are based on endeavors to come up with collections of risk types and the losses associated with these risks. Disaggregation involves separating out the different components of a risk cluster into categories.

5.1.1 General principles

The classification of operational losses (resulting from exposure to operational risk) can be approached from three alternative angles: the causes of operational failure, the resulting loss events, and the legal and accounting forms of consequential losses (that is, cause, event, and effect as shown in Figure 4.5). An operational (loss) event is defined by Haubenstock (2004) as "an event due to failed or inadequate processes, people or systems, or exposure to external events that caused, or potentially could have caused, a material loss or adversely impacted stakeholders". The phrase "potentially could have caused" refers to "near-misses". The effects, according to the BCBS, are the direct losses resulting from (i) write-down of assets, (ii) regulatory compliance penalties, (iii) legal payments/settlements, (iv) customer restitution, (v) loss of recourse, and (vi) loss of physical assets. Out of these effects, the two that need explaining are customer restitution and loss of recourse (as the others are straightforward). Restitution refers to payments to third parties resulting from operational losses for which the firm is legally responsible. Loss of recourse refers to losses experienced when a third party does not meet its obligations to the firm, provided that the outcome is attributable to an operational event. Moreover, the causal relations between the three levels (causes, events, and effects) are complex and indeterminate.

At first sight, the BCBS's definition is more consistent with the first alternative: it purports to identify the ultimate sources of operational losses by pointing to four broad categories of causes (people, processes, systems, and external events). The problem is that these generic sources of operational risk cannot be linked in a straightforward manner to the general types of loss identified by the BCBS. However, event- and effect-based regulatory classifications also appear in various Basel papers including the Quantitative Impact Study 3. The logical reason for the three dimensions of cause, event, and effect is easy to understand. Every operational risk manager who wants to know how to reduce exposure needs causal disaggregation to identify areas where management actions will have the desired effect (avoiding the cause outright or reducing the influence of the causer on the frequency or severity of the resulting event). An event-based classification makes the operational risk manager's task easier, as losses can be considered to materialize in an event.

Peccia (2003) argues that what is needed is developing a framework for classifying the causes of operational risk, because the usual classification of the causes of operational risk as either system problems or poor controls is unsatisfactory, giving rise to the possibility of misclassification or double counting. A more appropriate schema, he suggests, is the classification of losses by the area of impact on the results, as the ultimate objectives is to explain the volatility of earnings arising from the direct impact of losses on the financial results. Another problem is that the causes and effects of operational events are still commonly confused. Operational risk types, such as human risk and system risk, constitute the cause (not the outcome) of risk, as the latter is the monetary consequence. Peccia concludes that a classification based on causes is prone to errors and misunderstanding.

5.1.2   The BCBS classification

The Basel Committee has proposed the categorization of operational risk into manageable units according to regulatory-specified business lines or functional units. This may not be satisfactory for banks because the structure of regulatory business lines for the standardized approach does not reflect the way in which banks are structured or managed. With the help of the industry, the BCBS developed a matrix of seven broad categories of loss events that are further broken down into sub-categories and related activity examples. This classification is similar to the typology of hazards used by the insurance industry. Table 5.1 shows a listing of operational loss events with definitions and examples. Here, it is possible to relate event types to departments. For example, litigation and settlements can be

Table 5.1 The BCBS taxonomy of operational loss events

Event	BCBS Definition	Sub-categories/Examples
Internal fraud (IF)	Losses due to acts of fraud involving at least one internal party.	• Account take-over and impersonation • Bribes and kickbacks • Forgery • Credit fraud • Insider trading (not on firm's account) • Malicious destruction and misappropriation of assets • Tax noncompliance • Theft • Extortion • Embezzlement • Robbery • Intentional mismarking of position • Unauthorized and unreported transactions
External fraud (EF)	Same as internal fraud except that it is carried out by an external party.	• Computer hacking • Theft of information • Forgery • Theft
Employment practices and workplace safety (EPWS)	Losses arising from violations of employment and health and safety laws.	• Discrimination • Compensation and termination issues • Health and safety issues General liability
Clients, products and business practices (CPBP)	Losses arising from failure to meet obligations to clients or from the design of a product.	• Disputes over advisory services • Violation of anti-monopoly rules and regulations • Improper trade • Insider trading on firm's account

(Continued)

Table 5.1 (*Continued*)

Event	BCBS Definition	Sub-categories/Examples
		• Market manipulation • Money laundering • Unlicensed activity • Product defects • Exceeding client exposure limits • Account churning Aggressive sales • Breach of privacy • Misuse of confidential information • Customer discloser violations
Damage to physical assets (DPA)	Losses arising from damage inflicted on physical assets by a natural disaster or another event.	• Terrorism • Vandalism • Natural disasters
Business disruption and system failures (BDST)	Losses arising from disruptions to or failures in systems, telecommunication and utilities.	• Hardware • Software • Telecommunications • Utility outage • Utility Disruption
Execution, delivery and process management (EDPM)	Losses arising from failed transaction processing with counter-parties such as vendors	• Incorrect client records • Negligent loss or damage of client assets • Unapproved access to accounts • Client permissions • Missing and incomplete legal documents • Failed mandatory reporting obligations • Inaccurate external reports Non-client counterparty disputes • Accounting errors • Collateral management failure • Data entry, maintenance or loading error • Delivery failure • Miscommunication • Missed deadlines • Vendor disputes

Source: BCBS (2004a)

related to the Legal Department, compensation claims can be related to Human Resources, system failures to IT, settlement failures to Treasury, and errors in the books to the Accounts Department.

An alternative classification structure is based on functional units but this is specific to an individual firm. For example, the term "legal department" can be expected to vary between firms according to their history and internal environment. In the same firm, the term may vary between countries in response to local requirements. Yet, there is clear added value in using this classification, as disaggregation empowers and encourages the functions to monitor and manage risk on a structural basis. Moreover, this approach emphasizes the role of the functional units as providers of proactive, rather than reactive, risk management support to the risk owners.

One problem with this classification is that some of the subcategories do not have precise meaning. Take, for example, "fraud", which does not have an exact legal or regulatory meaning. It is used as a generic term to designate a variety of forms of (mostly nonviolent) economic wrongdoing, whose commission constitutes a criminal offence and/or a civil wrong. Examples of fraud are theft, unauthorized withdrawal of money from ATMs, forgery of instruments, false accounting, fraudulent conveyance, and unauthorized trading. One should distinguish between three roles that a bank can play in fraud: perpetrator, vehicle, or victim. Tax fraud and money-laundering offences are common examples of economic crimes committed by banks. Fraud can be committed by banks and employees against clients and counterparties. In this sense, it is misleading to describe fraud as a risk faced by banks. Rather, the bank itself is the source of risk borne by outside parties (from the bank's perspective, it is legal risk). When the bank is a vehicle for fraud, it is not subject to the direct risk of loss, but reputational risk is present. There may be cases where the law reallocates financial risk, forcing banks to bear the loss and compensate the victims on the grounds of contributory negligence or some breach of conduct-of-business standards (for example, failure to cancel a reported stolen card on time, or not checking signatures). In cases where a bank is the victim or the vehicle, fraud can be internal or external. The BCCI, for example, was both the perpetrator (for example, money laundering) and the victim (fraudulent lending, theft, and other practices of its management).

It may also be the case that some important subcategories are missing. For example, should employment practices and workplace safety have a category called "employee offensive odour". This is not a joke. In a recent article in *Financial Times*, Sanghera (2005) concluded after some research that "dealing with smelly employees in these days of windowless workplaces and cubicles may be one of the biggest management challenges of our time". Indeed, a message on *workplace.net* says "any one who has an offensive body odour and works with other people who find it offensive is breaching health and safety law guidelines". This issue may lead to termination problems and people failure, as the message says that body odor can cause "disruption in the workplace". Sanghera (2005) says explicitly that "barely a month passes without some smell-related dispute hitting the headlines", referring to the "worker from Portsmouth getting sacked because his bosses claim he is too pongy".

5.1.3   Classification according to causes (sources)

The classification of operational risk according to the cause (the sources of risk) is consistent with Mestchaian's (2003) suggested decomposition of the BCBS's definition of operational risk. Table 5.2 reports the risk sources, their categories and examples. For instance, external risk includes external fraud (such as external money laundering), natural disasters (such as floods), and non-natural disasters (such as arson). This classification goes beyond the BCBS categories.

Table 5.2 Operational risk by cause

Risk	Category	Examples
People Risk	Disclosure-related issues	• Concealing losses • Misuse of important information • Non-disclosure of sensitive issues
People Risk	Employment, health and safety	• Employee actions • Compensation disputes • Employee defection • Labor disputes • Strikes • Employee illness • Employee injury • Forced retirement • Promotions related disputes • Discrimination and harassment issues • Infliction of distress
People Risk	Internal fraud	• Embezzlement • Money laundering • Unauthorized fund transfers • Accounting fraud • Credit card fraud • Tax fraud
People Risk	Trading misdeeds	• Insider trading • Market manipulation • Improper pricing • Unauthorized trading

(Continued)

Table 5.2 (*Continued*)

Risk	Category	Examples
Process Risk	Errors and omissions	• Employee error • Inadequate quality control • Inadequate security • Inadequate supervision • Failure to file a proper report
Process Risk	Transaction and business process risk	• Inadequate account reconciliation • Inadequate transaction completion • Inadequate transaction execution • Inadequate transaction settlement • Lack of proper due diligence • Loss of critical information
Technology Risk	General technology problems	• New technology failure • Technology-related operational errors
Technology Risk	Hardware	• System failure • Outdated hardware
Technology Risk	Security	• Computer virus • Data security • Hacking
Technology Risk	Software	• Inadequate testing • System failure • Incompatible software
Technology Risk	Systems	• Inadequate systems • System maintenance
Technology Risk	Telecommunications	• Fax • Internet • E-mail • Telephone
External Risk	External fraud	• Burglary • External misrepresentation • External money laundering • Robbery
External Risk	Natural disasters	• Flooding • Hurricane • Blizzard • Earthquake
External Risk	Non-natural disasters	• Arson • Bomb threat • Explosion • Plane crashes • War

5.2 FREQUENCY AND SEVERITY OF LOSS EVENTS

Operational risk events can be divided into high-frequency, low-severity events (which occur regularly) and low-frequency, high-severity events (which are rare but produce huge losses if they occur). The low-frequency, high-severity risks (such as internal fraud, which could jeopardize the whole future of the firm) are risks associated with loss events that lie in the very upper tail of the total loss distribution. High-frequency, low-severity risks (such as credit card fraud and some human risks) have high expected loss but relatively low unexpected loss.

The BCBS (2002b) has produced results on the frequency and severity of each type of risk event for a typical bank with investment, commercial, and retail operations. These are reported in Table 5.3, showing that internal fraud is a low-frequency, high-severity risk event. These are the kinds of event that can bring a major bank to its knees (for example, the Barings case). It is also shown that external fraud is less severe than internal fraud although it is more frequent. Damage to physical assets, on the other hand, is a low-frequency, low-severity event and so is business disruption and system failure. Exactly the opposite to internal fraud is execution, delivery, and process management, which is a high-frequency, low-severity event.

The frequency and severity of operational loss events depend on and vary with the business line, as shown in Table 5.4. For example, internal fraud is a low-frequency, high-severity event in corporate finance, trading and sales, commercial banking, and asset management, but it is a low-frequency, medium-severity event in retail banking, payment and settlement, and in agency and custody. Execution, delivery, and process management is a low-frequency, low-severity event in corporate finance, but it is a high-frequency, low-severity event in trading and sales, retail banking, and in payment and settlement. It is also a medium-frequency, low-severity event in commercial banking, agency and custody, and asset management.

Table 5.3 Frequency and severity of operational risk events

Risk Event	Frequency	Severity
Internal fraud	L	H
External fraud	H/M	L/M
Employment practices and workplace safety	L	L
Clients, products, and business practices	L/M	H/M
Damage to physical assets	L	L
Business disruption and system failures	L	L
Execution, delivery, and process management	H	L

Table 5.4 Frequency (top) and severity (bottom) by business line and risk type

	Internal fraud	External fraud	Employment practices and workplace safety	Clients, products and business practices	Damage to physical assets	Business disruption and system failures	Execution, delivery and process management
Corporate Finance	L / H	L / M	L / L	L / H	L / L	L / L	L / L
Trading & Sales	L / H	L / L	L / L	M / M	L / L	L / L	H / L
Retail Banking	L / M	H / L	L / L	M / M	M / L	M / L	H / L
Commercial Banking	L / H	M / M	L / L	M / M	L / L	L / L	M / L
Payment & Settlement	L / M	L / L	L / L	L / L	L / L	L / L	H / L
Agency & Custody	L / M	L / L	L / L	M / M	L / L	L / L	M / L
Asset Management	L / H	L / L	L / L	H / H	L / L	M / L	M / L
Retail Brokerage	L / M	M / M	L / L	L / M	L / L	L / L	M / L

Based on the frequency of loss events, Pezier (2003a) classifies operational risk into nominal, ordinary, and exceptional risks. Nominal operational risk is the risk of repetitive losses (say, losses that may occur on average once a week or more frequently) associated with an ongoing activity such as settlement risk, minor external fraud (credit cards), or human error in transaction processing. Ordinary operational risk is the risk of less frequent (say, between once a week and once every generation) but larger losses, yet not life-threatening for the firm. Exceptional operational risk produces losses that have no more than a few percent chance of occurrence over a year, but those losses may be life-threatening.

Examples of exceptional risk events are reported in Table 5.5. The majority of the institutions listed in the table went bankrupt, were taken over, or they

Table 5.5 Examples of exceptional operational loss events

Year	Company	Cause of Loss
1991	Salomon Brothers (U.S.)	Treasury bond primary market manipulation
1993	Bank of Commerce and Credit International (BCCI) (Luxembourg)	Illegal activities (drugs, arms)
1994	Kidder Peabody (U.S.)	Management Incompetence
1995	Barings Bank (U.K.)	Rogue trading and management incompetence
1995	Diawa Securities (Japan)	Involvement with gangsters
1996	Bankers Trust (U.S.)	Selling products that clients did not fully understand
1997	Morgan Grenfell (U.K.)	Unauthorized investment in illiquid assets
1997	NatWest Markets (U.K.)	Mispricing of derivatives
1998	Long-Term Capital Management (U.S.)	Lack of transparency, conflict of interest, model bias and uncontrolled leverage
2000	Equitable Life Assurance Society (U.K.)	Non-respect of guaranteed annuity contracts
2001	Cantor Fitzgerald and Others (U.S.)	Terrorist attack on World Trade Center
2002	Allied Irish Bank (U.S.)	Rogue trading
2002	Merrill Lynch (U.S.)	Biased analyst recommendations
2003	Central Bank of Iraq (Iraq)	External fraud (by the former President)
2004	Yukos Oil Company (Russia)	Internal fraud
2005	Central Bank of Brazil (Brazil)	External fraud (a brilliantly-executed bank robbery)
2006	Royal Bank of Scotland (U.K.)	External fraud

were forced to merge as a consequence of their losses (hence the characteristic of life-threatening loss events). These were all consequences of deliberate actions and not mere accidents. In most cases, these actions were unethical, illegal, or criminal. They were not necessarily initiated by senior management but they were at least allowed to endure by management incompetence and/or negligence. The root problem is individual or corporate greed. These loss events have been widely publicized and used as case studies.

Sometimes, of course, it may not be clear whether the failure of a firm is due to operational risk only or a multiplicity of risks (recall the discussion in Chapter 4 on distinguishing operational loss events from market and credit loss events). Take, for instance, the case of the most publicized hedge fund failures during the period 1994–2002, which are shown in Figure 5.1. These failures brought total losses of $12.8 billion caused by a variety of factors, as shown in Table 5.6. As we can see, the failure of the ten hedge funds is attributed to more than operational risk, but it is the diversity of operational risk that makes it appear more prominently in Table 5.6. In a Capco Research (2002) paper, these failures were attributed mostly (50 percent) to operational risk, followed by investment risk (38 percent) then business risk (6 percent) and multiple risks (6 percent). Presumably investment risk here means market risk and credit risk. Although one tends to think that market risk would be more important

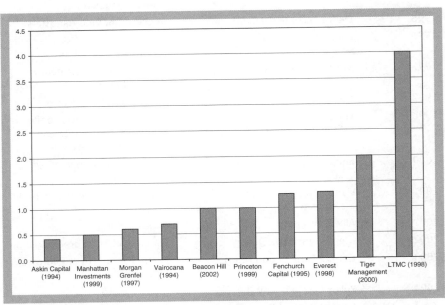

Figure 5.1 Losses incurred in the ten most publicized hedge fund failures ($billion)

Table 5.6 The risk factors responsible for hedge fund failures

Market Risk Factors	Credit Risk Factors	Operational Risk Factors
• Trading losses • Directional bets • Highly complex portfolios • Unfavorable market • conditions • High and uncontrolled leverage	• Post-Russian debt-default shock	• Weakness in the risk management systems • Misrepresentation of fund performance • Unauthorized holdings of unlisted securities • Pricing irregularities • Lack of liquidity • Conflict of interest • Collusion with a prime broker • Absence of adequate risk management system for new strategies • Lack of transparency to prime broker • Model bias in the risk management process

than operational risk in the case of hedge funds, this is obviously not the case here. Thus, the prominence of operational risk in Table 5.6 is not only due to its diversity but also to the fact that the failures are attributed mostly to operational risk.

5.3 A CLOSE LOOK AT OPERATIONAL LOSS FIGURES

To get a feel of the frequency and severity of operational loss events, we examine the loss data reported in BCBS (2003c) as a result of the 2002 data collection exercise. The BCBS asked participating banks to provide information on operational losses in 2001. A total of 89 banks participated in this exercise, reporting the number of loss events and the amounts involved (in millions of euros). The reported losses were classified by business lines and event types according to the BCBS's classification, but some reported losses were unclassified. As far as the number of losses is concerned, a total of 47,269 events were reported, 43 percent of which were events of external fraud (Figure 5.2) and more than 60 percent were in retail banking (Figure 5.3). As far as the loss amount is concerned, the total amount lost was EUR7.8 billion, 29 percent of which came under execution, delivery, and process management (Figure 5.4) and 290 percent was under retail banking and commercial banking (Figure 5.5). In terms of business line/event type combinations, the most frequent losses occurred

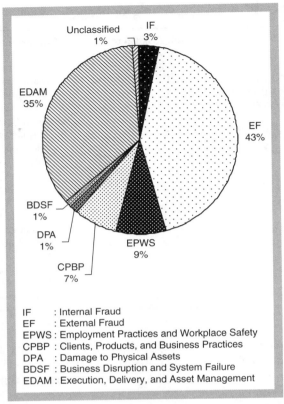

IF   : Internal Fraud
EF   : External Fraud
EPWS : Employment Practices and Workplace Safety
CPBP : Clients, Products, and Business Practices
DPA   : Damage to Physical Assets
BDSF : Business Disruption and System Failure
EDAM : Execution, Delivery, and Asset Management

Figure 5.2 Number of losses by event type (the BCBS (2003c) data)

in external fraud in retail banking, whereas the largest loss amounts occurred in damage to physical assets in commercial banking.

Switching now to the concepts of frequency and severity, the frequency is the number of loss events, whereas average severity can be calculated by dividing the total loss incurred under a certain loss event type or business line by the corresponding number of losses. Figures 5.6 and 5.7 report the severity of losses by event type and business line, respectively.

The operational loss events reported in Table 5.4 encompass mostly financial institutions. But all entities are exposed to operational risk in the course of their daily business, and for this reason, it may be useful to examine some operational risk events that span a wide variety of entities. Appendix 5.1 contains a table showing 62 randomly selected operational loss events that took place between 1984 and 2006. The reported operational losses were incurred by banks (including central banks), non-bank financial institutions, and firms operating in various sectors (manufacturing, utilities, transportation, food, mining, and entertainment), as well as universities, cities, and

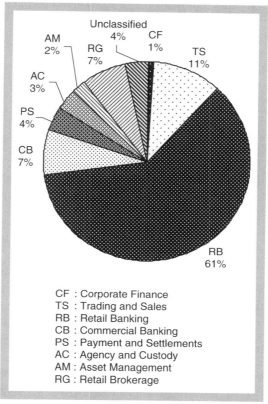

Unclassified
4%
AM
2%
RG
7%
CF
1%
TS
11%
AC
3%
PS
4%
CB
7%
RB
61%

CF : Corporate Finance
TS : Trading and Sales
RB : Retail Banking
CB : Commercial Banking
PS : Payment and Settlements
AC : Agency and Custody
AM : Asset Management
RG : Retail Brokerage

Figure 5.3 Number of losses by business line (the BCBS (2003c) data)

government entities. Because the BCBS's classification of operational loss events covers banks only, a large number of loss events appear as unclassified. The losses reported in the table range between the $9499 dollar incurred by the Yorkshire Building Society (as a result of an alleged sex discrimination case) and the $95 billion incurred by New York City as a result of the 9/11 terrorist attacks.

Table 5.7 shows a classification of the 62 events by type and business line, providing information on the number of events, the mean and the median values of the loss incurred, as well as the smallest and largest loss in each case. By event type, the most serious events (measured by the mean value of the loss) are damage to physical assets and internal fraud, with the former appearing more important because of the losses incurred by New York City as a result of the 9/11 attacks. By business line, the unclassified business lines are the ones where the big losses were incurred, this is mainly due to the fact that these losses were incurred by non-financial firms and other entities, which are not covered by the business line classification

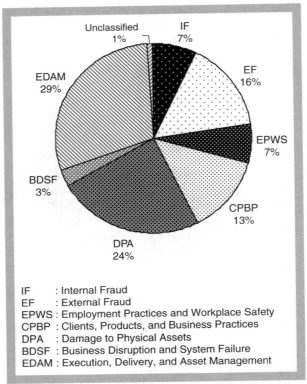

IF   : Internal Fraud
EF   : External Fraud
EPWS : Employment Practices and Workplace Safety
CPBP : Clients, Products, and Business Practices
DPA   : Damage to Physical Assets
BDSF : Business Disruption and System Failure
EDAM : Execution, Delivery, and Asset Management

Figure 5.4 Loss amount by event type (the BCBS (2003c) data)

of the BCBS. Naturally, the judgment changes if we consider the median loss as opposed to the mean loss: in this case, for example, external fraud appears to be more serious than internal fraud. In terms of the number of events (frequency), events related to clients, products, and business practices are the most frequent followed by internal fraud.

Table 5.8 shows a two-way classification of the same loss events by type and business line. If we exclude the events recognised by the unclassified business lines, we can see that the most common combination are loss events related to clients, products and business practices in corporate finance followed by internal fraud in commercial banking. While these tables provide some interesting information, one has to be careful about deriving some overall conclusions from a relatively small sample of events.

Finally, Appendix 5.2 presents a brief description of loss events organized by event type and business line as reported by the media. This is just a drop in the ocean compared to the universe of operational loss events. Operational losses are indeed more frequent than what one may believe, which is definitely the impression one gets by examining operational loss databases.

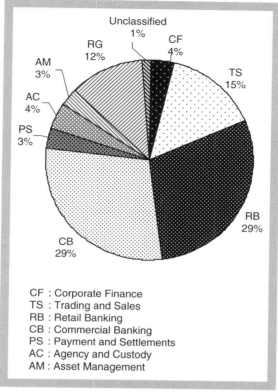

Figure 5.5 Loss amount by business line (the BCBS (2003c) data)

5.4 EXTERNAL OPERATIONAL LOSS DATABASES

In this section we deal with external databases as opposed to internal databases of individual firms (which we will deal with in the following section). External databases may take two forms. The first, such as the British Bankers Association's (BBA) database the global operational loss database (GOLD), is a contributory scheme where members contribute their own loss data in return for access to the loss data of other members, ending up with an industry-pooled database. The second type are the public databases that record publicly released loss events, including the databases of vendors such as OpRisk Analytics and OpVantage through the OpRisk Global Data and OpVar database, which are parts of the SAS Institute, Inc and a division of Fitch Risk Management, respectively. These vendors collect data from public sources, such as newspaper reports, court filings, and Securities and Exchange Commission (SEC) filings. As well as classifying losses by the Basel business line and causal type, the databases also include descriptive information on each loss event. A description of the GOLD database can be found on the BBA's website (www.bba.org.uk).

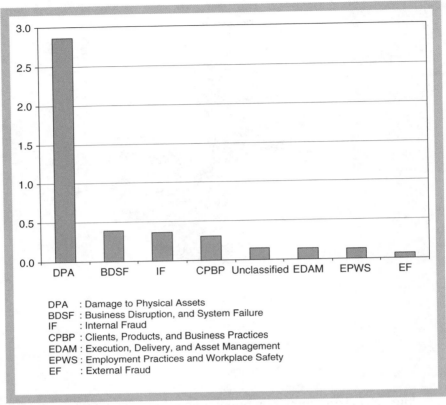

Figure 5.6 Severity by event type

Imeson (2006a) describes GOLD and similar databases by pointing out that these databases allow firms to consider the following questions: (i) What are typical loss events? (ii) Could loss circumstances occur in my firm? (iii) Would we see similar loss amounts? (iv) Which operational risks are subject to the highest losses? (v) How do loss events impact on the business? (vi) Which business areas suffer most losses? (vii) Are my controls or risk indicators appropriate? and (viii) Is reputational risk associated with loss events?

Baud, Frachot, and Roncalli (2002) identify two differences between the public databases and the industry-pooled databases, the first of which is the threshold for the recorded losses, as the threshold is expected to be much higher in the case of public databases than in the industry-pooled database. The second difference is the level of confidence one can place on the information provided by the database. For example, nothing ensures that the threshold declared by an industry-pooled database is the actual threshold, as banks are not necessarily prepared to uncover all losses above this threshold even though they pretend to do so.

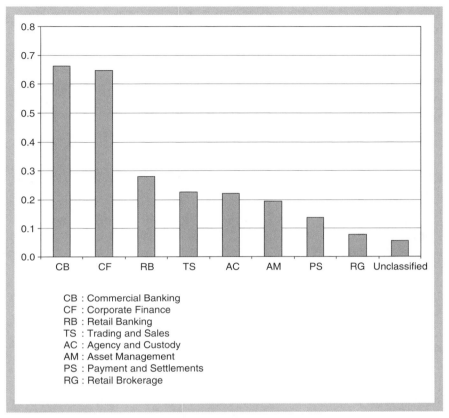

CB : Commercial Banking
CF : Corporate Finance
RB : Retail Banking
TS : Trading and Sales
AC : Agency and Custody
AM : Asset Management
PS : Payment and Settlements
RG : Retail Brokerage

Figure 5.7　Severity by business line

An operational loss database must include, as a minimum, information on (i) the business line recognizing the loss; (ii) the unit in the business line recognizing the loss; and (iii) the function/process within the unit recognizing the loss. The information provided on each loss event include: (i) the firm incurring the loss; (ii) the amount; (iii) the start, end, and settlement dates; (iv) the type of entity incurring the loss; (v) the event type; and (vi) the business line. Also reported is a description of the event. Most of the information is obtained from the media.

Cagan (2001) argues that collecting data according to less optimal standards can misinform the decision-making process. Therefore, she recommends the following criteria for proper data collection:

▪ Data must be collected according to the reasons for (sources of) the losses.

▪ Data records should include contributory factors (such as the lack of controls), although these factors may not be the cause. This is because

Table 5.7 Loss events (million dollars) by event type and business line (62 events)

	Number	Mean	Median	Minimum	Maximum
Event Type					
Internal fraud	15	677.0	9.1	0.38	9,300.0
External fraud	5	225.0	50.4	0.15	1,000.0
Employment Practices and Workplace safety	7	17.2	1.2	0.95	100.0
Clients, products and business practices	22	72.9	8.3	0.44	925.0
Damage to physical assets	9	10,700.0	41.3	1.0	95,000.0
Business disruption and system failures	1	175.0	175.0	175.0	175.0
Execution, delivery and process management	3	48.5	20.0	0.75	125.0
Business Line					
Corporate Finance	9	138.0	20.0	0.9	925.0
Trading & Sales					
Retail Banking	2	7.5	7.5	0.01	15.0
Commercial Banking	9	189.0	50.4	0.28	1,000.0
Payment & Settlement	1	88.0	88.0	88.0	88.0
Agency & Custody					
Asset Management	3	14.1	7.3	1.3	33.6
Retail Brokerage					
Unclassified	38	2.8	9.5	0.1	95,000.0

the contributory factors may intensify the severity of the loss. It was Leeson's activities that brought the demise of Barings, but inadequate supervision contributed to the severity of the loss. With adequate supervision, it is likely that his activities would have been put to an end at an earlier stage and a lower level of losses.

Table 5.8 Classification by event type and business line (million dollars)

	Internal fraud	External fraud	Emp practices and workplace safety	Clients, products, and business practices	Damage to physical assets	Business disruption and system failures	Execution, delivery, and process management
Corporate Finance							
Number	1			7			1
Mean	127.5			156.2			20.0
Trading & Sales							
Number							
Mean							
Retail Banking							
Number			1		1		
Mean			0.1		15.0		
Commercial Banking							
Number	6	3					
Mean	96.5	37.4					
Payment & Settlement							
Number	1						
Mean	88.0						
Agency & Custody							
Asset Management							
Number	2			1			
Mean	20.5			1.3			
Retail Brokerage							
Unclassified							
Number	5	2	6	14	8	1	2
Mean	1,887.4	3.3	20.1	98.0	12,035.0	174.6	62.7

■ Each data record should include the type of loss incurred or the loss effect for the purpose of proper risk quantification.

■ Loss events should be tracked over their life cycles, as they are often not one-time events. This is why a database may show dates for the beginning, end, and settlement of loss events.

■ The scaling of data should be based on asset size "buckets" to avoid revealing the identity of the firm enduring operational loss.

Thrilwell (2003) describes how an operational loss database should be constructed and run with reference to the BBA's GOLD, where members of the BBA pool their operational loss data. The main driving force behind the willingness of banks to take part in this venture is their desire to benchmark their performance against their peers. In his analysis, Thirlwell talks about some general issues pertaining to the construction of an operational loss database, including confidentiality, anonymity, trust between participants, consistency, and flexibility/evolution. On the general issues he suggests the following:

1. The key factor in developing a database is confidentiality between the providers and the holder of the data.

2. Anonymity means that there are no clues that could trace a loss back to a particular participant unless the event is publicized in the media.

3. Trust is a fundamental factor if the participants are to report their loss events.

4. Consistency means that those reporting loss events should place similar losses in the same categories (that is, consistency in classification).

5. The database must be structured in such a way as to be easy to modify, should the need arise (for example, the emergence of new kinds of risk).

Thirlwell (2003) also talks about what he calls specific issues that include (i) operational loss versus operations loss; (ii) the classification of losses; (iii) the distinction between hard losses, soft losses, and near misses; (iv) the choice between cause/event and impact/event; (v) the reporting threshold; and (vi) scaling. On these issues he makes the following points:

1. Operational risk covers a far broader category of risk than simply operations risk (hence the distinction between operational risk and operations risk).

2. For the purpose of constructing a database, it is best to identify generic causes of losses since they can apply to a number of business activities.

3. Soft losses, contingent losses, and near misses are excluded from the database because they are difficult to quantify.

4. The database should identify the number or size of the events that give rise to a loss, then the cause is identified by a narrative field.

5. Establishing a threshold for reporting is determined by two factors: the purpose of the database and the cost/benefit balance.

6. One bank's minor event is another bank's catastrophe, which requires some scaling factor, such as assets, transaction volume, income, expenses, etc.

While operational risk databases are a useful means of providing information, Thirlwell (2003) identifies some of their limitations, including the following:

1. The data are not independently audited.

2. The database does not provide information on the quality of controls in the reporting banks.

3. The choice of the reporting threshold affects the quantity of data reported.

4. There are some data reporting problems, including the double counting of operational risk, credit risk, and market risk, as well as some legal and other reasons that prevent reporting.

5.5 INTERNAL OPERATIONAL LOSS DATABASES

The Basel II Accord places significant emphasis on the construction of internal loss databases for the purpose of measuring and managing operational risk. The BCBS (2003a) stipulates that data on operational losses is a tool that can be used for validating risk estimates, being a component of risk reporting and a key input in any AMA model of operational risk. Cagan (2001) argues that internal databases resemble external databases in the sense that both need to be supported by a well-defined body of data standards, but they differ in the type of losses they cover. While internal databases record the high-frequency, low-severity losses that characterize daily operations, external databases tend to cover the low-frequency, high-severity losses.

Haubenstock (2004) argues that collecting operational loss data is more beneficial to the underlying bank than just the satisfaction of the regulatory requirements, including the very act of collecting the data and the calculation of regulatory capital. It is indeed a component of the risk management framework (see Chapter 8), which is implemented for the ultimate objective of reducing both the frequency and severity of operational losses. More specifically, Haubenstock (2004) lists the following advantages of operational loss data collection:

■ Increasing awareness of operational risk and its potential harm to the firm.

■ Quantifying exposure, which helps efforts to focus resources on risk mitigation where it is needed.

■ Analysis of the causes of events, which can be conducive to the improvement of controls.

■ Evaluating the self-assessment process, because actual loss events can be used as a quality check over self-assessment. For example, a department that endures 100 operational loss events with an average severity of $50,000 cannot (without proper justification) make the prediction that it will only endure five loss events with an average severity of $10,000 over the following year.

An important question that crops up in any endeavor to construct an operational loss database is what constitutes an operational loss event (that is, what to record and what to leave out). According to the Basel II Accord, only direct losses are to be recorded, which encompass categories ranging from the write-down of assets to the loss of physical assets. The justification for this restriction is that these effects are objective and can be measured directly and consistently. Just like the choice of the definition of operational risk, this choice is rather narrow for a pragmatic reason, to facilitate the measurement of operational risk and hence regulatory capital. However, Haubenstock (2004) argues that firms should define their own data collection policies, which may mean going beyond Basel II. As a matter of fact, some external databases go beyond the Basel II recommendations by recording events that are not recognized by the Accord for the purpose of calculating regulatory capital. Why? Because the collection of operational loss data has more benefits than the mere regulatory compliance, and because (as we will see in Chapter 8) it is an integral part of the operational risk management framework. Likewise, Cagan (2001) argues that although it makes sense to adopt a definition for quantifying capital that excludes items that cannot be easily calculated, it is important to collect softer and less quantifiable losses for the sake of qualitative analysis.

In addition to the direct losses identified by Basel II, Haubenstock (2004) recommends that firms should collect data on near misses, which are events where some type of failure occurred without incurring financial loss, and indirect losses (or associated costs), which include items like business interruption, forgone income, loss of reputation, and poor quality. He also recommends the inclusion of strategic or business risk events. We have already seen that the exclusion of business risk from the definition of operational risk is a controversial issue, which Haubenstock (2004) capitalizes upon in his defense of the inclusion of business risk. For example, he takes the difficulty of attributing the following costs to either operational risk or business risk to mean that the line between operational risk and strategic risk is not clear at all: pulling out of a country, a failed product introduction, restructuring costs after layoff and excess real estate capacity due to inaccurate estimation.

Another important issue is the determination of the loss threshold, which is the amount below which the underlying loss event will not be recorded. The answer is simply that the choice of a threshold is a matter of costs and benefits, which means that it should vary across firms and activities. Some guidance can be obtained from the external databases. For example, the Riskdata Exchange Association, the American Bankers Association, and the BBA use thresholds of $25,000, $10,000, and $50,000, respectively. Roehr (2002) argues that the threshold, which is necessary to make the task of data collection manageable and cost effective, may change over time, depending on the business line and event type. He also argues that thresholds are likely to be much higher in external than in internal databases.

In addition to these issues, other related issues are confidentiality of the data and the mechanics of the collection process, including roles and responsibilities. We will have more to say about the modes of operational loss data collection in Chapter 8, so we close this chapter by saying a few words about confidentiality. In general, operational losses and events are regarded as very sensitive information, which means that there should be some standard for disclosure within and outside the firm. Firms, therefore, design their own confidentiality and data access restriction policies with the objective of striking a balance between security and transparency.

APPENDIX 5.1   SELECTED OPERATIONAL LOSS EVENTS

Table 5A1.1 contains 62 randomly selected operational loss events organized chronologically, spanning the period 1984–2006. The table reports the settlement date (when the case is closed), the name of the entity incurring the loss, the loss amount in million US dollars, the business line and event type. When no specific business line appears (–), this means that it is unclassified by the BCBS. This is because the BCBS classification is designed for banks only, whereas this table reports loss events endured by a variety of entities, including cities and universities. The source of information is various media outlets.

Table 5A1.1 Selected operational loss events reported by the media

Settlement Date	Firm	Loss (US$ million)	Business Line	Event Type
23/05/1984	Nestle S.A.	41.3	–	Damage to Physical Assets
01/05/1988	Nissan Motor Company	4.9	–	Clients, Products, and Business Practices
12/07/1989	Walt Disney Company	100.0	–	Employment Practices and Workplace Safety
01/10/1990	Eastman Kodak	92.5	Corporate Finance	Clients, Products, and Business Practices
01/02/1991	Mobil Oil Company	1.0	–	Clients, Products, and Business Practices
20/12/1991	Apple Computers	19.8	–	Clients, Products, and Business Practices
01/01/1992	Kuwait Oil Tankers Company	100.0	–	Internal Fraud
01/02/1992	Motorola Inc.	15.1	–	Clients, Products, and Business Practices
01/02/1992	Xerox Corp.	2.5	–	Clients, Products, and Business Practices
22/07/1992	Midland Bank	6.0	Commercial Banking	Internal Fraud
01/10/1992	Caterpillar Inc.	15.7	–	Employment Practices and Workplace Safety
20/05/1993	Nippon Steel	127.5	Corporate Finance	Internal Fraud
01/07/1993	Louisiana Interstate Gas Company	35.0	–	Clients, Products, and Business Practices
01/09/1993	Yamaichi Securities Co.	96.0	–	Clients, Products, and Business Practices
28/10/1993	Land Bank of Taiwan	4.0	Commercial Banking	Internal Fraud

(Continued)

Table 5A1.1 (*Continued*)

Settlement Date	Firm	Loss (US$ million)	Business Line	Event Type
01/01/1994	British Gas	1.2	–	Employment Practices and Workplace Safety
01/01/1994	Sao Paulo State Electricity Company	1.0	–	Damage to Physical Assets
01/02/1994	Air France	131.5	–	Damage to Physical Assets
01/02/1994	US Airways	8.1	–	Damage to Physical Assets
01/10/1994	Stanford University	3.2	–	Internal Fraud
01/01/1995	Lockheed Martin Corporation	24.8	–	Internal Fraud
10/03/1995	Kraft Foods Inc.	75.3	Corporate Finance	Clients, Products and Business Practices
01/12/1995	University of Wisconsin	3.5	–	Damage to Physical Assets
01/01/1996	Coca-Cola	2.0	–	Clients, Products, and Business Practices
01/01/1996	University of California at Berkley	1.0	–	Employment Practices and Workplace Safety
01/01/1996	Yorkshire Building Society	0.01	Retail Banking	Employment Practices and Workplace Safety
08/03/1996	Nike Inc.	15.0	–	Clients, Products, and Business Practices
31/12/1996	Bangkok Bank of Commerce	88.0	Payment and Settlement	Internal Fraud
01/02/1997	Toyota Motor Corporation	200.0	–	Damage to Physical Assets
01/01/1998	National Mortgage Bank of Greece	4.0	–	Clients, Products and Business Practices
01/01/1998	PepsiCo Inc.	2.4	–	Clients, Products, and Business Practices
17/02/2000	Singapore Airlines	9.1	–	Internal Fraud
15/06/2000	Amsterdam Stock Exchange	65.0	Corporate Finance	Clients, Products, and Business Practices
11/09/2001	New York City	95,000.0	–	Damage to Physical Assets
11/09/2001	Zurich Financial Services Group	900.0	–	Damage to Physical Assets

(Continued)

Table 5A1.1 (*Continued*)

Settlement Date	Firm	Loss (US$ million)	Business Line	Event Type
31/12/2001	Agricultural Development Bank of China	1.7	Commercial Banking	Internal Fraud
11/02/2002	British Airways	6.5	–	External Fraud
31/10/2002	Municipal Credit Union of New York City	15.0	Retail Banking	Damage to Physical Assets
19/03/2003	Central Bank of Iraq	1,000.0	Commercial Banking	External Fraud
25/03/2003	Commerzbank	33.6	Asset Management	Internal Fraud
01/04/2003	Yale University	0.15	–	External Fraud
31/05/2003	UK Inland Revenue	174.6	–	Business Disruption and System Failure
28/08/2003	Central Bank of Sweden	0.1	–	Employment Practices and Workplace Safety
19/03/2004	Bank of India	82.2	Commercial Banking	Internal Fraud
05/07/2004	Merchant Bank of Central Africa	19.0	Corporate Finance	Clients, Products, and Business Practices
06/09/2004	New Zealand Stock Exchange	0.44	–	Clients, Products, and Business Practices
20/10/2004	KPMG International	10.0	–	Clients, Products, and Business Practices
20/12/2004	Yukos Oil Company	9,300.0	–	Internal Fraud
31/12/2004	Bank of China	485.0	Commercial Banking	Internal Fraud
12/04/2005	New York Stock Exchange	20.0	Corporate Finance	Execution, Delivery, and Asset Management
10/05/2005	Banca Nazionale del Lavoro	1.3	Asset Management	Clients, Products, and Business Practices
18/05/2005	Morgan Stanley	1.6	Corporate Finance	Clients, Products, and Business Practices
08/08/2005	Central Bank of Brazil	70.0	Commercial Banking	External Fraud
29/08/2005	Lloyds of London	300.0	–	Clients, Products, and Business Practices
03/09/2005	State Bank of India	0.3	Commercial Banking	Internal Fraud
24/01/2006	Lloyds of London	124.6	–	Execution, Delivery, and Asset Management

(*Continued*)

Table 5A1.1 (*Continued*)

Settlement Date	Firm	Loss (US$ million)	Business Line	Event Type
15/03/2006	Commonwealth Bank of Australia	7.3	Asset Management	Internal Fraud
25/04/2006	British Petroleum	2.4	–	Employment Practices and Workplace Safety
12/07/2006	Bank of America	0.75	–	Execution, Delivery, and Asset Management
24/07/2006	Credit Suisse First Boston	6.7	Corporate Finance	Clients, Products, and Business Practices
24/07/2006	Lehman Brothers	0.88	Corporate Finance	Clients, Products, and Business Practices
02/08/2006	Royal Bank of Scotland	50.4	Commercial Banking	External Fraud

APPENDIX 5.2 A DESCRIPTION OF SOME OPERATIONAL LOSS EVENTS BY TYPE AND BUSINESS LINE

Tables 5A2.1 and 5A2.2 contain a brief description of selected loss events, as reported by the media, classified by event type and business line, respectively.

Table 5A2.1 A description of some operational loss events by type

Event Type	Company	Description of Event
Internal Fraud (Robbery)	Westpac Banking Corporation (Australia)	A senior bank customer relations manager stole more than AUD3.5 million between February 2003 and December 2004 from 15 customers' accounts. He was arrested in July 2006 and charged with obtaining money by deception and several counts of signature forgery.
Internal Fraud (Tax Evasion)	GlaxoSmithKline plc (U.S.A.)	In September 2006, a settlement was reached between the company and the U.S. Internal Revenue Service, whereby the Company agreed to pay $3.4 billion to settle a dispute over the taxation dealings between the British parent company and its U.S. subsidiary over the period 1989-2005.
Internal Fraud (Robbery)	JP Morgan Chase & Co (U.S.A.)	At a hearing in a U.S. federal court held on 21 August 2006, a former mailroom employee pleaded guilty to the theft of some $100 million in corporate cheques from a lock-box facility in New York.

(Continued)

Table 5A2.1 (*Continued*)

Event Type	Company	Description of Event
Internal Fraud (Credit Fraud)	Agricultural Bank of China (China)	In June 2006, China's Audit Office announced that it had discovered cases of criminal activity and fraudulent loans worth 51.5 billion yuan ($6.45 billion) at the Agricultural Bank of China.
Internal Fraud (Credit Fraud)	Universal Corporation (U.S.A.)	In September 2006, a California court ordered Universal Corporation to pay two of its employees $25 million in compensation for retaliation against them after they had reported fraudulent insurance claims.
Internal Fraud (Credit Fraud)	ANZ (Australia)	In June 2006 charges were brought against a former employee of the ANZ following an investigation by the Australian Securities and Investment Commission into unauthorized loans totaling AUD14.5 million.
External Fraud (Robbery)	Shanghai City Pension Fund (China)	A 33 year old Shanghai tycoon was arrested in October 2006 following an investigation of his role in the disappearance of 3.2 billion yuan ($400 million) from the Shanghai City Pension Fund.
Internal Fraud (Robbery)	Kuwait Oil Tankers Company (Kuwait)	In March 1992, two of four former executives of the Kuwait Oil Tankers Company were accused of embezzling $100 million from the state-owned company in the 1980s and during the 1990-91 Gulf crisis (war).
External Fraud (Forgery)	Macquarie Bank Limited (Australia)	In June 2006, four people were charged over Macquarie Bank's loss of about $4.5 million in margin loans obtained from the bank by them on behalf of investors.
BDSF (Hardware Failure)	Sony Corporation (Japan)	In August 2006, Apple Computer and Dell Inc recalled a total of 5.9 million notebook-computer batteries made by Sony, which can overheat and cause fire hazard. The loss amount was estimated at $225 million.
BDSF (Software)	Anthem Inc (U.S.A.)	In November 2005, the state government of Kentucky ordered Anthem Inc to refund $23.7 million to customers who were overcharged for Medicare Supplement coverage as well as fining it $2 million. The company stated that the faulty numbers resulted from a computer processing error.
BDSF (Software)	National Australia Bank (Australia)	In November 2004, the National Australia Bank announced that it had written off AUD409 million in impaired software.

(*Continued*)

Table 5A2.1 (*Continued*)

Event Type	Company	Description of Event
BDSF (Software)	ING Groep NV (Netherlands)	In June 2005, the ING Groep NV announced that it would compensate some 500,000 customers who were provided with incorrect calculations for personal insurance policies at a cost of 65 million euros.
BDSF (Systems)	JPMorgan Chase & Co (U.S.A.)	In 1998, Chase Manhattan Bank identified inaccuracies in its bond recording system, but nothing was done about it until it merged with JP Morgan in 2000. As a result, the bank lost $46.8 million as the glitch in the system caused funds to be transferred to bondholders who were not entitled to them.
EDPM (Data entry or maintenance errors)	Universal Health Care Services Inc. (U.S.A.)	In August 2006, Universal Health Care Service Inc announced that a U.S. government glitch caused a hold up of members' promised refunds, thus costing the company $3 million.
EDPM (Failed reporting obligation)	Morgan Stanley (U.S.A.)	In September 2006, the National Association of Securities Dealers fined Morgan Stanley $2.9 million for a variety of trading and trade-reporting violations over the period 1999-2006.
EDPM (Inaccurate reporting)	Banesto (Spain)	In April 2001, a court case between Carlisle Ventures and Banesto was settled when the latter paid the former $13.5 million in compensation for false reporting. According to Carlisle, Banesto portrayed itself as being in a better financial position than it was in reality.
EDPM (system misoperation)	Royal Bank of Canada (Canada)	In December 2005, the Royal Bank of Canada announced that it would refund CAD25 million to customers who were paid simple rather than compound interest as a result of a calculation error.
EPWS (Discrimination)	FedEx Corporation (U.S.A.)	In June 2006, a court awarded two Lebanese-American drivers $61 million in damages for suffering from racial discrimination by their supervisor.
EPWS (Loss of staff)	Benfield Group (U.K.)	In October 2006, the Benfield Group (a reinsurance brokerage firm) declared that its results would be sharply worse than expected due to the departure of key staff members. The firm also declared that it would spend some GBP10 million to retain the remaining staff.
EPWS (Termination Issues)	Microsoft Corp. (U.S.A.)	In October 2005, Microsoft paid $97 million to settle a lawsuit to compensate workers who were employed and paid by temporary agencies while they worked for Microsoft for long periods.

(*Continued*)

Table 5A2.1 (*Continued*)

Event Type	Company	Description of Event
EPWS (Termination Issues)	Commertzbank (U.K.)	In November 2000, Commerzbank reached a GBP5 million settlement with the former chairman of a company that Commerzbank had acquired. He was dismissed over a dispute over the valuation of certain assets.
EPWS (Discrimination)	Merrill Lynch and Company (U.K.)	In July 2004, a former employee of Merrill Lynch received a GBP550,000 compensation from the employer following comments about her physique and sex life at a Christmas lunch.
DPA (Natural Disasters)	Murphy Oil Corporation (U.S.A.)	In August 2005, Hurricane Katrina resulted in a major leak in Murphy's oil refinery in Louisiana, spilling over 85,000 barrels of oil. The company had to pay $330 million in compensation to the residents of St Bernard Parish in New Orleans.
DPA (Natural Disasters)	Allianz AG (Germany)	In July 2002, Allianz AG declared losses of 550 million euros as a result of severe flooding in Europe that summer.
CPBP (Guideline Violation)	FleetBoston Financial Corporation (U.S.A.)	In October 2006, FleetBoston Financial Corporation agreed to pay $19.75 million for failure to prevent the collapse of Enron Corporation.
CPBP (Money Laundering)	Bank of America	In September 2006, Bank of America agreed to pay $7.5 million to settle a money-laundering case involving $3 billion from South America.
CPBP (Market Practices)	Deutsche Bank Group (U.S.A.)	In September 2006, Deutsche Asset Management, a U.S. arm of Deutsche Bank, agreed to pay $19.3 million in settlement after failure to disclose conflict of interest.

Table 5A2.2 A description of some operational loss events by business line

Business Line	Company	Description of Event
Corporate Finance	JPMorgan Chase & Co (U.S.A.)	In September 2006, the New York Stock Exchange fined JPMorgan Chase $400,000 for violation of short-selling rules.
Corporate Finance	General Electric Co. (U.S.A.)	In August 2006, General Electric paid Canatxx Energy Ventures $136.1 million in damages for breaching a contract pertaining to a joint industrial project.

(*Continued*)

Table 5A2.2 (*Continued*)

Business Line	Company	Description of Event
Corporate Finance	Canadian Imperial Bank of Commerce (U.S.A.)	In July 2006, the Canadian Imperial Bank of Commerce agreed to pay $16.5 million as its share of the settlement over a case involving the underwriting of securities prior to the bankruptcy of Global Crossing in January 2002.
Corporate Finance	Grand Tobidabo (Spain)	In 1994 the former president of Grand Tibidabo was arrested for misappropriating $1 billion pesetas from a government-guaranteed loan to the company received from Chase Manhattan Bank.
Commercial Banking	Bank Islam Malaysia (Malaysia)	In 2005, Bank Islam Malaysia recorded losses of 480 million ringgit due to higher provisions for nonperforming loans made on operations conducted by the bank's offshore unit in Labuan.
Commercial Banking	ABN Amro Bank (U.K.)	In March 1999, ABN Amro declared losses of $30 million due to fraud related to letters of credit.
Retail Banking	Wells Fargo & Co. (U.S.A.)	In October 2006, Wells Fargo & Co. reached a $12.8 million settlement in an overtime pay lawsuit with employees.
Retail Banking	Visa International (U.S.A.)	In July 2006, Visa agreed to pay $100 million as its share of a settlement regarding fees charged to cardholders for foreign currency denominated transactions.
Retail Banking	ANZ (New Zealand)	In March 2006, the ANZ pleaded guilty to 45 charges of breaching the new Zealand Fair Trading Act by failing to disclose fees charged for overseas currency transactions on its credit cards.
Payment and Settlement	Credit Lyonnais (Belgium)	In March 1997, a former employee of Credit Lyonnais Belgium was arrested for embezzling BEF3.5 billion from the bank's offices in Ghent.
Agency Services	Dresdner Bank (U.K.)	In July 2004, Dresdner Bank was told by a London court that it must repay EUR49.2 million to the Saudi Arabia Monetary Agency.

CHAPTER 6

Modeling and Measuring Operational Risk: General Principles

6.1 INTRODUCTION

More than a century ago, the Irish mathematician and physicist Lord Kelvin (1842–1907) made the following statement (cited in King, 2001):

> I often say when you can measure what you are speaking about, and express it in numbers, you know something about it; but when you cannot measure it, when you cannot express it in numbers, your knowledge is of a meager and unsatisfactory kind.

Lord Kelvin's remarks relate to science, which is naturally more precise than trying to measure the "ghost" of operational risk. But before talking about the measurement of operational risk, it may be worthwhile to go back to 1707 when Britain, then the supreme naval force, lost four ships and 2000 sailors because of inadequate measurement. That happened on a foggy night of October that year, but there was no battle at sea then. Not knowing exactly where they were, the four ships under the command of Admiral Clowdisely Shovell smashed into the rocks of the Scilly Isles off the Southwest Atlantic coast of England. How did that happen under the watch of such an experienced admiral? He simply miscalculated his position (longitude and latitude) in the Atlantic because he did not have the instruments to do that, basing his calculations instead on an intellectual guess of the average speed of his ship.

Although Edward Smith, the captain of the Titanic, had better instruments to calculate his position, he still lacked the instruments to tell him how far away an iceberg was, in which case he had to depend on the eyes of two young sailors to look for icebergs. Smith was also an experienced captain, but unlike Shovell, he was under pressure to sail too far north at a high speed to make it to New York by a certain time. While more blame can be put on Smith than Shovell (although the former was acting on orders from his boss), inadequate measurement led to a disaster (a catastrophic loss event) in both cases.

6.1.1   Measurement or assessment?

Going back to operational risk, it is arguable that the accuracy of operational risk measurement will never be achieved (Dowd, 2003). In relation to operational risk, the word "measurement" means something closer to the word "assessment", although Knot et al. (2006) distinguish between risk measurement and risk assessment by arguing that risk measurement refers to the quantification of risk, whereas risk assessment is a broader concept in the sense that it also entails the interpretation of nonquantitative pieces of information. Whether we call it measurement or assessment, this rather difficult task remains a crucial one for the purpose of developing the knowledge necessary for its proper management. Because risk cannot be eliminated completely, risk measurement is the key to, and an essential prerequisite for, effective risk management. And it is not only about the amount of risk (whatever this means) but also where it resides, what contributes to it and the impact of mitigation strategies. All of these dimensions are important for the risk manager who aspires for the implementation of effective risk management practices. And while there is nothing wrong in principle with using a capital buffer for any sort of risk, the resulting capital charge will only create unsound incentives if the calculation method is poor.

Current efforts to quantify operational risk follow more than a decade of immense changes in risk management practices. During this time, the emergence of new quantitative techniques and computational resources has greatly enhanced our ability to measure, monitor, and manage risk. The new techniques (starting with value at risk, VAR) were first applied to market risk. Credit risk management has also been greatly enhanced, as banks have been utilizing credit risk models to calculate the probability of default, loss given default, and exposure at default. Currently, efforts are directed at the improvement of the techniques used for operational risk measurement and consequently management.

6.1.2 Why modeling operational risk is necessary

A question may arise as to why modeling operational risk is necessary, given that banks appear to have been managing it successfully? The very survival of banks (and firms in general) would suggest that they have the skills and procedures for managing operational risk without measurement, let alone modeling. Peccia (2003) responds to the question about the need for operational risk measurement by arguing that modeling operational risk has become important because the environment in which banks operate has changed dramatically. To remain fit, he argues, banks must adapt to the new reality, given that the new environment is much more complex in terms of product offerings, delivery channels, and jurisdictions. Peccia (2003) argues that a model is "simply a telescope and compass" that banks need to navigate in a rapidly shifting environment. But there is also the regulatory requirement of the Basel II Accord that an operational risk model is needed to be in a position to use the AMA, which is attractive because it results in lower regulatory capital than under the other two approaches. Indeed, it is arguable that one advantage of operational risk modeling is that the resulting models allow the firm to meet the regulatory requirements.

Operational risk modeling is also needed to provide the management of a firm with a tool for making better decisions about the desirable level of operational risk to take (risk appetite or risk tolerance). Bocker and Kluppelberg (2005) argue that the only feasible way to manage operational risk successfully is by identifying and minimizing it, which requires the development of adequate quantification techniques. An operational risk model creates the common language of VAR for operational risk, enhancing senior management to set consistent operational risk tolerance and guiding the management of operational risk. One may argue that the appropriate level of operational risk should be 0, in which case no model is required: simply avoid risk altogether. But this does not make sense, because it may require closing down the business, particularly in the case of payments systems, asset management, trading, and other advisory business. If a bank implements many controls on the activities of traders, the risk of rogue trading can be reduced significantly, but such a drastic action makes it prohibitively expensive to trade. At present, most banks put in controls that allow for some level of rogue trading, but it is not straightforward to tell if the level of the risk of rogue trading is acceptable. The same can be said about information security, identity theft, aggressive selling, and various other forms of operational risk. By running these businesses, banks operate within certain implicit operational risk tolerance.

An operational risk model makes risk tolerance explicit and transparent, allowing the possibility of determining whether or not the risk-return trade off is acceptable. After all, a bank should allocate capital to support the risks that produce the highest return–risk ratio, and this principle is valid for operational risk as much as it is valid for market risk and credit risk. The only difference is that the risk–return trade off associated with market risk and credit risk is more conspicuous than that associated with operational risk.

Fujii (2005) argues that quantifying operational risk is a prerequisite for the formulation of an effective economic capital framework. Indeed, a model designed to measure operational risk should provide answers to some vital questions pertaining to (i) the most significant operational risks facing the firm; (ii) the impact of the most significant risks on the firm's financial statements; (iii) the worst the impact can be; (iv) the weight of the impact in stress situations; (v) how the impact is affected by changing the business strategy or control environment; and (iv) how the impact compares with the experience of similar firms. Furthermore, Consiglio and Zenois (2003) emphasize the importance of operational risk models by attributing some widely publicized loss events to the use of inadequate models rather than anything else. For example, they wonder whether the collapse of Long-Term Capital Management was due to liquidity risk or the inappropriate use of models. They also wonder whether the demise of Barings was due to the "tail below its value at risk exposure". And they wonder whether the bankruptcy of Nissan Mutual was due to declining interest rates in Japan or inadequate models for pricing the options embedded in its policies. Actually, Giraud (2005) attributes the collapse of Long-Term Capital Management in 1998 (with a total loss of $4 billion) in large part to "model bias in the risk management process".

One has to bear in mind that models are used to support (rather than replace) management judgment. This is because judgment is sometimes inadequate, particularly in the case of certain types of operational risk, and when it comes to dealing with unexpected losses. While it is relatively easy for the management to make judgment about frequent events, such as credit card fraud, it is rather difficult and hazardous to make judgment about rare events. Models are used to extend business judgment about expected losses to the unknown territory of unexpected losses.

6.1.3 The origin of operational risk modeling

Although Bocker and Kluppelberg (2005) trace operational risk modeling to the insurance risk theory of the early 20th century, interest in this topic has grown tremendously in the last 10 years or so, and not only for regulatory purposes. Indicative of the fact that financial institutions were interested in operational risk measurement prior to the advent of Basel II is that some major banks have made some early attempts in this direction. Cruz (2003a) describes the early attempts to measure operational risk by Bankers Trust, Barclays, Touche Ross, Bank of America, the Commonwealth Bank of Australia, and Chase. The following is a brief account of these early attempts.

Bankers Trust, which is currently part of the Deutsche Bank Group, attempted to measure the level of economic capital required to support operational risk, relying heavily on external historical data. Barclays Bank was motivated to indulge in this exercise because the management attributed 30 percent of earnings volatility to business and operational risk, viewing operational risk as being made up of a large number of very specific risks that are not correlated and so tend to cancel out each other. The model developed by Barclays for this purpose relied strongly on controls and insurance for operational risk management. Actually, Barclays was one of the first financial institutions to establish an operational risk team with a responsibility for all global operations. In 1995 Touche Ross (now Deloitte Touche Ross) used a qualitative approach based on a risk assessment matrix that categorized operational risk across all activities. Bank of America focused on a set of eight operational risk key ratios (such as the ratio of operating expenses to fixed costs) for the purpose of comparing businesses and individual business lines, as well as internal surveys on the riskiness of their business. The Commonwealth Bank of Australia developed an earnings volatility approach, encompassing a hybrid calculation methodology that involved quantitative volatility analysis and a qualitative risk estimation process.

Chase used the Capital asset pricing model (CAPM) to measure operational risk, assuming that the difference between total return for the bank and investment return arises from operational risk. It followed that the required earnings against operational risk was equal to the rate of return on operational risk multiplied by the book value of the firm. The final step in this approach was to calculate the capital required to cover operational risk as the required earnings on operational risk divided by the rate of return on the firm.

6.2 THE PROBLEMS OF MEASURING AND MODELING OPERATIONAL RISK

Measuring risk is problematical, and measuring operational risk is even more so. In a particular reference to operational risk, Pezier (2003b) argues that risk cannot be measured, which is contrary to popular opinion. Risk, he argues, "is not like the length of hosepipe that can be checked by anyone with a measuring tape and which can be connected to other lengths of hosepipe to reach the back of the garden". Because risk is about the future, it can be assessed only by using a model that represents future realizations. Measuring operational risk, it seems, is yet another difficult exercise that we have to indulge in, just like when we indulge in exchange rate forecasting. Crouchy (2001) argues that the difficulties encountered in measuring operational risk do not imply that it should be ignored. Indeed, Crouchy uses the difficulty of identifying and measuring operational risk as a reason why this kind of risk should be paid more attention. In this section, we discuss the problems associated with measuring and modeling operational risk, which is a prerequisite for its management.

Perhaps it is useful at this stage to distinguish between the modeling and measurement of operational risk. Modeling operational risk is essentially an exercise that is conducted with the objective of arriving at the best-fit distribution for potential operational losses over a given period of time (normally a year). Typically, the distribution of operational losses is obtained by combining the loss frequency and loss severity distributions. The measurement of operational risk amounts to arriving at a single figure that tells us how much the underlying firm is likely to lose with a certain probability, so that a correspondingly adequate amount of capital is held for the purpose of protecting the firm from insolvency. In the advanced measurement approach, measurement is based on modeling, for example, by using a given percentile of the total loss distribution. However, measurement can be based on *ad hoc* methods (and so it is measurement without modeling) as in the basic indicators approach and the standardized approach. The link between modeling and measurement is viewed by van Lelyveld (2006) as a common pattern underlying all state-of-the art models in that they ultimately determine a number called the "economic capital".

6.2.1 The problems of definition and data availability

The first problem encountered by any endeavor to model operational risk pertains to the conceptual issue of finding a proper and universally accepted definition of operational risk. It is the unavailability of such a definition that creates the first problem. Peccia (2004) expresses this view by describing the BCBS's definition of operational risk as being "too elastic to be useful for developing a useful measurement model".

The second problem is data availability (or rather unavailability). Muzzy (2003) highlights this problem by arguing that "anyone venturing into operational risk management has quickly learned that the process is doomed without robust data", but he describes the gathering of operational loss data as "a high-wire act with no safety net". This is because there is in general an absence of reliable internal operational loss data, which has impeded progress in measuring and managing operational risk. The available databases that are dominated by high-frequency, low-severity events and by few large losses. But with the impetus of Basel II, banks and vendors have begun collecting reliable data on operational losses. The problem, however, is that publicly available operational loss data pose unique modeling challenges, the most important of which is that not all losses are reported in public. de Fontnouvelle et al. (2003) argue that if the probability that an operational loss is reported increases as the loss amount increases, there will be a disproportionate number of very large losses relative to smaller losses appearing in external databases. Allen and Bali (2004) suggest that operational risk databases tend to suffer from underrepresentation of low-frequency, high-severity events. Haas and Kaiser (2004) note that low-frequency, high-severity events, which by definition are much less likely to occur, are often kept confidential (therefore, unreported or misclassified under credit or market risk losses). Another bias inherent in the databases stems from the minimum loss requirement for inclusion in the database. Haas and Kaiser (2004) and Kalhoff and Haas (2004) discuss the issue of how truncated databases yield biased VAR estimates.

One solution to the data availability problem is to augment internal data with external data on the operational losses incurred by other firms. Frachot and Roncalli (2002) discuss why and how internal and external data on operational loss are mixed by distinguishing between frequency data and severity data. They, for example, argue that mixing internal and external frequency data can be based on the credibility theory, which is the root of insurance theory. One problem here is that external data must be scaled to fit the size and business mix of the underlying firm to make it suitable for the estimation of operational risk for that firm. Pezier (2003b) casts considerable doubt on the usefulness of external operational loss data by wondering about the relevance of an exceptional loss incurred by a broker in Bombay (currently known as Mumbai) to the operational risk distribution of an asset manager in Manhattan. He concludes that the mere recording of a loss amount in one firm cannot be translated mechanically into the probability and severity of loss in another firm. Peccia (2004) argues on similar lines by saying that pooling data should be done only for firms that share the same risk factors (business activity, size, business environment, and control environment). Frachot and Roncalli (2002) put forward the view that mixing internal and external severity data is "almost an impossible task" because no one knows which data generating process is used to draw external severity data. They further argue that merging internal and external data gives spurious results that tend to be over-optimistic regarding the actual severity distribution.

Alexander (2003b) suggests that internal data should be augmented by "soft data" obtained from scorecards, expert opinions, publicly available data, and operational risk data from an external consortium. However, she admits that soft data have a subjective element, which means that they must be distinguished from the more objective operational risk hard data that are obtained directly from the historical loss experience of the underlying firm. She also suggests that the external loss data must be scaled by the ratio of a particular firm's capitalization to total capitalizations of all firms in the data sample. New methods are being developed for combining internal and external data in response to the BCBS's (2001a) recommendation that banks must establish procedures for the use of external data as a supplement to its internal loss data. As for the data obtained from "expert opinion", Peccia (2004) argues that there is a problem here because the experts typically have little or no experience in the low-frequency, high-severity events.

Scaling external data is a problem because it is not clear if an increase in the scale of operations results in a proportional increase in operational risk, which leads to the issue of size and how to measure size. Smithson (2000) argues that a simple benchmark measure of operational risk could be based on an aggregate measure of the size of the firm. As possible measures of size, he suggests gross revenue, fee income, operating costs, managed assets, and total assets adjusted for off-balance sheet exposures. The problem is that while the relation between size and operational risk has some intuitive appeal and is easy to calculate, it does not capture the connection between operational risk and the nature of the business. Shih, Samad-Khan, and Medapa (2000) have shown that little of the variability in operational losses can be explained by the size of a firm (revenue, assets, number of employees, etc.). Moreover, this approach is likely to set up perverse incentives in the sense that a firm that does a good job of operational risk management will have to hold more capital if the improvement in operational risk management leads to an increase in the volume of business.

6.2.2 The cyclicality of risk and loss events

Another problem associated with the measurement and modeling of operational risk arises from the cyclicality of risk and loss events. Allen and Bali (2004) argue that extrapolating the past to measure future risk may be flawed if there are cyclical factors that impact operational risk measures. Historical data on operational risk gathered during an economic expansion may not be relevant for a period of recession. Loss events incorporate cyclical components that are correlated with systematic risk factors such as macroeconomic fluctuations and regulatory shifts. It is typical, however, to ignore cyclical factors and extend an unadjusted trend line into the future. Allen and Bali demonstrate the importance of developing models to adjust for systematic and cyclical risk factors.

The neglect of the cyclical components of risk is not the result of an oversight, and it is indeed arguable that one of the major impediments to the adoption of Basel II is the Accord's apparent neglect of cyclical factors. Allen and Bali (2004) put forward the view that the risk-adjusted requirements of Basel II are procyclical. For example, if the risk models overstate (understate) risk in bad (good) times, then capital requirements will be too high (low) in bad (good) times, which forces capital-constrained banks to retrench on lending during recessions and expand during booms. Banks are typically subject to the same macroeconomic cyclical fluctuations, which means that the overall effect of the Accord would be to increase the amplitude of the business cycle, making recessions more severe and overheating the economy excessively during the expansion phase of the cycle. The importance of cyclical factors in the business measures of risk has been acknowledged by Allen and Saunders (2002, 2004). Empirically, Allen and Bali (2004) show that cyclical factors are significant components of both catastrophic and operational risk.

6.2.3   The problem of correlation

Yet another problem is the assumption to be made about the correlation of operational loss events. Frachot, Moudoulaud, and Roncalli (2004) cast doubt on the validity of the proposition that operational risk losses occur simultaneously, describing it as being "rather dubious and hardly supported by empirical evidence". They also argue that common sense suggests that operational risk events are uncorrelated. If the proposition of perfect correlation across risk types and business lines is accepted, capital charges by risk type and/or business lines should be summed, leading to a higher capital charge than in the standardized approach as proposed by Basel II. As regulators intend to promote the use of the AMA, the perfect correlation assumption would be a disincentive and would go against the stated objectives of the Basel II Accord.

However, it is difficult to assess the level of correlation between different risk types and/or business units because of the lack of historical data. Powojowski, Reynolds, and Tuenter (2002) express the view that although some correlation exists between operational losses, modeling this correlation is not an easy task. Frachot et al. (2004) show that reliable estimations of correlation can be done by using data-independent theoretical calculations, producing weak correlation between the loss events corresponding to various risk types and business lines. They conclude that there are strong arguments in favor of low levels of correlation between aggregate losses, suggesting that capital charge summation is exaggeratedly conservative. Powojowski et al. (2002) suggest that including correlations in the calculation of regulatory capital requirements can have a significant effect on the calculation. Of course, one must not overlook the fact that correlation is only a measure of linear dependence, whereas loss events may be interdependent in other ways that cannot be captured by correlation. It is for this reason that operational risk modeling is making increasing utilization of the concept of the copula, which will be described in Chapter 7.

6.2.4 General problems and conclusion

In general, statistical/actuarial approaches to the measurement of operational risk create many challenges for the user, including the following:

1. The size of internal loss data necessary to develop a risk profile for a business line or the whole firm.

2. How to combine internal and external data, and should external data be scaled?

3. How to fit loss data to a distribution, particularly when the data are not collected from a zero loss level (for practical reasons all loss data are collected above a threshold level, the choice of which can be rather subjective).

4. How are loss frequencies estimated, particularly when data are collected from different sources over different time periods and with different threshold levels?

5. How to conduct mathematical backtesting?

Notwithstanding these (serious) problems (or perhaps because of them), major banks are actively indulging in (and spending a lot of money on) operational risk modeling. If for nothing else, they are required to do so by the regulators responsible for the implementation of the Basel II Accord.

6.3 EMPIRICAL STUDIES OF OPERATIONAL RISK

In this section, some empirical studies of operational risk are reviewed, starting with de Fontnouvelle et al. (2003) who address the problem of sample selection bias using an econometric model in which the truncation point for each loss (that is, the dollar value below which the loss is not reported) is modeled as an unobserved random variable. To model the underlying loss distribution, they rely on the extreme value theory (EVT), which suggests that the logarithm of losses above a high threshold should have an exponential distribution. They conclude the following:

■ While some have questioned the need for four explicit capital requirements for operational risk, the estimates indicate that operational losses are an important source of risk for banks. In fact, the capital charge for operational risk will often exceed the charge for market risk. They produce figures of the same order of magnitude as those reported by Hirtle (2003) for market risk capital requirement for top US banks.

■ Reporting bias in external data is significant. Accounting for bias reduces significantly the estimated operational risk requirement.

■ The distribution of observed losses varies significantly by business line. It is not clear, however, whether this is driven by cross-business line variation in operational risk or by variation in the sample selection process.

■ Supplementing internal data with external data on extremely large events could improve models of operational risk significantly.

To deal with the data problem, Allen and Bali (2004) estimate an operational risk measure for individual financial institutions using a monthly time series of stock returns over the period 1973–2003. The model is represented by the following OLS regression

$$r_t = \alpha_{0,t} + \alpha_{1,t}\Delta x_{1t} + \cdots + \alpha_{22,t}\Delta x_{22t} + \beta_t r_{t-1} + \sum_{i=1}^{4} \gamma_{i,t} FF_{it} + \sum_{i=1}^{3} \pi_{i,t} R_{i,t} + \varepsilon_t \quad (6.1)$$

where r_t and r_{t-1} are the monthly current and lagged equity returns; Δx_{it} ($i = 1,2,\ldots 22$) is the first difference of the 22 variables used to represent credit risk, interest rate risk, exchange rate risk, and market risk; FF_{it} represents the three Fama–French (1993) factors (overall excess return on the market, a measure of the performance of small stocks relative to big stocks, and a measure of the monthly stock returns on a portfolio of value stocks relative to growth stocks), as well as a momentum factor (measured as the average return on the two highest prior return portfolios minus the average return on the two lowest prior portfolios); R_{it} represents three alternative industry factors measured as the average monthly return for each industry sector: depository institutions, insurance companies, and securities firms. The 22 Δx_{it} variables are reported in Table 6.1.

The residual term from equation (6.1) is taken to be a measure of operational risk. The coefficients are estimated using a rolling window of 50 months to yield results indicating that the ratio of the residual (operational risk) to total stock return is 17.7 percent, with considerable monthly variance. This suggests that financial firms have considerable levels of residual operational risk exposure that has been left relatively unmanaged. They attribute this finding to the lag in the development of operational risk measurement models, as well as the less developed state of the catastrophic and operational risk derivatives market. Furthermore, the residuals are then used to estimate operational risk VAR, while cyclicality is taken care of through the use of the GJR–GARCH model of Glosten, Jagannathan, and Runkle (1993). They conclude that macroeconomic, systematic, and environmental factors play a considerable role in influencing the risk to which financial institutions are exposed and that models ignoring cyclical factors are flawed.

Table 6.1 The risk variables used by Allen and Bali (2004)

Risk measures	Variables
Overall credit risk measure	• The spread between the AAA and BBB corporate bond yields
Firm-specific credit risk measures	• Market value of equity/book value of assets=1-leverage ratio • Net income/sales • Log of book value of total assets
Interest rate risk measures	• 3-month U.S. Treasury bill rates • 10-year U.S. Treasury bond rates • 3-month Eurobond rates • 10-year German Treasury bond rates • Discount rate in Japan • Long Japanese bond rates • 91-day U.K. Treasury bill rates • 10-year U.K. Treasury bond rates
Exchange rate risk measures	• DEM/USD exchange rate • GBP/USD exchange rate • JPY/USD exchange rate
Market risk measures	• Stock price index (Canada) • Stock price index (France) • Stock price index (Italy) • Stock price index (Japan) • Stock price index (Germany) • Stock price index (France)

de Fontnouvelle, Rosengren, and Jordan (2004) used loss data covering six large internationally active banks (as part of the BCBS's (2003c) operational risk loss data exercise) to find out if the regularities in the loss data make consistent modeling of operational losses possible. They find similarities in the results of models of operational loss across banks and that their results are consistent with the publicly reported operational risk capital estimates produced by banks' internal economic capital models. Moscadelli (2005) analyzed data from the BCBS's exercise, performing a thorough comparison of traditional full-data analyses and extreme value methods for estimating loss severity distributions. He found that EVT outperformed the traditional methods in all of the eight business lines proposed by the BCBS. He also found the severity distribution to be very heavy-tailed and that a substantial difference exists in loss severity across business lines. One major difference between these two studies is that while Moscadelli (2005) aggregated data across all banks, de Fontnouvelle et al. (2004) used data at the individual bank level. Furthermore, de Fontnouvelle et al. used the technique of Huisman et al. (2001) to correct for potential bias in the tail parameter estimate. They also explored several models of the loss frequency distribution, which makes it possible to obtain indicative estimates of economic capital for operational risk.

Wei (2003) conducted an empirical study of operational risk in the insurance industry to test the following hypotheses:

1. Operational loss events do not lead to significant changes in the stock prices of insurance companies.

2. No relation exists between operational losses and changes in stock prices.

3. Operational losses resulting from market conduct problems and those resulting from other types of events have the same effects on the change of stock prices.

4. The insurance industry is not affected by the operational loss events of a few insurers.

5. Operational loss events due to firm-specific problems and events due to common problems within the industry have the same effect on the industry as a whole.

6. Nonannouncing insurers are affected in a similar manner, regardless of differences in firm characteristics by operational loss events.

In general, these hypotheses fall under two groups: the information effect hypothesis and the contagion effect hypothesis. By using data from the OpVar operational loss database, he found results indicating that operational loss events have a significant negative effect on the market value of the affected insurers and that the effect of operational losses goes beyond the firm that incurs them. The conclusion derived from this study is that "the significant damage of market values of both the insurers and the insurance industry caused by operational losses should provide an incentive for operational risk management in the U.S. insurance industry".

In a more recent study, Wei (2006) examined the impact of operational loss events on the market value of announcing and nonannouncing US financial institutions using data from the OpVar database. The results reveal significantly negative impact of the announcement of operational losses on stock prices. He also found that the declines in market value significantly exceed the operational losses causing them, which supports the conjecture put forward by Cummins et al. (2006), and that there is a significant contagion effect. By using data from the same source, Cummins et al. (2006) conduct an event study of the impact of operational loss events on the market values of US banks and insurance companies, obtaining similar results to those obtained by Wei (2006). They found losses to be proportionately larger for institutions with higher Tobin's Q ratios, which implies that operational losses are more serious for firms with strong growth prospects.

6.4   THE TAXONOMY OF OPERATIONAL RISK MODELS

An operational risk model should help identify operational risk exposures, as well as the financial impact of these exposures. Since firms constantly change their strategies, product offering and distribution channels, the management of the firm should also be interested in what will be, which is another aspect of the issue that the model should deal with. Last, but not least, the model should provide information that enables the management to compare the situation with those of other firms.

6.4.1   Top-down versus bottom-up models

In general, operational risk models are classified into top-down models and bottom-up models, both of which rely on historical data. Bottom-up models are based on an analysis of loss events in individual processes, whereas top-down models require the calculation of the capital charge at the firm level and subsequently allocating it to the business lines, often using a proxy such as expenses or a scorecard approach. Haubenstock and Hardin (2003) argue that the bottom-up approach is preferred because of the degree of subjectivity in the allocation process and the lack of a good risk proxy across businesses. Likewise, Gelderman et al. (2006) argue that a limitation of the top-down approach is that it does not clearly indicate how to manage and control the outcomes of the model, and this is why the bottom-up approach tends to be more prevalent in practice.

Allen and Bali (2004) argue that many of the bottom-up models that are designed to measure operational risk from a cost perspective can produce spurious results. For example, if a firm institutes operational risk managerial controls, costs will generally increase thereby leading the bottom-up model to generate estimates of increased risk, but if the managerial controls are effective, operational risk should actually decrease. Moreover, bottom-up models often suffer from overdisaggregation in that they break production processes into individual steps that may obscure the broader picture. Finally, bottom-up models rely on the subjective data provided by employees who are under scrutiny and therefore have little incentive to be forthcoming. They further note that whereas bottom-up models may be appropriate for the purpose of risk diagnostics and the design of internal managerial controls, top-down models may be effective in estimating economic capital requirements. Currie (2004) calls for the concurrent use of top-down and bottom-up models to calculate operational risk capital requirements.

6.4.2 Process, factor, and actuarial approaches

Smithson (2000) classifies operational risk models under three approaches: (i) the process approach, (ii) the factor approach, and (iii) the actuarial approach. In the process approach, the focus is on the individual processes that make up operational activities, which means that models falling under the process approach are necessarily bottom-up models. The processes are decomposed into components (for example, a foreign exchange transaction is decomposed into processes ranging from the initial price discovery to the final settlement of the deal). Each component is examined to identify the operational risk associated with it, and by aggregating the operational risk inherent in the individual components, one can arrive at a measure of operational risk for the whole process. This approach encompasses the techniques described in Table 6.2.

The second approach is the factor approach, whereby an attempt is made to identify the significant determinants of operational risk, either at the institution level or lower levels (individual business lines or processes). Hence, operational risk is estimated as

$$OR = \alpha + \sum_{i=1}^{m} \beta_i F_i + \varepsilon \tag{6.2}$$

where F_i is risk factor i. The factor approach covers the techniques described in Table 6.3.

Table 6.2 The techniques of the process approach

Technique	Description
Causal Networks	Historical data are used to work out statistics for the behaviour of the components in the past, which makes it possible to identify the problem areas. Then it is possible to use scenario analysis or simulations to predict how the process works in the future.
Statistical Quality Control and Reliability Analysis	This technique is rather similar to causal networks, used widely to evaluate manufacturing processes.
Connectivity Analysis	The emphasis here is on the connections between the components of the process. A connectivity matrix is used to estimate potential losses arising from the process. For the whole institution, failure in one component propagate throughout the process and the institution.

Table 6.3 The techniques of the factor approach

Technique	Description
Risk Indicators	A regression-based technique that is used to identify the risk factors such as the volume of operations, audit ratings, employee turnover, employee training, age and quality of the systems used, and investment in new technology. Once an equation has been estimated, it can be used to calculate expected losses.
CAPM-like Models	More precisely known as arbitrage pricing models or economic pricing models, they are used to relate the volatility of returns (operational risk earnings) to operational risk factors.
Predictive Models	In this case, discriminant analysis and similar techniques are used to identify the factors that lead to operational losses.

The third approach is the actuarial approach, whose focus is the loss distribution associated with operational risk. This approach covers the following techniques: (i) the empirical loss distributions technique, (ii) the parameterized explicit distributions approach, and (iii) the EVT. The empirical loss distributions technique involves the collection of data on losses and plotting them in a histogram. Since individual firms typically have own data on high-frequency, low-severity losses but not much on low-frequency, high-severity losses, the histogram is constructed using internal data and external data after scaling. The problem with this technique is that even after utilizing external data, it is likely that an empirical histogram will suffer from limited data points, particularly in the tail of the distribution. The solution to this problem can be found in the parameterized explicit distributions technique, which is used to smooth the distribution by choosing an explicit distributional form. It has been suggested that it is more useful to specify a distribution for the frequency of losses and another different distribution for the severity of losses. Smithson (2000) argues that this has two advantages: (i) it provides more flexibility and more control; and (ii) it results in an increase in the number of useable data points. For frequency, the Poisson distribution is normally used, whereas for severity various distributions are used, including the lognormal distribution and the Weibull distribution. Once the two distributions have been parameterized using historical data, it is possible to combine the two distributions, using a process called convolution, to obtain a loss distribution. This exercise will be described in detail in Chapter 7.

The EVT is used to describe the distribution of extreme values in repetitive processes (Gumbel, 1958; Embrechts, Resnick, and Samorodnitsky, 1997). It indicates that, for a large class of distributions, losses in excess of a high enough threshold follow the same distribution (a generalized Pareto distribution). One advantage of EVT is that it can be used to predict the probability of events that have never happened, which can be done by extrapolating the stochastic behavior of past events. This, according to Cruz (2003b), is very useful for measuring operational risk when the experience with very large losses is limited or nonexistent (these are very hard to predict, but there is a small possibility that they would occur). This claim, however, does not seem to be supported by Embrechts, Kaufmann, and Samorodnitsky (2004) who argue that EVT cannot predict exceptional operational losses. In Embrechts, Kluppelberg, and Mikosch (1997), it is stated very clearly that EVT is not "a magical tool that could produce estimates out of thin air", but it makes the best use of the available data. Hence, according to Embrechts et al., (2004) EVT offers a very powerful statistical tool when data on sufficient normal and few extreme events are available, in the sense that it makes it possible to extrapolate from normal to the extreme.

Neslehova, Embrechts, and Chavez-Demoulin (2006) argue that "what EVT is doing is making the best use of whatever data you have about the phenomenon". They warn, however, that EVT should not be used "blindly", warning of the hazards of not choosing the "right" threshold (that is, not too low and not too high) and bringing attention to the requirement of the EVT of (close to) independently and identically distributed (IID) data, an assumption that may be too restrictive for practical applications. Likewise, Coles (2001) points out that "notwithstanding objections to the general principle of extrapolation, there is no serious competitor models to those provided by the extreme value theory".

Another advantage of the EVT, according to Moscadelli (2005), is that it has solid foundations in the mathematical theory of the behavior of extremes, which makes it (as indicated by many applications) a satisfactory scientific approach to dealing with rare, large losses. Embrechts et al. (1999) speak for EVT by saying that "EVT offers an important set of techniques for quantifying the boundaries between the different loss classes" (that is, expected loss, unexpected loss and catastrophic loss), and that it "offers a scientific language for translating management guidelines on these boundaries into actual numbers".

Hubner et al. (2003) are very critical of the use of EVT for this purpose by referring to the "myth that EVT can make an important contribution to the assessment of exceptional operational risk". While the EVT has been successful in describing extremes of physical processes where a theory gives some indication about the underlying distribution and the observations are IID, Hubner et al. argue that any attempt to apply EVT to a small set of unrelated operational losses in different firms around the globe is "another triumph of wishful thinking over reason".

6.4.3 Evaluating the probability of a loss event

Sometimes, the operational risk literature describes approaches to the evaluation of the probability of a loss event, which is another way of talking about models. These approaches form the basis of the advanced measurement approach to the measurement of operational risk as suggested by the Basel II Accord. To start with, there is the historical analysis approach, which is based on the assumption that the driving force of loss events do not change over time. Measurement in this case is based on internal and external loss data. The advantages of this approach is that (i) it captures the idiosyncratic features of a firm's own controllable risk and provides (by using external data) a larger sample to capture catastrophic risk. The disadvantages of this approach are that it is backward-looking, and there is the problem of data limitation.

The second approach is the subjective risk assessment approach, which is a combination of interviews, scorecards, and self-assessments, as well as workshops. The advantages of this approach is that it gets business managers involved, it leverages a broad ranger of experience/expertise, and it is more forward-looking than the historical approach. The disadvantages of this approach is that the generated data are subject to individual and group cognitive biases, as well as the possibility of inconsistencies.

The third approach is the causal approach, whereby the factors causing high-risk events that need to be explained are identified. It is simply based on a model in which an event is explained by a number of independent factors (the explanatory variables). This approach is appropriate for causally dependent but relatively rare events for which other approaches are inappropriate. The disadvantage of this approach is that it is used to estimate frequency rather than severity.

6.5 EXPECTED AND UNEXPECTED LOSS

Let n be the frequency exposure, p the probability of a loss event, E the severity exposure, and r the loss rate when a loss event occurs. Therefore, the expected number of losses is $N = np$, the expected severity is $S = Er$, and the expected total loss is NS.

For the purpose of measurement, Peccia (2003) defines operational risk as the unexpected total loss to some confidence level, which is related to the standard deviation of the total loss distribution. The unexpected loss is the potential loss, from all possible losses contained in the total loss distribution, at some confidence level. For a confidence level of 99 percent, there is 0.99 probability that all losses will be less than the expected loss plus the unexpected loss, or that there is a probability of 0.01 that losses will be more than the expected loss plus the unexpected loss. To arrive at the unexpected loss, the loss distribution must be constructed, which requires Monte Carlo simulations for combining frequency and severity distributions into a loss distribution. Klugman, Panjer, and Willmont (1998) show how this can be done.

Unexpected loss can be expressed as a multiple of the expected loss, which (following the regulatory nomenclature), is referred to as the gamma. Gamma is an easy way to represent the different levels of riskiness. For example, credit card fraud losses may have a gamma of 5, whereas rogue trading may have a gamma of 100. Gamma is essentially the ratio of unexpected loss to expected loss. An associated concept is that of vega, which defines the loss rate for each business line/event type combination under normal circumstances. It is essentially beta, which measures the loss rate for each business line, divided by the number of event types (7). For example, the beta for retail banking is 12 percent, which makes the vega $12/7 = 1.7$ percent.

The loss distribution can be obtained by using extreme value simulation (EVS), which is described by Pezier (2003a) (in a rather skeptical manner) as follows. The starting point is a large external operational risk losses database that contains all sorts of loss events. This database is then "purified" by screening out the events that could not occur in the firm under consideration (for example, rogue trading in a firm that is not involved in trading). The severities of the remaining events are scaled to the relative size of the firm, for example, by using the number of transactions as a measure of size. The following step is to scale the number of loss events to one year for the firm under consideration. For example, if N loss events remain in the revised database distributed over Y years by banks with adjusted total capital C (capital corresponding to relevant activities of the target firm), and if the underlying firm's capital is c, the expected number of loss events in one year is $E(n) = Nc/CY$. By picking at random n loss events among the N events in the database where n is a random variable (perhaps following the Poisson distribution) with mean $E(n)$), the sum of all n losses gives a realization of operational losses for the target firm over one year. This sampling exercise is repeated some 10,000 times to create a histogram of losses with about 10 or more occurrences beyond the 99.9th percentile.

Having described it, Pezier (2003) is very critical of this procedure, not only because of the difficulty of making external data relevant to a specific firm. The main problem, he argues, is confusing the observation of a few rare loss events with a model of extreme losses. The extreme tail (the 99.9th percentile of an operational loss distribution) is dominated by a few high-severity but highly improbable losses. The largest industry-wide database contains just a few examples of these exceptional losses and therefore can only lead to highly unreliable estimates of their probabilities. Pezier describes the EVS as a blind approach, giving as an example the difficulty of extrapolating what happened to the Titanic (a combination of rare events) to a modern ocean liner.

6.6 CALCULATING THE CAPITAL CHARGE

In general, the capital charge (that is, regulatory capital or the regulatory capital requirement) is calculated from the total loss distribution by using the concept of VAR. Cruz (2003b) identifies two fundamental differences between market and operational VAR models. The first is that by applying EVT to operational loss events, we can relax the assumption of normality on which market VAR models are based (at least when the parametric approach is used to calculate market VAR). The second difference is that, unlike market prices that follow a continuous stochastic process, operational losses follow a discrete stochastic process.

Frachot, Moudoulaud, and Roncalli (2004) argue that there is ambiguity about the definition of the capital charge, hence suggesting three alternative definitions. The first definition is that it is the 99.9th percentile of the total loss distributi on, which means that the probability of incurring a loss bigger than the operational value at risk (OpVAR) is 0.1 percent, or

$$Pr(L > OpVAR) = 0.001 \tag{6.3}$$

which means that regulatory capital should cover both expected and unexpected losses. The second definition pertains to the unexpected loss only, which is the OpVAR given in equation (6.3) less the expected loss, which gives

$$Pr(L > OpVAR + EL) = 0.001 \tag{6.4}$$

where EL is the expected loss. The Basel II Accord seems to accept this definition as long as the underlying bank can demonstrate that it has adequately provided for expected losses. Recall from Chapter 3 that one of the quantitative standards that the users of the AMA must satisfy is that regulatory capital must be calculated as the sum of the expected loss and unexpected loss unless it can be demonstrated that the expected loss is adequately captured in the internal business practices, in which case regulatory capital is meant to cover the unexpected loss only.

The third definition considers only losses above a threshold, which gives

$$Pr\left(\sum_{i=0}^{N} JL_i > OpVAR\right) = 0.001 \tag{6.5}$$

where N is the number of loss events, L is the loss amount and J takes the value of 1 if $L_i > H$ and 0 otherwise, where H is the threshold. This is probably the least acceptable definition of the capital charge.

The use of the concept of value at risk to measure operational risk capital charges has not escaped criticism. For example, Hubner et al. (2003) argue against using a "VAR-like figure" to measure operational risk, stipulating that although VAR models have been developed for operational risk, questions remain about the interpretation of the results. Another problem is that VAR figures provide an indication of the amount of risk but not of its form (for example, legal as opposed to technology).

Moreover, some doubts have been raised about the use of the 99.9th percentile. For example, Alexander (2003b) argues that the parameters of the total loss distribution cannot be estimated precisely because the operational loss data are incomplete, unreliable and/or subjective. This makes the estimation of risk at the 99.9th percentile implausible. Alexander argues that regulators should ask themselves very seriously if it is sensible to measure the capital charge on the 99.9th percentile.

6.7 THE CONCEPT OF RISK MAP

A risk map is a plot of expected loss frequency against expected severity for the firm as a whole, individual risk types, individual business lines, or combinations thereof. Often the variables are plotted on a logarithmic scale, because of the wide range of frequency and severity. The diagram is a useful visual aid that can be used to identify the risks that should be the main focus of management control. Figure 6.1 shows a risk map plotted on a log–log scale, where severity is measured in terms of the minimum regulatory capital (MRC) such that if log severity is 0 the total MRC will be lost. On the other hand, frequency is measured as the number of loss events per year, so that a log frequency of 0 implies the occurrence of one event in a year. Furthermore, Figure 6.2 shows a risk map that divides the severity–frequency space into three zones for the purpose of risk monitoring and control: (i) acceptable zone, (ii) warning zone, and (iii) main focus zone. Risk maps can also be plotted in such a way as to distinguish among business lines and loss events as shown in Figure 6.3 and Figure 6.4, respectively. Figure 6.5, on the other hand, shows a risk map by combinations of event types/ business lines (56 combinations). The combinations appear mostly in the low-frequency, low-severity category, whereas none appears in medium-frequency, high-severity; high-frequency, medium-severity; and high-frequency, high-severity categories.

The risk map shown in Figures 6.1–6.5 are theoretical, in which case it would be useful to see how a risk map would look like using the loss data reported by the BCBS (2003c) for 2002. Figure 6.6 is the risk map for a total of 72 observations (7 event types plus the unclassified times 8 business lines plus the unclassified). We can see the clustering of the observations at

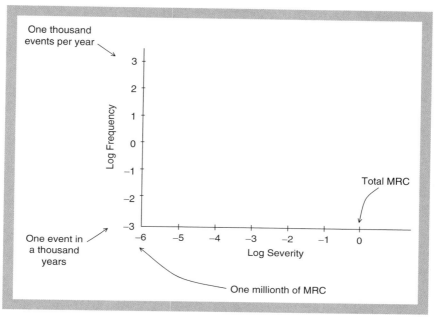

Figure 6.1 A risk map on a log–log scale

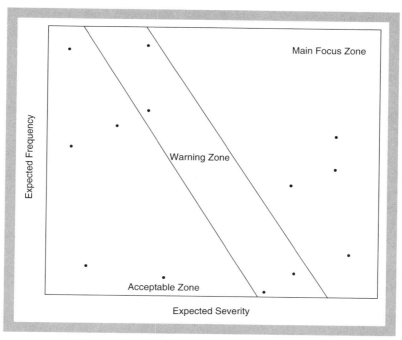

Figure 6.2 A risk map showing risk zones

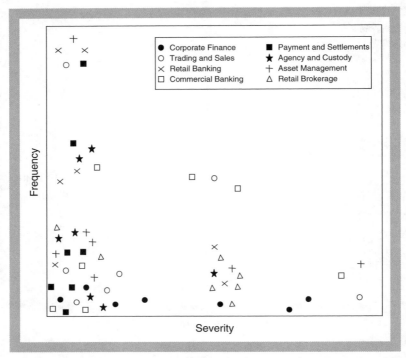

Figure 6.3 A risk map by business line

the low-frequency, low-severity zone. In Figure 6.7, the risk map is plotted on a log–log scale, showing a better picture than Figure 6.6, but we can again see the clustering of points. Figure 6.8 shows the risk map by event type (total), whereas Figure 6.9 shows the risk map by business line. In both cases, we can see that most points represent low-frequency, low-severity events but there are also low-frequency, high-severity and high-frequency, low-severity events. There are no high-frequency, highly-severity events, which is indicated by the correlation coefficient between frequency and severity, turning out to be −0.35 (by event type) and −0.33 (by business line).

An alternative form of a risk map is the so-called heat map, which is shown in Figure 6.10. The severity–frequency space is divided into five risk zones with different shades, such that the darker the zone the greater the implied risk. The white zone encompasses the (very) low-frequency, (very) low-severity events, whereas the darkest zone is the (very) high-frequency, (very) high-severity zone. In between, there are three zones with increasing darkness, as we move toward the (very) high-frequency, (very) high-severity zone.

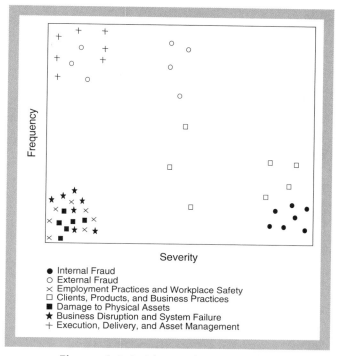

Figure 6.4 A risk map by event type

6.8   BAYESIAN ESTIMATION

Bayesian estimation, which is useful for modeling operational risk, is a parameter estimation technique that can be used to combine hard data (recent and relevant internal data) and subjective soft data (data from an external consortium or from risk scores based on the opinions of industry experts or the owner of the risk). Soft data can also be past internal data that, following a merger, acquisition or the sale of assets. Alexander (2003b) argues that when a bank's operations undergo a significant change in size, it may not be sufficient simply to scale the capital charge by the size of its current operations because the internal system processes and people are likely to have changed considerably, which makes the historical loss data irrelevant.

The Bayesian estimation of the mean and standard deviation of a loss severity distribution works as follows. Suppose that we have n observations of hard data, $L_1^h, L_2^h, \ldots L_n^h$, and m observations on soft data, $L_1^s, L_2^s, \ldots, L_m^s$. The means and standard deviations are:

$$\bar{L}^h = \frac{1}{n} \sum_{j=1}^{n} L_j^h$$

(6.6)

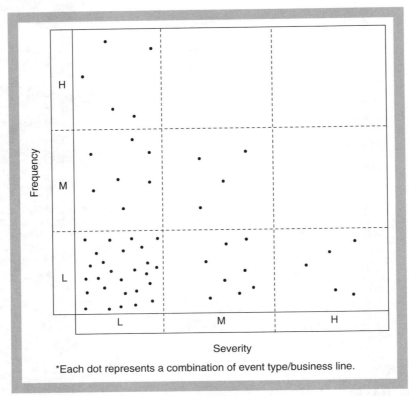

*Each dot represents a combination of event type/business line.

Figure 6.5 A risk map by business line and event type*

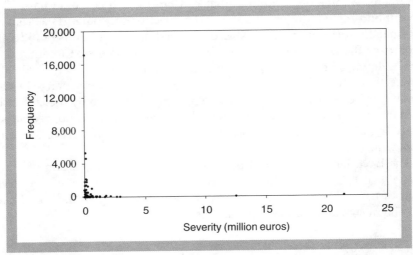

Figure 6.6 A risk map in linear scale (the BCBS (2003c) data)

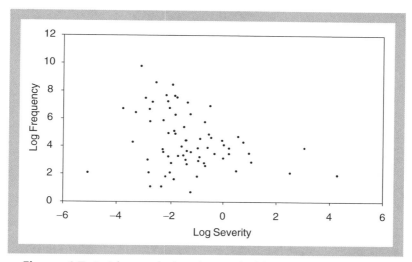

Figure 6.7 A risk map in log–log scale (the BCBS (2003c) data)

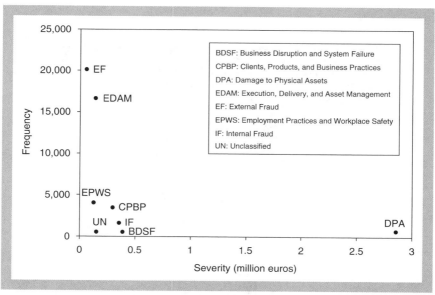

Figure 6.8 A risk map by event type (the BCBS (2003c) data)

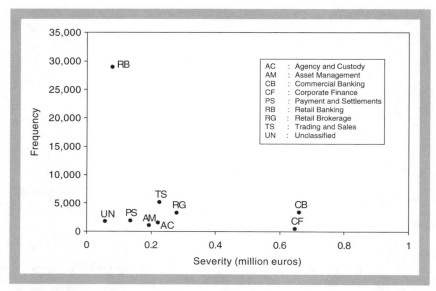

Figure 6.9 Risk map by business line (the BCBS (2003c) data)

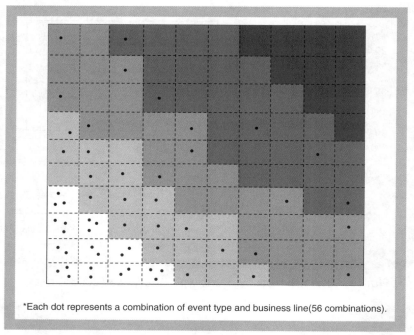

*Each dot represents a combination of event type and business line(56 combinations).

Figure 6.10 A heat map in terms of frequency and severity*

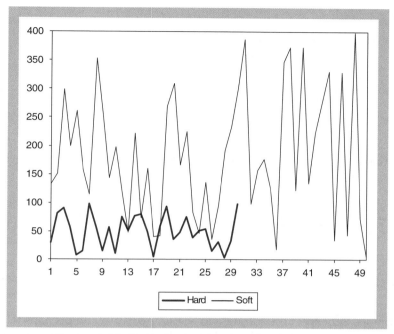

Figure 6.11 Hypothetical hard and soft loss data

$$\bar{L}^s = \frac{1}{m}\sum_{j=1}^{m} L_j^s \tag{6.7}$$

$$\sigma^2(L^h) = \frac{1}{n-1}\sum_{j=1}^{n} (L_j^h - \bar{L}^h)^2 \tag{6.8}$$

$$\sigma^2(L^s) = \frac{1}{m-1}\sum_{j=1}^{m} (L_j^s - \bar{L}^s)^2 \tag{6.9}$$

where $\bar{L}^h$ is the mean of the hard data, $\bar{L}^s$ is the mean of soft data, $\sigma^2(L^h)$ is the variance of the hard data and $\sigma^2(L^s)$ is the variance of the soft data. Alexander (2003b) shows that the Bayesian estimates of the mean and variance of total loss severity, L, are calculated as

$$\bar{L} = \frac{w^h \bar{L}^h + w^s \bar{L}^s}{w^h + w^s} \tag{6.10}$$

where w^h and w^s are the weights assigned to hard data and soft data, respectively.

Hence

$$\bar{L} = \frac{[1/\sigma^2(L^h)]\bar{L}^h + [1/\sigma^2(L^s)]\bar{L}^s}{[1/\sigma^2(L^h)] + [1/\sigma^2(L^s)]} \tag{6.11}$$

The combined variance is calculated as

$$\sigma^2(L) = \frac{1}{1/\sigma^2(L^h) + 1/\sigma^2(L^s)} \tag{6.12}$$

The maximum likelihood estimates of the mean and variance that are based on the combined sample are

$$\bar{L} = \frac{1}{n+m} \left[\sum_{j=1}^{n} L_j^h + \sum_{j=1}^{m} L_j^s \right] \tag{6.13}$$

$$\sigma^2(L) = \frac{1}{n+m-1} \left[\sum_{j=1}^{n} (L_j^h - \bar{L})^2 + \sum_{j=1}^{m} (L_j^s - \bar{L})^2 \right] \tag{6.14}$$

One should expect the soft data to be more volatile, and perhaps to have a higher mean value, than the hard data. If this is the case, then we should expect the Bayesian mean and variance to be lower than the maximum likelihood estimates. For the purpose of illustration, consider the following numerical example, using 30 observations of hard data and 50 observations of soft data, which are shown in Figure 6.11. As we can see, the soft data series is much more volatile than the hard data series. Figure 6.12 shows the means and standard deviations of the hard data, soft data, the combined sample estimated by maximum likelihood and the Bayesian mean and standard deviation. We can readily observe the following:

1. The hard data series has lower mean and standard deviation than the soft data series.

2. The maximum likelihood estimates of the mean and standard deviation are closer to those of the soft data.

3. The Bayesian estimates of the mean and standard deviation are lower than the maximum likelihood estimates.

Another application of Bayesian statistics in operational risk modeling is Bayesian networks. Neil, Fenton, and Tailor (2005) show how Bayesian networks are used to model statistical loss distributions in financial operational loss scenarios. The focus is on modeling the long tail events using mixtures of appropriate loss frequency and severity distributions, where these mixtures are conditioned on causal variables that model the

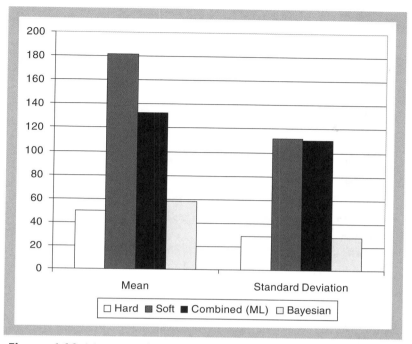

Figure 6.12 Means and standard deviations of hard and soft data

capability or effectiveness of the underlying controls process. We will have more to say about the concept of risk controls in Chapter 8.

6.9 RELIABILITY THEORY

Reliability theory is used in operational research to measure the impact of failure of components in mechanical and electronic systems. This theory stipulates that the failure rate at a particular point in time follows a bathtub shape, as shown in Figure 6.13, which is a representation of the reliability function. The bathtub function has three phases: the learning phase, the maturity phase, and the wear-out phase. In the learning phase, failures occur frequently because of lack of experience. In the maturity phase, failures occur infrequently after the completion of the learning process. In the wear-out phase, failures occur because the components are worn out or become obsolete. The reliability function can be written as

$$h(t) = k\lambda c t^{c-1} + (1-k)bt^{b-1}\beta e^{\beta t^b} \tag{6.15}$$

where $h(t)$ is the failure rate, c and λ are the parameters defining the learning phase, b and β are parameters that define the wear-out phase and k is

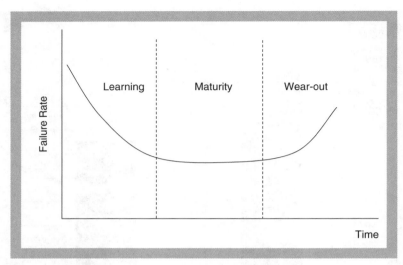

Figure 6.13 The phases of the reliability function

the parameter that determines the length of the maturity phase. The restrictions imposed on the values of these parameters are $b>0$, $c>0$, $\beta>0$, $\lambda>0$, and $0\le k\le 1$. Figure 6.14 shows a reliability curve for specific values of the parameters, whereas Figure 6.15 shows the corresponding percentage cumulative number of failures corresponding to the reliability curve shown in Figure 6.14.

McConnell (2003) argues that reliability theory can be used to model the occurrence of failures/errors in operational processes. Failures occur frequently in a new project due to factors such as lack of experience, incomplete knowledge of the process, lack of controls, and bad employment decisions. With the passage of time, these problems are overcome as the project moves along the learning phase, resulting in a reduction in the number of failures. After some time, the underlying process diverges from the industry's best practices and become out of date, leading to a rise in the failure rate. If suitable parameters for a particular operational process can be determined, it should be possible to use the reliability function to estimate the number of failures that are likely to occur over a particular period of time.

Reliability theory deals only with the probability of a failure event, not with the size of the financial loss resulting from the event. To estimate the distribution of losses we need some more information, particularly on the clustering factor of an event. Clustering refers to the idea whether the failure event affects a single transaction or a cluster of transactions. McConnell (2003) suggests that it is possible to construct a loss function that can be used to estimate the loss that would be incurred as a result of a particular event at some time in the future. Following Cruz (2002), he

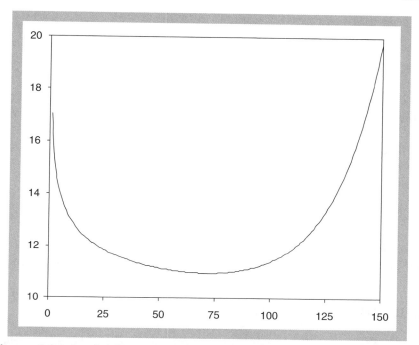

Figure 6.14 A reliability curve ($b = 0.1$, $c = 0.8$, $\beta = 0.5$, $\lambda = 0.2$, $k = 0.9$)

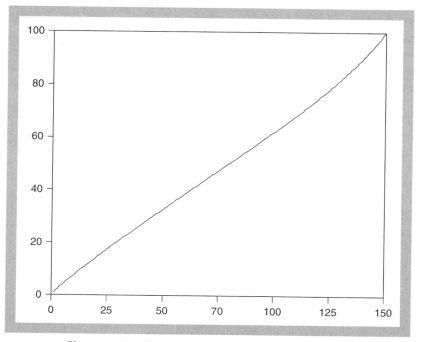

Figure 6.15 The cumulative percentage failures

suggests that if a process p is normally distributed with mean μ_p and standard deviation σ_p, then the expected loss at a specified confidence level α is

$$LF(\alpha,t) = K_p g(\mu_p + \alpha\sigma_p) \tag{6.16}$$

where K_p is a cluster factor for process p and g is some growth function that estimates a particular loss at a specific point in time. When the underlying process is discrete, we have $K_p = 1$.

Once we have a reliability function and a loss distribution for a process p, we can calculate the VAR of a portfolio of processes as

$$VAR_p = \sum_{p=1}^{P}\sum_{1}^{n} h_p(t)LF_p(\alpha,t) \tag{6.17}$$

where P is the number of processes, $t = 1$ is the starting period, $t = n$ is the end period, h_p is the reliability function and LF_p is the loss distribution.

6.10   THE LEVER METHOD

The abbreviation LEVER stands for loss estimated by validating experts in risk, which is a method for estimating operational loss based on the work of Cooke (1991). This method is used as an alternative to the statistical models when adequate data are not available. The method amounts to constructing a weighted combination of subjective probability assessments of experts to arrive at a rational consensus. The process of combining the subjective assessments is based on testing the expertise of the experts using the so-called seed questions, the answers to which are known to the analysts but not to the experts.

The subjective probability assessments are obtained by using questionnaires covering target variables and seed variables, for which the experts should give quintile assessments. The difference between the target variables and the seed variables is that the former are the variables of interest whereas the latter are of known values. Bakker (2005) presents a case study on their use of the LEVER method to evaluate the operational risk facing a bank. He makes the following recommendations when the LEVER method is used:

■ The questionnaire should be designed in such a way as to contain questions that are univocal.

■ The experts should be comfortable with expressing their assessments in numbers.

■ Before using the LEVER method, research should be done to assess the correlations of operational risks.

■ Experts should not be able to differentiate between the seed questions and the target questions.

6.11   WHAT IS NEXT?

In this chapter, we examined some principles and described the general techniques used in modeling operational risk. Chapter 7 will take us from the generals to the specifics, as it deals with the implementation of the three approaches of the AMA. We actually came across some elements of the AMA in this chapter by considering the problems of data and correlation, EVT, simulations, expected and unexpected loss, and the calculation of the capital charge. In Chapter 7, we will see how these elements are combined systematically to measure operational risk and calculate the capital charge by using the AMA.

CHAPTER 7

Modeling and Measuring Operational Risk: Implementing the AMA

7.1 CONSTRUCTING THE TOTAL LOSS DISTRIBUTION

The total loss distribution, from which the capital charge is calculated, is obtained by combining, using Monte Carlo simulations, the loss frequency distribution and the loss severity distribution. The following is a simple description of Monte Carlo simulations.

7.1.1 A description of Monte Carlo simulation

Andres (2003) likens Monte Carlo simulations to "a big dice-rolling exercise where the dice are shaped so that their different sides fall with different likelihoods". Each iteration starts with a roll of the frequency die because the number that falls determines how often the severity die is rolled. The severities resulting from the individual rolls of the severity die are added up to obtain the potential loss for this iteration. This procedure is carried out thousands of times to create a histogram, which is an empirical probability distribution function. In practice, this exercise is carried out by using a computer program such as *Crystal Ball*. Formally, the total loss distribution is obtained by conducting Monte Carlo simulations as follows:

1. A random draw is taken from the frequency distribution to produce the simulated number of loss events per year.

2. A number of random draws that is equal to the simulated number of loss events is taken from the severity distribution.

3. The annual loss amount is obtained by summing the simulated losses obtained in step 2.

4. Steps 1, 2, and 3 are repeated a large number of times to obtain a large number of values (amounts) of the annual loss, which are used to plot a histogram representing the distribution of the total annual loss.

5. A capital charge is then calculated using one of the definitions we came across in Chapter 6. If the definition is that given by equation (6.4), then the capital charge is the difference between the 99.9th percentile and the mean of the total loss distribution.

6. The process is repeated for each event type and business line.

The description of Monte Carlo simulations can be represented schematically by Figure 7.1, which shows an exercise that consists of n iterations. Starting with iteration 1, the draw from the frequency distribution gives an annual loss frequency f_1. The severity distribution is then used to generate f_1 losses per year, $L_{1,j}$, where the subscript $1,j$ refers to the iteration number and the number of draws $j = 1,2,...,f_1$. The total annual loss derived from iteration 1 (L_1) is the sum of $L_{1,1}, L_{1,2},..., L_{1,j}$. The process is repeated in iteration 2 to obtain another figure for the annual loss, L_2, and so on until we get L_n from iteration n. The observations $L_1, L_2 ,..., L_n$ are then used to plot a histogram that represents the distribution of the annual loss.

7.1.2 Frequency and severity distributions

For a given type of operational risk in a given business line, a discrete probability density $b(n)$ is chosen to represent the number of loss events n in one year, while loss severity is represented by a continuous conditional probability density, $g(L \mid n)$. The annual loss has the combined density

$$f(L) = \sum_{n=0}^{\infty} b(n) g(L \mid n) \tag{7.1}$$

Figure 7.2 is a schematic representation of the process of combining the (discrete) frequency and (continuous) severity distributions to obtain the total loss distribution.

The question that arises here is about the functional form to be assigned to the frequency and severity distributions. Loss frequency can be represented by a binomial distribution $B(N,p)$ where N is the total number of events that are susceptible to operational loss and p is the probability of a

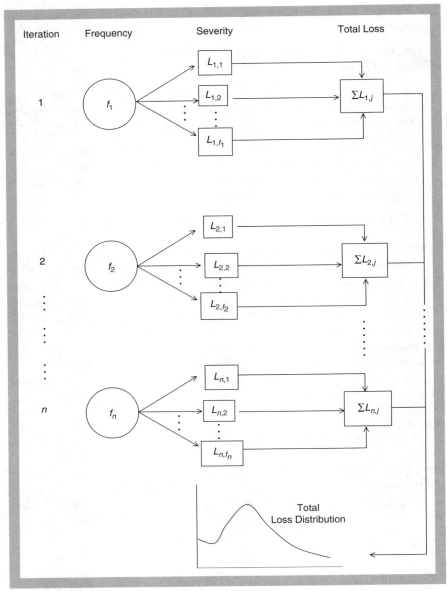

Figure 7.1 Using Monte Carlo simulations to obtain the
total loss distribution

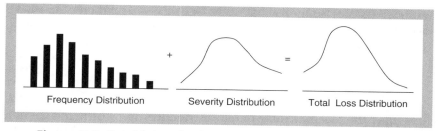

Figure 7.2 Combining the frequency and severity distributions

loss event. If events are assumed to be independent, the density function of the frequency distribution is

$$b(n) = \binom{N}{n} p^n (1-p)^{N-n}$$

(7.2)

where $n = 0,1,..., N$. The problem with the binomial density function is the need to specify the total number of events, N. When p is small, the binomial distribution can be approximated by the Poisson distribution, which has a single parameter, the expected frequency of loss events, $\lambda = Np$ (because the mean and variance are equal). The Poisson distribution density function is specified as

$$b(n) = \frac{\lambda^n e^{-\lambda}}{n!}$$

(7.3)

where $n = 0,1,... $.
Alexander (2003b) suggests that a better representation of the loss frequency is the negative binomial distribution, which allows for variances that are greater than the mean. The negative binomial distribution has the density function

$$b(n) = \binom{\alpha + n - 1}{n} \left(\frac{1}{1+\beta} \right)^{\alpha} \left(\frac{\beta}{1+\beta} \right)^{n}$$

(7.4)

The functional form for the severity distribution may be different across different risk types. High-frequency risks can have a lognormal severity distribution of the form:

$$g(L) = \frac{1}{\sqrt{2\pi}\sigma L} \exp \left[-\frac{1}{2} \left(\frac{\log (L) - \mu}{\sigma} \right)^{2} \right]$$

(7.5)

for $L > 0$. Andres (2003) suggests that the results of research conducted at Dresdner Bank support the proposition that the lognormal distribution is very well suited to internal historic operational loss data. However,

Alexander (2003b) suggests that some severity distributions may have substantial leptokurtosis and skewness, in which case a better fit would be a two-parameter density such as the gamma density, which is given by

$$g(L) = \frac{x^{\alpha-1} \exp(-L/\beta)}{\beta^{\alpha} \Gamma(\alpha)} \tag{7.6}$$

where $\alpha\beta$ is the mean of the gamma distribution and $\Gamma(.)$ is the gamma function. Otherwise, we may use the two-parameter hyperbolic density function, which is given by

$$g(L) = \frac{\exp(-\alpha\sqrt{\beta^2 + L^2})}{2\beta B(\alpha\beta)} \tag{7.7}$$

where $B(.)$ denotes the Bessel function. Other possibilities include, among others, the extreme value distribution. The suitability of these distributions for the representation of loss severity is due to the fact that they are fat-tailed and asymmetrical. A fat tail means that high-severity losses occur with a much higher likelihood than a normal distribution would suggest (the tail is fatter), while asymmetry means that low-frequency, high-severity losses are not symmetrical to the high-frequency, low-severity losses.

Having chosen the distributions, they must be parameterized by assigning numerical values to the mean, variance, and other parameters if necessary. For this purpose, historical loss data and evaluations from experts within the firm are used. While historical loss data are a valuable source for analyzing operational risk, they only represent the past and they are not always complete. It is also unclear how external loss amounts can accurately represent an internal risk situation. The alternative is to use the opinions of the experts in the firm based on loss history, the insurance cover, their understanding of the processes, banking and industry experience, and knowledge of embedded controls. Expert evaluations are then translated into the parameter values of the severity and frequency distributions.

7.1.3   Modeling risk dependence to calculate the firm-wide capital charge

When the frequency and severity distributions for each cell (where a cell is a combination of event type and business line) are created, the capital charge for the whole firm can be calculated in three ways, depending on the assumptions we make about correlation among various risk categories. If we assume perfect correlation among risk categories (that is, losses occur at the same time) the capital charge for the whole firm is calculated by adding up the individual capital charges for each risk type/business line combination. This is shown in Figure 7.3, where (1,1), (1,2), ... (7,8) are 56

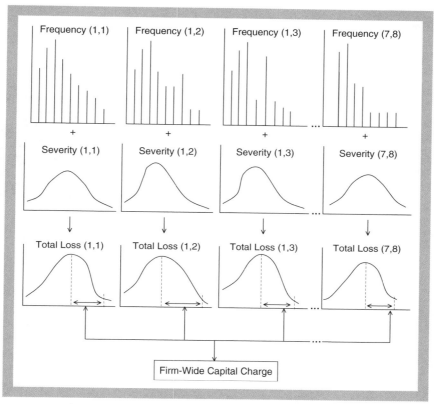

Figure 7.3 Calculating the firm-wide capital charge
(assuming perfect correlation)

combinations of seven event types and eight business lines. On the other extreme, the assumption of zero correlation among risk categories (that is, they are independent of each other), the firm-wide capital charge is calculated by compounding all distribution pairs into a single loss distribution for the firm. This is done by calculating the total loss produced by each iteration of the Monte Carlo simulations. Figure 7.4 shows how the total loss distribution is obtained from Monte Carlo simulations involving two risk categories (A and B). Figure 7.5, shows how the firm-wide capital charge is calculated in this case.

In between the two extremes of assuming perfect correlation and zero correlation, we could allow for the explicit modeling of correlations between the occurrences of loss events. This is indeed is the most difficult procedure. The problem here is that correlation, which is a simple form of the first moment of the joint density of two random variables, does not capture all forms of dependence between the two variables (it is a measure of linear association between the two variables). Everts and Liersch (2006) argue that

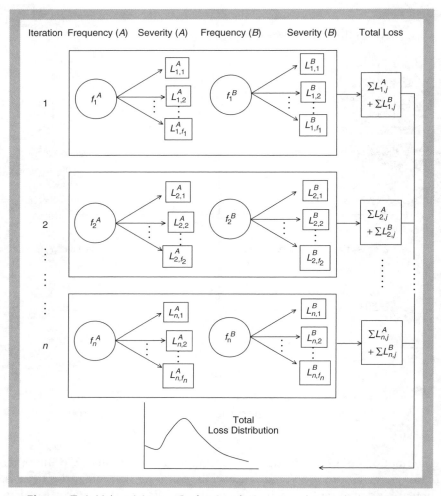

Figure 7.4 Using Monte Carlo simulations to obtain the total loss distribution (two risk categories)

the crucial assumption behind the use of correlation for this purpose is the assumption of multivariate normal distribution, which means that if this assumption is violated (which is invariably the case with the total loss distribution), then correlation is not an appropriate measure of dependence. Another problem with correlation is that it varies over time. This is why it is more appropriate to use the copula for this purpose (a copula is an expression of a bivariate or multivariate distribution in terms of the marginal distributions). Copulas are used to combine two or more distributions to obtain a joint distribution with a prespecified form of dependence.

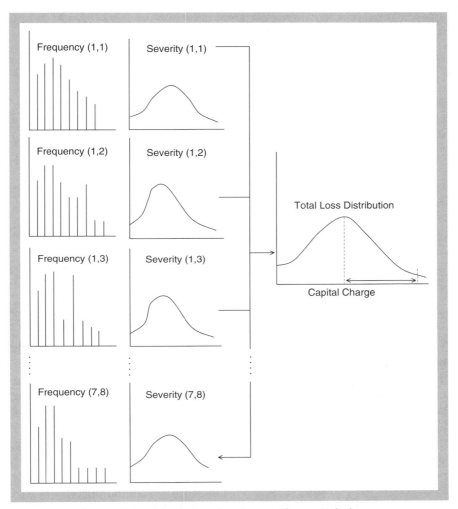

Figure 7.5 Calculating the firm-wide capital charge
(assuming zero correlation)

Assume that the two random variables X_1 and X_2 have the marginal distribution functions $F_1(X_1)$ and $F_2(X_2)$. The joint distribution of X_1 and X_2 can be written as

$$J(X_1, X_2) = C[F_1(X_1), F_2(X_2)] \qquad (7.8)$$

where $C[.,.)]$ is the copula. The joint density is given by

$$b(X_1, X_2) = f_1(X_1) f_2(X_2) c[X_1, X_2] \qquad (7.9)$$

where $f_1(X_1)$ and $f_2(X_2)$ are the marginal density functions of X_1 and X_2 and $c[X_1 X_2]$ is the probability density function of the copula, which is given by

$$c(X_1, X_2) = \frac{\partial^2 C[F_1(X_1), F_2(X_2)]}{\partial F_1(X_1) \partial F_2(X_2)} \tag{7.10}$$

Now, consider two total loss distributions for two different event type/business line combinations, L_1 and L_2. Given a certain form of dependence, the joint density is

$$b(L_1, L_2) = f_1(L_1) f_2(L_2) c(L_1, L_2) \tag{7.11}$$

Let $L = L_1 + L_2$. If $b(L_1, L_2)$ is discrete, the probability density of L is the convolution sum

$$S(L) = \sum_{L_1} b(L_1, L - L_1) = \sum_{L_2} b(L - L_2, L_1) \tag{7.12}$$

If, on the other hand, $b(L_1, L_2)$ is continuous, the probability density of L is the convolution integral

$$S(L) = \int_{L_1} b(L_1, L - L_1) = \int_{L_2} b(L - L_2, L_1) \tag{7.13}$$

The case can be extended for several combinations of loss event types and business lines. An appropriate copula must be chosen to generate the joint density as defined in equation (7.11). Figure 7.6 shows how copulas are used to combine the loss distributions of the 56 combinations of event type/business line (from (1,1) to (7,8)) to arrive at the firm-wide loss distribution, which is subsequently used to calculate the capital charge. Notice that we start by combining (1,1) and (1,2), then we combine the convulsion sum of (1,1) and (1,2) with (1,3) and so on until we get to (7,8), at which point we obtain the total risk distribution for the firm.

What procedure is used to select the appropriate copula? This is done by looking at the sources of risk (the so-called risk drivers). For example, if two operational risk types are believed to be positively related, because a set of operational risk sources tends to boost these risks while another set of risk sources tends to bring them down, then a copula with a positive dependence structure should be used for aggregation. If, for example, a decision is taken to reduce the number of staff in the back office, this would lead to an increase in the risk event of employment practices and those of internal fraud and external fraud. If, on the other hand, the management of a firm decides to outsource its IT systems, business disruption and system failures become less risky but the risk of execution, delivery, and process management, as well as the risk of employment practices and workplace safety, will increase. This seems to be a more sensible procedure than attempting to specify a correlation matrix involving each and every combination of loss event and business line.

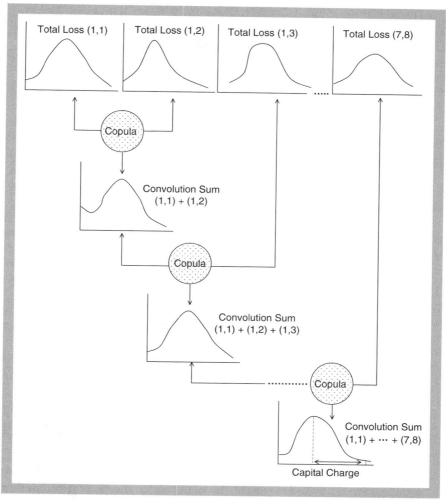

Figure 7.6 Calculating the firm-wide capital charge
by modeling dependence

It is also important to remember that, because we are talking about combined frequency–severity distributions, any correlation or dependence between two risks can be traced to frequency dependence and severity dependence. For example, positive dependence between internal fraud and external fraud would result if the number of internal fraud events is positively correlated with the number of external fraud events and/or the internal fraud loss amounts is positively correlated with the external loss amounts.

Following Saita (2004), Everts and Liersch (2006) identify the advantages and disadvantages of using correlation and copulas for the purpose of aggregation. Starting with correlation, it is simple, intuitive and easy to explain to people without formal training in statistics. It is also simple with respect to parameter estimation while allowing the calculation of the regulatory capital analytically. The disadvantages of correlation are the problems arising from the assumption of normality, its changing pattern (over time) and that it can be underestimated if too short data series are used. The advantages of the copulas, on the other hand, are that they do not require the assumption of a particular joint distribution and, if the right copula is used, dependence can be captured accurately while maintaining the original distribution. The copulas, however, are difficult to explain to people without formal training in statistics, and the calculated capital charge will be sensitive to the copula used for the purpose of aggregation. Furthermore, choosing the right copula may require a time series of considerable length.

7.1.4 Approaches to the AMA

The AMA encompasses a range of approaches, including the loss distribution approach (LDA), the internal measurement approach (IMA), the scenario-based approach (SBA), and the scorecard approach (SCA). All of these approaches could involve simulation:

1. In the IMA, the gamma factor relating expected to unexpected losses has to be calibrated, which can be done by simulation.

2. In the LDA, there is scope for the direct application of simulation to the calculation of capital in much the same way that market risk and credit risk capital are calculated.

3. In the SCA, the initial calculation of capital must be supported by the same data and methodologies as the LDA, which means that simulation can play an important rule.

In general, the first step in determining the annual loss distribution is to choose and calibrate the most appropriate models, which requires a large amount of data. Several different types of input data are available, including internal loss data, risk indicators, near-misses data, scenarios, and external public-domain loss data. The risk indicators, which are time series of internal or external numerical factors that might influence losses, can be used as predictors of operational risk. For example, if the volume of transactions increases while the number of staff and the availability of new technology decreases, the number of losses per period will increase. Indicators are seen as having predictive power for the frequency and severity, which means that they can be useful for calibrating the loss distribution.

Near-miss data represent losses that could have been incurred in certain events (but they were not). A scenario is a set of estimated frequency and approximate amounts of hypothetical events from a self-risk assessment. We will elaborate on the concepts of indicators and scenarios later on.

7.2   A SIMPLE EXAMPLE

In this simple example, we calculate the capital charge against two kinds of operational risk, A and B, under the extreme assumptions of perfect correlation and zero correlation. For this purpose, *Excel* was used to generate 200 frequency observations for risk A and risk B, followed by the generation of the corresponding severity observations, producing 928 loss events for A and 1547 loss events for B. The frequency observations were generated from a Poisson distribution, whereas the severity observations were generated from a normal distribution (not that this is the most appropriate choice). Figures 7.7–7.10 show the distributions of frequency and severity for the two kinds of risk. Figures 7.11 and 7.12 show the total loss distributions for risks A and B, respectively.

Table 7.1 reports the means and standard deviations of the frequency, severity and total loss distributions. It also shows the 99th percentile for the loss distributions. By taking the capital charge to be the difference between the 99th percentile and the mean of the distribution, we can calculate capital charges against risks A and B, which turn out to be 373.17 and 384.72, respectively. If we make the assumption of perfect correlation, the total capital charge is the sum of the capital charges against risks A and B, which gives 757.89. If, on the other hand, we make the assumption of zero correlation, we must work out a combined total loss distribution, which is shown in Figure 7.13. This distribution has a mean value of 635.82 and a 99th percentile of 1305.46, which gives a total capital charge of 669.63. This obviously shows that the assumption of perfect correlation produces a higher capital charge.

7.3   THE LOSS DISTRIBUTION APPROACH

The standard LDA model expresses the aggregate loss as the sum of individual losses, which gives

$$L = \sum_{j=1}^{n} L_j \qquad (7.14)$$

where L is the aggregate loss, n is the number of losses per year (the frequency of events) and Lj is the loss amount (the severity of event).

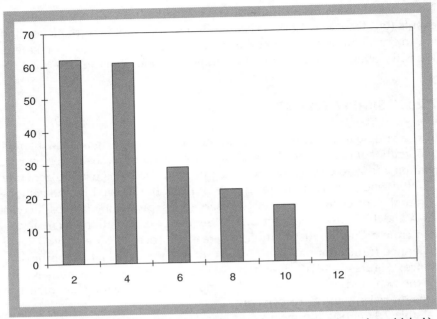

Figure 7.7 The frequency distribution of hypothetical loss data (risk A)

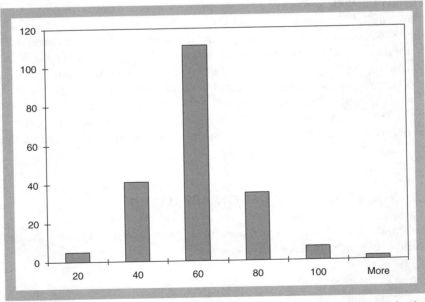

Figure 7.8 The severity distribution of hypothetical loss data (risk A)

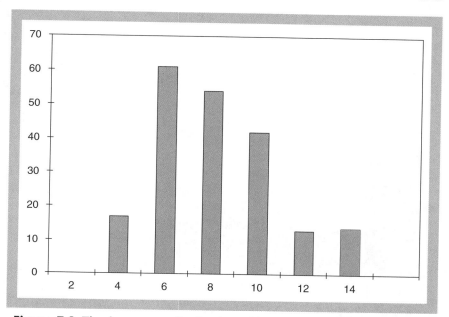

Figure 7.9 The frequency distribution of hypothetical loss data (risk B)

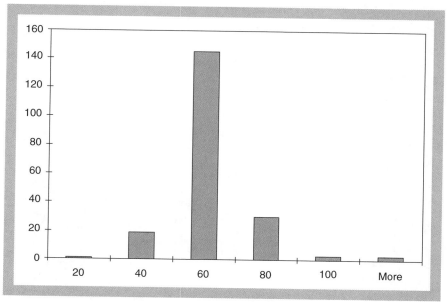

Figure 7.10 The severity distribution of hypothetical loss data (risk B)

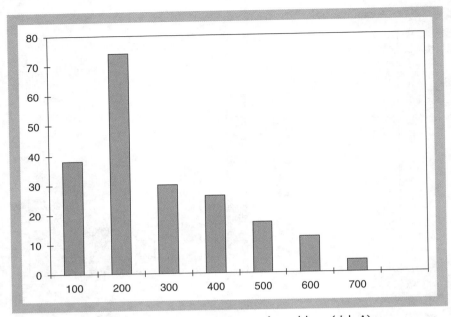

Figure 7.11 The distribution of total loss (risk A)

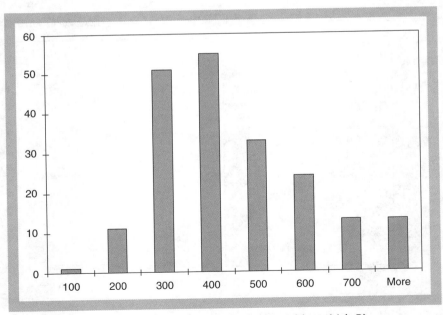

Figure 7.12 The distribution of total loss (risk B)

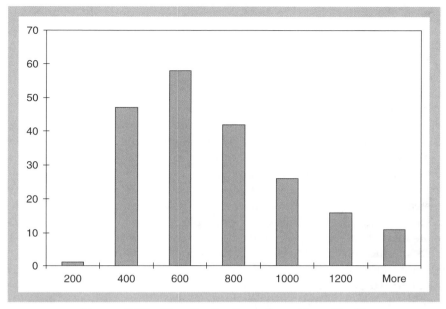

Figure 7.13 The distribution of total loss (A+B)

Table 7.1 Calculating capital charges with perfect and zero correlations

	Mean	Std Dev	99th Percentile	Capital charge
A (Frequency)	4.61	2.78		
A (Severity)	51.44	24.78		
B (Frequency)	7.70	2.67		
B (Severity)	52.80	15.47		
A (Total Loss)	233.55	153.34	606.72	373.17
B (Total Loss)	402.29	161.89	786.99	384.72
A+B (Perfect)				757.89
A+B (Zero)	635.82	285.93	1305.46	669.63

The aggregate loss is defined by Frachot, Roncalli and Salmon (2004) as the loss incurred in a class of risk, where a class refers to one cell and a cell is any element in 7 types of risk times 8 business lines as defined by the Basel Committee. Hence, losses arise from two sources of randomness, frequency and severity, both of which have to be modeled as described in the general framework. Two assumptions are used in the LDA model: (i) frequency and severity are independent and (ii) two different losses within the same class are independently and identically distributed, which means that $L_1, ..., L_n$ are independent random variables following the same distribution. Banks that wish to quantify their regulatory capital using a loss distribution model need to use historical data based on actual loss experience, covering a period of at least three years that are relevant to each line of business.

Haubenstock and Hardin (2003) put forward a schematic representation of the LDA, using a step-by-step procedure. This presentation involves three primary steps and additional steps with their components, which are defined in Table 7.2. They argue that while the LDA has several advantages, it also has some limitations. The advantages of the LDA, according to them, are: (i) the results are based on the unique characteristics of each firm instead of relying on a proxy operational risk industry averages; (ii) the results are based on mathematical principles similar to those used to estimate market and credit risk capital; (iii) the effect of insurance can be modeled specifically; (iv) the costs and benefits of the change in frequency or severity can be measured; and (v) the results evolve over time. On the other hand, they argue that it has the following limitations: (i) it is data-intensive, requiring a loss history or a set of scorecard data; (ii) it is potentially backward-looking, because it is based on historical data; (iii) data are too sparse to determine frequency and severity at lower levels, and so modeling is typically performed for business units one or perhaps two levels below the firm-wide results; and (iv) it does not capture the impact on revenue or margin from operational causes (these risks are excluded from the Basel definition).

Table 7.2 The steps involved in the LDA

Step	Components
Determining Rules and Parameters	• Defining each organizational component for which capital will be estimated. • Grouping events in categories for the purpose of analysis (for example, the Basel categories). • Determining parameters, such as the desired level of confidence, time horizon and correlation assumptions. • Estimating maximum loss per event category (worst case losses).
Collecting and Validating Data	• Collecting, categorizing cleansing and reconciling internal data. • Validating the quality of the data. • Compiling external data.

(Continued)

Table 7.2 (*Continued*)

Step	Components
Calculating Capital and Calibrating	• Establishing a consistent basis for the data to be modeled. • Modeling severity. • Modeling frequency. • Monte Carlo simulations across the frequency and severity distributions to produce a total loss distribution. • Validating results in the sense that each risk modeled should be reviewed for its reasonableness.
Additional steps	• Modeling insurance coverage (the impact of insurance can be estimated directly by altering the severity distributions and expanding the simulation model). • Developing scenarios for stress testing. • Incorporating scorecards and risk indicators (qualitative adjustments are made to the capital calculations based on some combination of qualitative assessments, risk indicators and audit results).

7.4   THE INTERNAL MEASUREMENT APPROACH

A variant of the LDA is the IMA. The difference between the LDA and the IMA is that in the former unexpected losses are estimated directly without an assumption about the ratio between expected and unexpected losses. In the LDA, simulation is used to estimate the entire loss distribution, whereas the IMA provides an analytical approximation to the unexpected loss.

The basic IMA formula, as suggested by the BCBS (2001a) is

$$K = \gamma(NpL) \tag{7.15}$$

where K is the capital charge, N is a volume indicator, p is the probability of a loss and L is the loss given event for each event type/business line combination. Alexander (2003b) argues that NpL corresponds to the expected total loss when the loss frequency follows a binomial distribution, while severity is not regarded as a random variable in the basic form of the IMA. To follow this approach, a value that is approved by the regulators must be assigned to γ. Alexander suggests a simple way of calibrating the model by rewriting equation (7.15) in such a way as to relate K to the standard deviation of the total loss. Hence

$$K = \phi\sigma(NpL) \tag{7.16}$$

where $\sigma(NpL)$ is the standard deviation of the total loss. Since the capital charge is aimed at covering unexpected loss, which is the 99.9th percentile of the total loss, we have

$$K = T - \mu(NpL) \tag{7.17}$$

where T is the 99.9th percentile and $K = \mu(NpL)$ is the mean value of the total loss. It follows that

$$\phi = \frac{T - \mu(NpL)}{\sigma(NpL)} \tag{7.18}$$

Given that the basic IMA formula assumes a binomial frequency distribution with no variability in severity, the standard deviation of the total loss is $L\sqrt{Np}$, which gives

$$K = \phi L \sqrt{Np} \tag{7.19}$$

By calculating the value of ϕ from equation (7.18), the capital charge can be obtained from equation (7.19). Alexander (2003b) shows how equation (7.18) can be modified to calculate the value of ϕ when the loss frequency has a normal, Poisson and negative binomial distribution. For example, under Poisson distribution, $j = Np$, which gives

$$K = \phi L \sqrt{\lambda} \tag{7.20}$$

Alexander also shows how equation (7.18) is modified to allow for random severity. Finally, she shows how to include insurance in the general IMA formula. Once the capital charge has been calculated for all business lines/event types, the firm-wide capital charge can be calculated by summing up the individual capital charges (assuming perfect correlation).

7.5   THE SCENARIO-BASED APPROACH

For low-frequency events, a very long observation period (greater than ten years) may be required to estimate the expected frequency, let alone other parameters such as the mean and standard deviation of the severity of operational risk. One way to fill the data gap is to create synthetic data by using scenario analysis, which is a rigorous process carried out by the risk management team with the active participation of business line managers. This approach is similar to the LDA, which is used when there are sufficient operational loss data, except that only the inputs are different. In scenario analysis, the inputs are derived from expert opinions, all available internal loss data and relevant examples from the industry.

7.5.1   What is a scenario?

Scenarios are descriptions of alternative hypothetical futures that allow us to assess potential developments (for example, with respect to operational loss events). They do not describe what the future will look like but rather what possible futures one might expect. One reason for contemplating various scenarios is that the process sets no boundaries for thinking.

According to the *Concise Oxford Dictionary*, a scenario is "an imagined sequence of future events". There are two popular definitions of scenario, which are used primarily in the forecasting literature. Khan (1965) defines scenarios as "hypothetical sequences of events constructed for the purpose of focusing attention on causal processes and decision points". The second definition is suggested by Mitchell, Tydeman, and Georgiades (1979). According to the second definition, a scenario is "an outline of one conceivable state of affairs, given certain assumptions about the present and the course of events in the intervening period". Jungermann and Thuring (1987) distinguish between the two definitions on the basis of their emphasis on the course of events between the initial state and the final state. In Khan's definition the emphasis is on the explication of the chain of actions and events and their causal relations. The definition of Mitchell et al., on the other hand, emphasizes the depiction of the situation at the time horizon, given certain assumptions about the preceding period. Hence, Jungermann and Thuring call the first definition a "chain scenario" and the second definition a "snapshot scenario". Furthermore, they list the following properties of a scenario:

1. It is hypothetical in the sense that it describes some possible future.

2. It is selective in the sense that it represents one possible state of some complex state of affairs.

3. It is bound in the sense that it consists of a limited number of states, events, actions and consequences.

4. It is connected in the sense that its elements are conditionally or causally related.

5. It is assessable in the sense that it can be judged with respect to its probability and/or desirability.

Ducot and Lubben (1980) have suggested the following three criteria for classifying scenarios:

1. Scenarios are either explanatory or anticipatory. Explanatory scenarios are forward-directed, in the sense that they start from some assumed final state of affairs and explore what consequences might result.

Anticipatory scenarios are backward-directed, in the sense that they start from a final state of affairs and ask for the possible events that could produce these effects.

2. Scenarios are either descriptive or normative. Descriptive scenarios present potential futures irrespective of their desirability or otherwise. Normative scenarios take an explicit account of values and objectives.

3. Scenarios are trend or peripheral. A trend scenario extrapolates the normal surprise-free course of events or state of affairs that one might expect if no particular action is taken. A peripheral scenario depicts trend-breaking surprising or unsurprising developments.

7.5.2 Writing scenarios

Geschka and Reibnitz (1983) have suggested a scenario writing process that consists of the following steps:

1. Defining and structuring the task, specifying the area of interest and identifying the major relevant features of this area.

2. Describing important external factors and their influence on the area of interest. These factors form the influence fields.

3. Identifying major descriptors for each field and making assumptions about their future trends.

4. Checking the consistency of possible combinations of alternative assumptions regarding the critical descriptors and identifying assumption bundles.

5. Combining assumptions with the trend assumptions regarding the uncritical depicters, resulting in a scenario for each field.

6. Making assumptions with respect to possible interfering events and their probabilities as well as their impacts on the field.

7. Assessing the impact of the field scenarios on the area of interest and its depicters. Respective scenarios are constructed.

8. Identifying strategies that could promote or impede the developments described in the scenarios.

Jungermann and Thuring (1987) assume the following steps in the cognitive activity of a person embarking on the task of writing scenarios:

1. The relevant problem will be activated within the world knowledge of the individual.

2. A mental model is constituted on the basis of the activated problem knowledge that includes those elements and relations of the domain that are needed for the specific task.

3. Inferences are drawn by simulating the mental model.

4. Scenario knowledge is composed by selecting those inferences that seem most relevant, probable, interesting or whatever criteria might be used.

7.5.3   Scenario-based analysis of operational risk

The frequency and severity distributions are guesstimated using all available quantitative and qualitative information, including the subjective judgment of business line and senior management. Once the simulated loss distribution is obtained, the expected and unexpected losses should be compared against similar businesses and evaluated for reasonableness by the risk management team and business line managers. If adjustment is required for the initial guesstimates, the whole process should be repeated.
    The SBA consists of the following steps:

1. Scenario generation, which is the process of writing scenarios for operational risk. It is important here to make sure that scenarios are consistent, relevant and that they capture all kinds of operational risk.

2. Scenario assessment, which is the process of evaluating the scenarios.

3. Ensuring data quality (for example, by deleting the data points that do not make sense).

4. Determination of the parameter values, including the mean and standard deviation (as well as higher moments) of the loss distribution.

5. Model application, which is the choice of the model (statistical distribution) that fits the data.

6. Model output, which is the final step of using the loss distribution to calculate regulatory capital.

    Fujii (2005) argues that scenario analysis is much more than just a method to supplement the actual operational loss distribution. According to him, the SBA has two advantages: (i) the creation of scenarios incorporating loss events from near misses is necessary to measure the operational risk capital charge for future events; and (ii) the SBA creates the ability to respond to changes of business.
    Table 7.3 displays nine scenarios pertaining to the joint occurrence of operational losses from internal fraud and external fraud. The probability

Table 7.3 An example of operational risk scenarios

Scenario	Internal Fraud	External Fraud	Total Loss	Probability	Statistics
1	200	100	300	0.20	
2	200	50	250	0.18	
3	200	20	220	0.16	
4	100	100	200	0.13	
5	100	50	150	0.11	
6	100	20	120	0.09	
7	50	100	150	0.07	
8	50	50	100	0.04	
9	50	20	70	0.02	
Expected Value					208.7
Variance					4264.5
Standard Deviation					65.3

distribution can be used to calculate the expected value (mean) and standard deviation (as well as higher moments), which can be used to simulate the total loss distribution and then calculate regulatory capital. Scenarios can be generated for frequency and severity separately. The basic difference between this approach and the LDA is whether the distribution parameters are estimated from historical data or scenarios (hence, the LDA is backward-looking whereas the SCA is forward-looking).

7.6 THE SCORECARD APPROACH

The name "scorecard approach" is derived from the fact that the results of the risk evaluation process are reported on scorecards, which typically show scores for operational risk. In retail banking, scorecards have been used for a long time to assign customers to classes, depending on whether a customer's score is above or below a given threshold (see, for example, Hand, 2005). One of the most widely known operational risk scorecard systems has been developed by the Australia New Zealand Bank (Lawrence, 2000). The scores are expressed in monetary terms for potential loss severities, in the number of times per year for potential loss frequencies, and in the form of ratings for operational qualities (excellent, good, poor). Blunden

(2003) describes a scorecard as "simply a list of a firm's own assessment of its risks and controls, containing the risk event, risk owner, risk likelihood, risk impact, controls that mitigate the risk event, control owner, control design and control impact". As a minimum, the scorecard must contain the risk event, risk likelihood and risk impact, but may also contain commentary and/or values for action plans to enhance controls or reduce (optimize) risk. As the firm becomes more familiar with loss data, scorecards will also record the losses incurred in each event.

Take, for example, the frequency of loss events as the variable of interest. A scorecard may specify a range of expected frequency, whereas the exact point on the range would be fixed by scenario analysis, using comparison with actual loss data, if available, or external data otherwise. The frequency may be defined in relation to frequency classes corresponding to certain probability ranges. For example, an event that is considered to be "almost impossible" has a probability range of 0–0.0001, whereas an event that is considered to be "very likely" falls in the probability range 0.90–1.0. Figure 7.14 defines the frequency classes and the corresponding probability ranges.

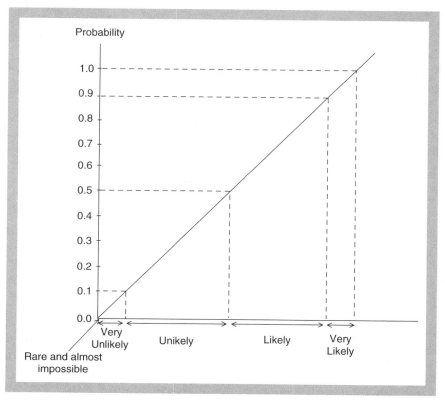

Figure 7.14 Frequency classes and corresponding probability ranges

7.6.1   Risk drivers and indicators

The SCA depends heavily on the concept of risk classes, key risk drivers (KRDs) and key risk indicators (KRIs). The best way to understand the concept of risk class is to use, as an example, the insurance industry, where it is common to create risk classes by classifying individuals or entities into groups sharing the same expected loss distribution. In car insurance, there is a set of risk characteristics (including age, marital status, the condition of the car and the accident record) that determine the classes. The same is true for life insurance where the historical loss experience is not available by definition. Mortality rates are assigned to individuals based on certain mortality risk indicators, such as age, parental history, occupation, and life style.

The same procedure can be used to analyze operational risk. For each operational risk type, the industry loss data can be grouped into several distinct loss distributions, each of which is uniquely characterized by the operational risk parameters (such as the probability of a loss event and the expected loss given event). Each set of parameters defines a particular risk class, in which case clusters of banks (risk classes) that share the same risk characteristics emerge. Changes in the business and control environment of a bank (measured by its KRDs) can be used to reclassify the risk classes.

KRDs, therefore, are the risk characteristics that distinguish the level of operational risk in one firm or business line from others. These include the complexity of the product, the complexity of the delivery system, the growth rate of the firm or the business line, the frequency of the system downtime, capacity usage and the skill level of the staff. KRDs are obtained from performance measures and from intuition, based on deep knowledge of the business activity. KDRs are defined by the BCBS (2002a) as "statistics and/or metrics, often financial, which can provide insight into a bank's risk position". These include "the number of failed trades, staff turnover rates and the frequency and/or risk severity of errors and omissions". Peccia (2004) relates the KRIs to what he calls the key risk factors. More specifically, he argues that the KRIs are the components of the following risk factors: (i) the type of business activity, (ii) the size of the activity (also called the exposure index), (iii) the business environment (for example, product complexity), and (iv) the control environment (for example, procedures and limits).

Alexander (2003a) gives examples of KRDs and KRIs for various operational risk types. In the case of credit card fraud, for example, a KRD is the quality of the authentication process, whereas a KRI is the number of unauthorized credit card transactions. Another example is the risk of employment practices and workplace safety where KRDs include recruitment policy with respect to discrimination, pay structure and safety measures whereas the KRIs include the number of employee complaints, staff turnover and time off work. More will be said about KRDs and KRIs in Chapter 8.

7.6.2 Risk controls

A related concept is that of a risk control, which is any measure that is taken to reduce operational risk of a certain type, typically measured in monetary terms because they constitute cost to the underlying firm. For example, to eliminate the risk of rogue trading completely, a firm will abandon its trading activity and put an end to trading operations. In this case, the control is completely effective but the cost is the trading profit forgone as a result of the action. In a less dramatic case, controlling the risk of rogue trading may be achieved partially by putting stringent limits on the traders and subjecting them to scrutiny. This will reduce the risk of rogue trading but at the cost of forgone trading profit, albeit smaller than the cost in the previous case. Likewise, the risk of system failure and the risk of credit card fraud can be eliminated completely by switching to manual processing of transactions and abandoning the use of credit cards. These controls are measured by the cost of inconvenience to customers and inefficiency. The risks can be eliminated partially by being very selective in granting credit cards and more severe authentication measures, and by using partial decentralized data processing systems. Again, the controls are measured by inconvenience and inefficiency. Peccia (2004) identifies seven control drivers, including the following: (i) policy and directives, (ii) qualified personnel, (iii) risk limits, (iv) procedures, (v) independent reporting/MIS, (vi) communication, and (vii) monitoring. The control environment is evaluated by assigning scores to the control drivers (say 1 to 5), then adding them up.

Related to the concept of control are the concepts of gross risk and residual risk (or net risk). If, for example, we expect the loss from rogue trading to be $1 million, but this amount can be reduced by half by imposing controls that will cost $200,000, then the gross loss (risk) is $1 million, the control is worth $200,000 and the residual loss (risk) is $500,000.

7.6.3 Constructing scorecards

Scorecards are constructed on the basis of expert evaluations and self-assessment exercises, the latter taking the form of well-designed questionnaires. Alexander (2003b) lists the information items required to determine potential severity and frequency. To determine potential severity, information must be obtained on (i) loss history, (ii) insurance cover, (iii) industry data, and (iv) banking experience. To determine potential loss frequency, information must be available on (i) KRIs, (ii) quality of controls, and (iii) business continuity planning. Table 7.4 shows an example of estimating potential severity and frequency for a particular type of operational risk based on the estimated KRDs, KRIs and control drivers. Experts can be asked to assign scores to these items where 1 is very low (very weak).

Peccia (2004) uses what he calls a risk rating system in terms of the business environment and control environment. Figures 7.15 and 7.16, respectively show risk rating by the business environment and control environment. For the business environment, six environmental drivers are used (product complexity, process complexity, system complexity, geography, legal complexity, regulatory complexity, and the speed of change). Combinations of event type/business line are classified according to these drivers as very low, low, medium, high, and very high. For the control evironment, the control drivers suggested by Peccia (2004) are classified as very weak, weak, moderate, strong and very strong.

Peccia also suggests the use of a heat map to represent both the control environment and the business environment, an example of which is shown in Figure 7.17. The control environment is plotted on the horizontal axis, such that a weak control environment shows high risk and vice versa. It is also possible to express the control environment in terms of control gaps, such that big control gaps imply more risk. The business environment is represented on the vertical axis, ranging from the very simple to the very

Table 7.4 Estimating potential severity and frequency based on scores

	1	2	3	4	5
Key Risk Driver 1		√			
Key Risk Driver 2				√	
Key Risk Driver 3			√		
Key Risk Indicator1	√				
Key Risk Indicator 2					√
Key Risk Indicator 3		√			
Control Driver 1	√				
Control Driver 2					√
Control Driver 3			√		
Potential Loss (Gross)			√		
Potential Loss (Net)		√			
Expected Frequency			√		

1: very low (weak), 2: low (weak), 3: medium/moderate, 4: high (strong), very high (strong).

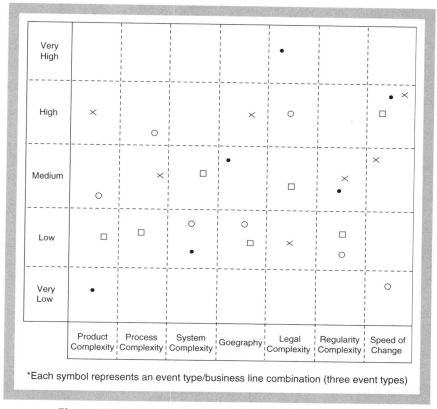

Figure 7.15 Risk rating by the business environment*

complex, such that a more complex business environment implies more risk. As we have seen before, the darker the shadow, the more risky the zone is. Such a heat map can be used to represent operational risk in event types, business lines or combinations thereof. In Figure 7.17, the dots represent 56 event type/business line combinations.

7.6.4   Processing the data

Once the experts have completed the questionnaires and the corresponding scorecard reports have been produced, the need arises for the validation of data. For this purpose, each expert's evaluation needs to be approved by a different person, whereas the internal audit reviews the evaluations. The independent oversight function ensures consistency across different questionnaires as well as the quality of the answers. Following validation, the data can be used to measure the capital charge against operational risk.

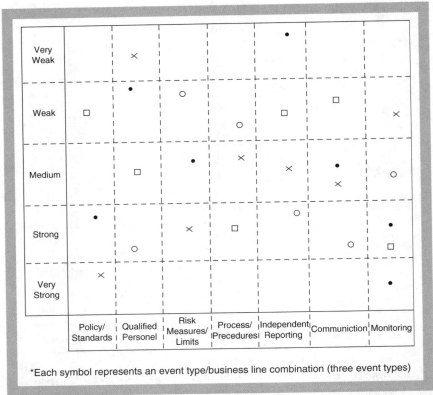

*Each symbol represents an event type/business line combination (three event types)

Figure 7.16 Risk rating by the control environment*

For this purpose, the occurrence of the risks and the failure of controls are simulated a considerable number of times to analyze the resulting distribution. To use the scorecard list of risks to run a model that produces a capital figure, it is necessary to assign values to the elements of the scorecard, such as the percentage of occurrence for the risk likelihood, a monetary value for the risk impact and the percentage of control failure (operational risk success) for the control design and performance.

Simulations are carried out on the risk and control profile. A decision has to be taken on the statistical distribution used for a particular data set. Although some risks appear to have complex distributions, Blunden (2003) suggests that a normal distribution can used for all simulations (which is strange, given that the normal distribution is symmetrical and does not have a thick tail). He also suggests that this can be done in three ways: (i) simulate the controls first and if a control fails, simulate the risks; (ii) simulate the risks first and if a risk happens (that is, a risk event materializes), then simulate the controls; and (iii) simulate both simultaneously. Correlations are important in this exercise, because risks are often

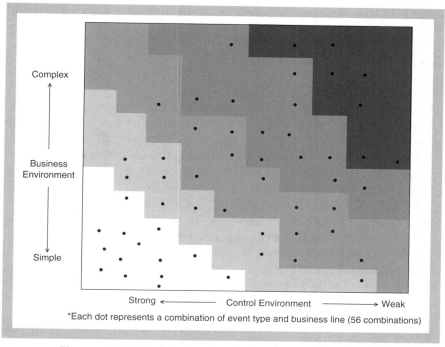

Figure 7.17 A heat map by the business environment and the control environment

correlated with other risks, and this should be reflected in the scorecard model. Blunden (2003) suggests various indicators for risk correlation: risk owners, geographical location of risks, and risks evolving from the same or similar causes. Controls are also correlated with each other. Sobehart (2006) considers a model of the severity of operational loss events whose distribution is determined by risk controls. He shows that ineffective controls can lead to a heavy-tailed distribution of operational losses. In the limit of highly effective controls, the model leads to normally distributed losses.

7.6.5   Allocating control resources

The ability to quantify, at an early opportunity, gross risk and the value of a control enables the firm to benefit by allocating control resources more efficiently, particularly if controls are more effective at a higher level of risk. By knowing the gross value of risk, a firm can start to rank risks by the likely monetary impact rather than by simple high, medium or low scores. By knowing the reduction in risk gained from the application of a control, it is possible to assess both the monetary value of the control and the percentage improvement in the risk exposure that the control produces. The quantification of gross risk and control values enables the management to see which risk is most susceptible to reduction, thus channeling more control resources to risks that are less effectively controlled rather than the biggest risks that are effectively under control.

To demonstrate how risk reduction can be more effective by channeling controls from one area to another, consider the loss data shown in Figure 7.18 and Figure 7.19. For this purpose we assume that controls are more effective at higher levels of risk. Specifically, it is assumed that the same amount of controls can reduce risk by 90 percent if it falls in the range 81–100, by 70 percent in the range 61–80, by 40 percent in the range 41–60, by 20 percent in the range 21–40 and by 8 percent in the range 0–20. If the controls are allocated evenly to the 56 business line/event type combinations, the relation between risk reduction and gross risk will be nonlinear, as shown in Figure 7.18. Suppose now, that the controls are reallocated as follows: 42.9 percent to the range 81–100, 24.1 percent to the range 61–80, 21.4 percent to the range, 41–60, 9.8 percent to the range 21–40 and 1.8 percent to the range 0–20. In this case, the relation between risk reduction and gross risk becomes staggered, represented by the dashed line in Figure 7.18. Notice, however, the improvement in risk reduction after the reallocation of controls. In terms of numbers, the total risk reduction when the controls are reallocated rises from 812 to 1320. Consider now Figure 7.19, which shows gross risk, residual risk when controls are distributed evenly and residual risk when controls are allocated according to the risk level. We clearly see that the residual risk is much lower when the controls are allocated according to the level of risk (1500, compared to 2008 when the controls are allocated evenly).

7.6.6 The pros and cons of the scorecard approach

Blunden (2003) lists the following advantages of the SCA:

1. The approach is flexible, as it fits with the underlying firm's identified risks and controls.

2. It does not require an external view of the risk categories faced by a firm.

3. It allows the firm to obtain skills and knowledge by starting operational risk capital calculation early rather than waiting to build up an internal database or using external data that may not be relevant to the firm.

4. It allows the quantification of net risk and therefore the ability to look at the risk exposure after control.

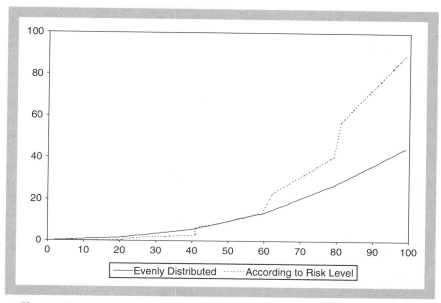

Figure 7.18 Absolute risk reduction as a function of the level of risk

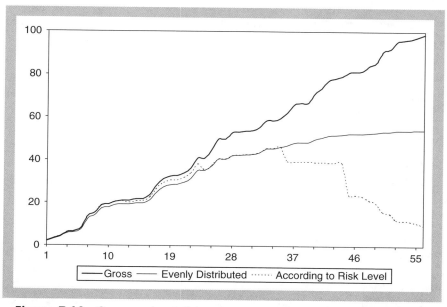

Figure 7.19   Gross and net risks when controls are distributed evenly and by risk level

5. By quantifying risks and controls, a firm can perform analysis on its risk inventory, which allows it to see (in monetary terms) the likely increase in the risk exposure resulting from the removal of a control or the likely reduction in exposure resulting from an increase in the quantity of control.

6. Unlike the LDA, the SCA is forward-looking. This is a useful property, particularly if we are trying to measure the operational risk associated with a new business line or activity, which has no history within the firm.

Furthermore, Lawrence (2000) puts forward a strong case for the SCA by arguing that if scorecards are deigned properly, business units will have sufficient incentive to take mitigating actions to control their risks. The motivation is that by controlling their risks, business units will improve their risk scores and reduce their capital allocation.

The main shortcoming of the SCA is that it is subjective. Rowe (2004a) cites a risk management specialist arguing that "psychological research reveals the existence of a number of systematic biases in people's subjective attempts to evaluate probabilities". Alexander (2003b) lists the following reasons why scorecards are subjective:

1. The industry standards for KRIs that should be used for each risk type have not been developed. The choice is, therefore, subjective.

2. Given a set of risk indicators, frequency and severity scores are usually assigned by the "owner" of the risk. Careful design of the management process is needed to avoid subjective bias (for example, a no-blame culture).

3. The scores need to be mapped in a subjective manner to monetary loss amounts, particularly with human risks (inadequate or failed people or management processes).

4. To use scorecard data in the AMA, the minimum requirement is to assess both expected frequency and expected severity quantitatively from scores that may be purely qualitative. For example, the score "very unlikely" for a loss event might translate into any probability depending on the scorecard design.

Furthermore, Knot et al. (2006) argue that the SCA leads to the creation of behavioral incentives to business units to manage and control their risks as a way to reduce their operational risk and to improve their risk scores. However, a major shortcoming is that it does not give any indication of the required capital, basically resulting in a relative risk comparison of the different activities. Holmes (2003) casts doubt on the ability of this approach to give reliable information about risk over time or rank the relative risk of two firms.

7.7 WHAT IS NEXT?

Following the definition of operational risk in Chapter 4, we examined the measurement and modeling of operational risk in Chapters 6 and 7. What follows should naturally be the management of operational risk, which is (or should be) the ultimate objective.

This chapter gave us a feel of some elements of operational risk management by introducing the concepts of risk drivers, risk indicators and risk controls. We have also seen the effect of executing a risk management task by reallocating the available control resources. Chapter 8 deals with operational risk management in detail.

The Management of Operational Risk

8.1 INTRODUCTION

The management of operational risk is not a new idea, neither is it an activity that firms have not indulged in. On the contrary, firms have always striven to manage the risk of fire through insurance and fire safety measures. Furthermore, they have always had specialists who managed other kinds of operational risk, such as the lawyers and other legal specialists who are involved in managing legal risk and the structural engineers who look after buildings and structures. This is typically done both proactively (for example, by providing advice to management prior to signing a contract and by maintaining buildings) and reactively (by providing legal representation in a court of law, representing the firm in out-of-court settlements of disputes, and doing repair work on damaged structures).

8.1.1 Operational risk management in financial institutions

On the issue of whether or not operational risk management has been practiced for some time, Kennett (2003) argues that operational risk has been managed (implicitly) since "year dot". Referring to banks specifically, he argues that "ever since they first opened their doors as banks, operational risk has been at the forefront of their activities". He even claims that most firms have managed operational risk pretty effectively over the years, although there are some obvious examples (most likely, this is reference to Barings Bank, Long-Term Capital Management and the like). Likewise, Buchelt and Unteregger (2004) argue that long before the advent of

Basel II, financial institutions had put in place various control mechanisms and procedures. To combat physical threats, for example, extensive security and safety measures, as well as security rules, have been put in place. They also mention the control roles of the human resources, legal and internal audit departments. A similar view has been put forward by Saxton (2002) who argues that operational risk is not new, but rather a concept that "banks have been struggling with for years with varying degrees of success".

Conversely, the management of market risk and credit risk, particularly by using the relatively recent invention of financial and credit derivatives as hedging devices, was virtually unknown for a long period of time, by a specific name or otherwise. Hence, operational risk management is older than either credit risk management and market risk management. But just like the terms "risk", "financial risk", "market risk", and "credit risk" appeared before the term "operational risk", the terms "risk management", "financial risk management", "market risk management", and "credit risk management" appeared before the term "operational risk management". However, it is not only the name because, unlike credit risk management and market risk management, operational risk management has never been (and it is still not) an integrated process, although it appears that things are moving this way. Rather, operational risk management has been a set of fragmented activities designed to deal with a wide variety of operational risks. We are still a long way away from the target of making operational risk management an integrated process that deals with operational risk as a generic kind of risk. This is not surprising, given that the concept of operational risk was unknown some ten years ago.

8.1.2   The operational risk management lag

What is new about operational risk management (as we know it now) is, according to Hubner et al. (2003), the objective of providing a structure that is comparable to those applicable to credit risk and market risk management. The lag in developing integrated operational risk management relative to credit risk management and market risk management is attributed by Hubner et al. (2003) to the need to bring together information from a range of existing functional units and the resources required for achieving that, as well as the lack of an organizational label (that is, operational risk management) under which these activities could be grouped. The functional units referred to by Hubner et al. include (i) management and financial accounting (information collection, analysis and reporting); (ii) purchasing (contractual terms, outsourcing); (iii) corporate security (the protection of corporate assets from harm); (iv) human resources (background checks on new staff, training in discrimination issues); (v) insurance; (vi) legal and intellectual property issues (trade marks, copyright, patents); and (vii) audit, both internal and external.

Indeed, Hubner et al. (2003) argue that even though operational risk has been managed inside banks for ever, the development of comprehensive systematic oversight is still at an embryonic stage. Kennett (2003) attributes the lag to several reasons, including the breadth of operational risk, the fact that it is already managed implicitly, the lack of data, the fact that it affects the whole firm, and the fact that a lot of tools and techniques are "more bleeding edges than cutting edges". Moreover, he argues that operational risk management is a "very complex undertaking", more so than either credit or market risk, which are not simple themselves.

Indicative of the lag in the development of operational risk management are the results of three surveys. The British Bankers' Association (1997) conducted a survey of its 300 members, which revealed that many banks had not thought through a definition of operational risk, few had anyone responsible for operational risk and very few attempts had been made to report operational losses in a systematic way. This was contrary to the way banks dealt with credit risk, in which case even relatively small losses were reported. The other survey was commissioned by the BBA together with ISDA and Robert Morris Associates in 1999 (BBA/ISDA/RMA, 1991). This survey, which was conducted on internationally active banks, showed that although much work had been done in the interim, there was still a lot of work to do. Marshall and Heffes (2003) report the results of a survey conducted by the Risk Water Group and SAS involving 400 risk managers at 300 financial institutions. The survey revealed that one in five financial institutions still does not have an operational risk management program although 90 percent of them lose more than $10 million a year due to the poor risk control practices. The survey also showed that a third of them expect to spend less than $1 million a year on the improvement of their risk management practices.

8.1.3   Operational risk management as an integrated process

A growing desire has emerged to organize the components of operational risk into what Hubner et al. (2003) call a "coherent structural framework". They explain the drive to orgainze the operational risk management process to: (i) shareholder value and competition, (ii) senior management and corporate governance issues, and (iii) regulatory issues. The rising importance of shareholders means that they can influence the way in which the firm conducts its affairs, which affects its competitive position. For an operational risk management framework to be effective, therefore, it is desirable to have the endorsement of shareholders. Senior management comes in to determine risk tolerance (or risk appetite) and formulate the corporate governance statement. For example, should operational risk management be reactive (such as fire fighting, crisis management and clean-up management) or proactive, consisting of data collection and risk assessment, risk control and mitigation and review of approach and enhancement? We have dealt, on more than one occasion, with the role of the regulators. The Basel II Accord is not only concerned with capital adequacy but also with sound risk (particularly operational risk) management.

There is definitely growing tendency to promote the perception of operational risk management as a discipline ranking alongside credit and market risk management and one that is necessary for an integrated risk management framework. This requires clear borders between operational risk, on the one hand, and credit risk and market risk on the other. One of the objectives of establishing the operational risk management function is to help the co-ordination of the application of specialist skills because co-ordination encourages greater communication and transparency.

8.2 WHO IS RESPONSIBLE FOR OPERATIONAL RISK?

A question arises as to who is responsible for operational risk, and this question might be interpreted to mean two different things. The first interpretation is that the question refers to the risk "owners", the risk takers who indulge in activities that lead to operational risk. The second interpretation is that it refers to who is responsible for managing operational risk, whether it is the risk owner or a more centralized corporate body. This is, therefore, a corporate governance issue.

In the broadest sense, risk management should be integrated into the activities of the risk-takers in the firm. But for an independent risk management structure to operate, there has to be an oversight activity that works independently of the risk takers. In the case of market risk and credit risk there is, as a result of many years of experience, a well-established concept of how the activity should function. For operational risk, the issue is somewhat more complicated because the ownership of, or responsibility for, operational risk is not clear. Hubner et al. (2003) put forward the view that the business lines are responsible for operational risk, which means that the responsibility is aligned with profit centers and risk takers. This is intuitively obvious for credit risk and market risk, as they are transaction-focused. The regulatory view embodied in Basel II appears to support the assumption that the business lines are responsible for its day-to-day management. But the problem with this view is that operational risk does not only pertain to profit centers, because it is a firm-wide kind of risk (recall the distinction between operational risk and operations risk).

This characteristic of operational risk creates some problems when we try to set a role for the support functional units (such as human resources management, IT, security, legal affairs and finance) in operational risk management. In practice, the functional units conduct activities on behalf of the risk owners and also act as advisors, providing not only reactive but also proactive support for the business units. The formalization of the operational risk management process means that there needs to be clarity over the interaction between risk owners and functional support units. The problem here is that functional support units are themselves exposed to operational risk. For example, the human resources department of a firm is a support unit that is exposed to operational risk (such as the legal risk of litigation against the firm by an unhappy employee). Moreover, it is sometimes not clear who the risk owner is. For example, who is responsible for the risk of the theft of information (stored electronically) that results in losses on some foreign exchange positions? Would it be the security department or the IT department (both of which are support units) or would it be the foreign exchange department (which is a business line or profit center)?

The concept of governance models invariably appears in any discussion of operational risk management. While the traditional view is that the responsibility for risk rests with line management, a new governance model is evolving in financial institutions. This model is characterized by having a central operational risk manager, most often reporting to the chief risk officer. The role is one of policy setting, development of tools, co-ordination, analysis and benchmarking, and integration and aggregation of the risk profile. The risk manager would be responsible for setting a common definition for operational risk, developing and facilitating the implementation of common risk management tools (such as risk maps, self-assessment programs and loss event databases), and developing measurement models along the lines described in Chapters 6 and 7. However, the line management remains responsible for the day-to-day risk management activities, since it is the business areas that face the customer, introduce products, manage the majority of people, operate processes and technologies, and deal with other external exposures. Support units develop specific policies and procedures, monitor emerging skills and advise senior management on risk as applicable to their areas.

In addition to the risk manager, line management and support units, risk committees may also be used. The role of a risk committee is to understand the risk profile, ensure that resources are properly allocated and that risk issues are addressed, as well as approving policies, including capital allocation. Haas and Kaiser (2005) suggest the introduction of an "operational risk coach", who would be neutral to all business lines, acting as a confidant, with whom employees could discuss operational loss events and possible solutions without having to fear layoff or negative reputation for themselves or the business line. They suggest that the operational risk coach can be either a member of the committee or reporting directly to it.

In short, therefore, two forms of integrated operational risk management have emerged. Some opt for a mix of the traditional siloed approach and a touch of firm-wide oversight. While business line managers are closest to the risks to be managed, they lack independence. Under this arrangement, a small corporate risk management department would be in charge of facilitating risk self-assessment. However, firm-wide risk management oversight may be largely absent. Alternatively, there is the centralized risk management approach where there is an established risk management group, which is in charge of (i) setting policies and facilitating the development of operational risk reporting, (ii) independent monitoring, and (iii) establishing key indicators and bottom up empirical capital allocation.

8.3   THE RISK MANAGEMENT FRAMEWORK: STRATEGY

Haunbenstock (2003) identifies the components of the operational risk framework as: (i) strategy, (ii) process, (iii) infrastructure, and (iv) the environment. This section is devoted to the strategy component, whereas the following section deals with the process. The infrastructure and environment are dealt with in a separate section that follows the section on the process.

The strategy involves determination of business objectives, the risk appetite, the organizational approach to risk management, and the approach to operational risk management. Naturally, the involvement of senior management in the formulation of the strategy is essential. The objective is to align the firm's risk profile (the risk that the firm wants to assume) with the selected risk appetite. The business objectives include targets like a market share or the introduction of new products and technology. Objectives are also stated for individual business units. The risk appetite does not only refer to the level of acceptable risk but also to the types of unacceptable risks. A risk map may be used as a quantifiable measure of the risk appetite that can be used to identify unacceptable risks.

The strategy also involves setting up an operational risk policy statement describing the overall approach and can be made specific to each business line as applicable. Policies often start with the objectives of operational risk management, which include increasing awareness and reducing operational losses. The statement of objectives can be complemented by a description of how the firm goes about the process and the agreed-upon definition of operational risk. The policy statement should also discuss the governance model and related roles and responsibilities. Also important are some general statements of risk management principles and a description of the expectations for the use of tools and reporting. For example, if there is a common self-assessment or database, the policy might state that every business area should implement it and maintain the information in an up-to-date manner.

In short, therefore, the strategy involves (i) setting effective operational risk policies and clear directions to follow, (ii) establishing an effective management structure and arrangement to deliver the policy, and (iii) implementing the policy through an effective operational risk management system. The following section deals with the second component of the risk management framework, which is the process.

8.4   THE RISK MANAGEMENT FRAMEWORK: PROCESS

The process involves the day-to-day activities required to understand and manage operational risk, given the chosen strategy. The process consists of (i) risk and control identification, (ii) risk measurement and monitoring, (iii) risk control/mitigation, and (iv) process assessment and evaluation. Peccia (2003) adds two more elements: capital allocation and loss management. We will deal with the components (i)–(iv) in turn.

8.4.1   Risk and control identification

Risk identification starts with the definition of operational risk to provide a broad context for potential threats. The best way to identify risk is to talk to people who live with it on a daily basis, people who can be found in the support functional units or in the business lines themselves. Peccia (2003) suggests that identification should begin with a rigorous self-assessment of the exposures, the control environment and key risk drivers. He further suggests that risk identification should be based on a well-defined and consistent classification of operational risk, otherwise similar risks within different business lines or different times may be identified as being different, whereas different risks may be identified as being similar. The product of risk identification may be a risk map detailing which risks, and to what degree, apply to any one business, process or unit. The degree of risk is typically defined as frequency and severity, rated either qualitatively (high, medium, low) or on a quantitative scale.

Mestchian (2003) suggests a decomposition of operational risk management along the lines used to decompose operational risk into process risk, people risk, technology risk, and external risk. Thus, operational risk management can be decomposed into the following: (i) people risk management, (ii) process risk management, (iii) technology risk management, and (iv) external risk management. If this is the case, then risk identification may be reported as in Table 8.1 where people risk, process risk, technology risk and external risk are classified into low, medium and high according to business activities. Alternatively, a risk map may appear as in Figure 8.1, which shows the frequency and severity of the risk embodied in individual activities.

Table 8.1 Risk identification

	People	Process	Technology	External
Activity 1	L	M	M	H
Activity 2	H	L	M	H
Activity 3	M	L	L	M
Activity 4	M	L	M	M
⋮	⋮	⋮	⋮	⋮
Activity n	M	M	L	M

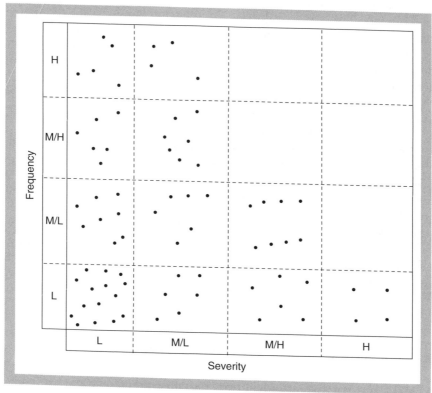

Figure 8.1 Risk assessment of activities

Risk identification should also include monitoring of the external environment and industry trends, as new risks emerge continuously, or it could be that risk may take on a new dimension. Internet security, privacy, patent risk, and discrimination are examples of risks that have increased dramatically over the past few years.

The identification of controls is part of the identification process, as it complements the identification of risk. Controls, a concept that we came across in Chapter 7, may reside at the business activity level, whereas others operate as part of the corporate risk management infrastructure. They include management oversight, information processing, activity monitoring, automation, process controls, segregation of duties, performance indicators, and policy and procedures. Risk mitigators include training, insurance programs, diversification and outsourcing. The control framework defines the appropriate approach to controlling each identified risk. Insurance, which is a means of risk control/mitigation, is typically applied against the large exposures where a loss would cause a charge to earnings greater than that acceptable in the risk appetite.

For the purpose of risk identification, the Federal Reserve System (1997) advocates a three-fold risk-rating scheme that includes (i) inherent risk, (ii) risk controls, and (iii) composite risk. Inherent risk (or gross risk) is the level of risk without consideration of risk controls, residing at the business unit level and is supervised through a review of significant activities. These activities are evaluated to arrive at the firm-wide inherent risk rating. Inherent risk depends on (i) the level of activity relative to the firm's resources, (ii) number of transactions, (iii) complexity of activity, and (iv) potential loss to the firm.

Composite risk (or residual risk or net risk) is the risk remaining after accounting for inherent risk and risk mitigating controls. The Federal Reserve System (1997) provides a matrix that shows composite risk situation based on the strength of risk management (weak, acceptable, strong) and the inherent risk of the activity (low, moderate, high). For example, when weak risk management is applied to low inherent risk, the resulting risk is low/moderate composite risk. On the other extreme, when strong risk management is applied to high inherent risk, the composite risk will be moderate/high. And when strong risk management is applied low risk, the composite risk will be low. Figure 8.2 provides an illustration of the Federal Reserve's classification of inherent and composite risk.

8.4.2 Risk measurement

As risks and controls are identified, risk measurement provides insight into the magnitude of exposure, how well controls are operating and whether exposures are changing and consequently require attention.

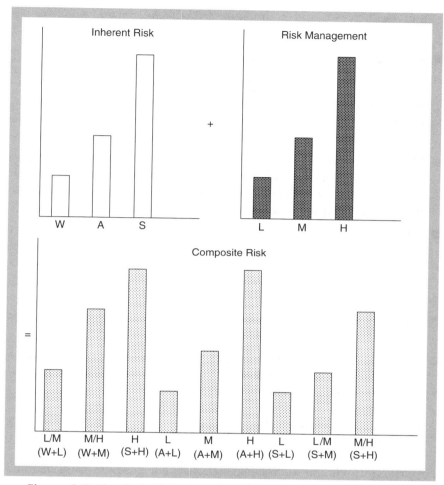

Figure 8.2 The Federal Reserve System's classification of inherent and composite risks

It remains true, however, that the borderline between identification and measurement is not well-defined and that there is some overlapping between the two. Haubenstock (2003) identifies the following items as relevant to the measurement of operational risk:

■ Risk drivers, which are measures that drive the inherent risk profile and changes in which indicate changes in the risk profile. These include (as we have seen) transaction volumes, staff levels, customer satisfaction, market volatility, the level of automation. According to Crouchy (2001), risk drivers are associated with change (for example, the introduction of new technology and new products), complexity (of products, processes and technology), and complacency (ineffective management of the business).

- Risk indicators, which are a broad category of measures used to monitor the activities and status of the control environment of a particular business area for a given risk category. The difference between drivers and indicators is that the former are *ex ante* whereas the latter are *ex post*. Examples of risk indicators are profit and loss breaks, open confirmations, failed trades and settlements and systems reliability.

- The loss history, which is important for three reasons: (i) loss data are needed to create or enhance awareness at multiple levels of the firm; (ii) they can be used for empirical analysis; and (iii) they form the basis for the quantification of operational risk capital.

- Causal models, which provide the quantitative framework for predicting potential losses. These models take the history of risk drivers, risk indicators and loss events and develop the associated multivariate distributions. The models can determine which factor(s) have the highest association with losses.

- Capital models, which are used to estimate regulatory capital as envisaged by Basel II.

- Performance measures, which include the coverage of the self-assessment process, issues resolved on time, and percentage of issues discovered as a result of the self assessment process.

Alexander (2003a) suggests three questions that are vital at this stage. These questions are:

1. What effect will the controls have on risk? For this purpose, a quantitative model is needed to relate risk to controls (a Bayesian network is recommended by Alexander).

2. Is it possible that by reducing one risk, another risk will increase? How can we quantify risk dependence, and how to control this dependence? Alexander argues that managing risk dependence is one of the main strengths of Bayesian networks.

3. What is the cost of controls, and is the likely reduction in risk worth the cost? This depends on the firm's utility function, which can be incorporated in the decision-making process.

Reporting is an important element of measurement and monitoring. Business lines perform the majority of data collection and reporting as part of their normal responsibilities. The central operational risk group adds value through benchmarking, analysis, and capital quantification. A key objective of reporting is to communicate the overall profile of operational risk across all business lines and types of risk. The risk profile is represented by a combination of risk maps, graphical results, issues, and initiatives. Loss events are also reported to provide the historical database for risk analysis and quantification. There are two alternative ways of reporting to a central database as shown in Figure 8.3. One way is indirect reporting where there is a hierarchy in the reporting process, which can be arranged on a geographical basis. Otherwise, direct reporting is possible where every unit reports directly to a central database.

Risk assessment is a qualitative process that complements the measurement process because not all risks can be measured quantitatively. Checklists are probably the most common approach to self-assessment. Structured questionnaires are distributed to business areas to help them identify their level of risk and related controls. The response would indicate the degree to which a given risk affects their areas. It would also give some indication of the frequency and severity of the risk and the level of risk control that is already in place. The narrative approach is also used to ask business areas to define their own objectives and the resulting risks. The workshop

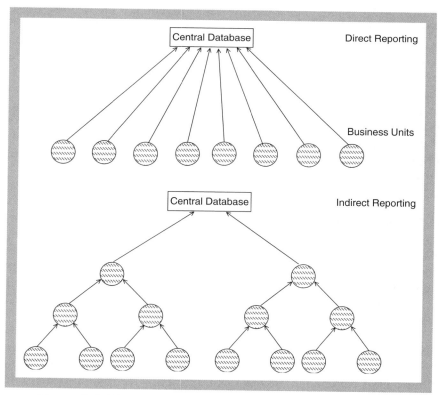

Figure 8.3 Direct vs. indirect reporting to a central database

approach skips the paperwork and gets people to talk about their risks, controls, and the required improvements.

Lam (2003b) argues for the use of elements of quantitative and qualitative approaches to the measurement of operational risk. In this respect, he identifies what he calls two schools of thought: (i) the one believing that what cannot be measured cannot be managed, hence the focus should be on quantitative tools; and (ii) the other, which does not accept the proposition that operational risk can be quantified effectively, hence the focus should be on qualitative approaches. Lam (2003b) warns of the pitfalls of using one approach rather than the other, stipulating that "the best practice operational risk management incorporates elements of both". Even the most quantitative experts of operational risk believe that a combination of quantitative and qualitative techniques and approaches is the way forward. For example, Chavez-Demoulin, Embrechts, and Neslehova (2006) admit that a full quantitative approach may never be achieved. However, they argue that some sophisticated techniques (such as advanced peaks over threshold modeling, the construction of dependent loss processes and the establishment of bounds for risk measures under partial information) are very powerful quantitative techniques.

Currie (2004) identifies what she calls "potentially unintended consequences" that arise from the use of operational risk models for practical risk management purposes. First of all, attempting to summarize all operational risk into a single measure could be "misleading and dangerous". The second consequence is that emphasis may be placed on the management of the model rather than reality. Currie argues that senior management may, on the basis of the model's output, take actions to reduce the model's estimate of operational risk rather than address the real core issues. There could also be misdirected focus and misdirected resources, the former with respect to the risks that can be quantified rather than major risks, and the latter with respect to the resources needed to maintain the model.

8.4.3   Risk control/mitigation

We now come to risk control/mitigation. When risk has been identified and measured, there are a number of choices in terms of the actions that need to be taken to control or mitigate risk. These include (i) risk avoidance, (ii) risk reduction, (iii) risk transfer, and (iv) risk assumption (risk taking). Sometimes, the notion of risk sharing is also suggested.

Risk avoidance can be quite difficult and may raise questions about the viability of the business in terms of the risk-return relation. Recall that the "most effective" way to eliminate the risk of rogue trading is to stop trading altogether. A better alternative is risk reduction, which typically takes the

THE MANAGEMENT OF OPERATIONAL RISK

form of risk control efforts as it may involve tactics ranging from business re-engineering to staff training as well as various less extensive staff and/or technical solutions. Reducing risk can raise a number of issues, including not only the risk-return relation of the activity but also the availability of resources. Cost-benefit analysis may be used to assist in structuring decisions and to prevent the business from being controlled out of profit. It is, therefore, a matter of balancing the costs and benefits of risk reduction.

Risk reduction can be illustrated with the aid of Figure 8.4, which shows a heat map by the business environment and the control environment. Suppose that the risk appetite of the firm allows it to be in the lowest three risk zones. This firm then attempts to move points (activities) falling in the high risk zones to the low risk zones by spending more money to strengthen controls (which may take the form of reduced return) and/or reducing the complexity of the business environment (if this is at all possible). Risk reduction may be represented, as shown in Figure 8.5, by a downward shift in the total loss distribution as a result of applying risk controls.

Risk transfer is what Mestchian (2003) calls "the external solution to operational risk". Insurance is typically described as a key tool of risk transfer, as some kinds of operational risk have been insured for some

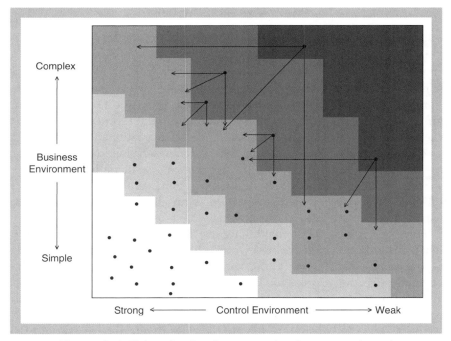

Figure 8.4 Risk reduction by strengthening controls and reducing complexity

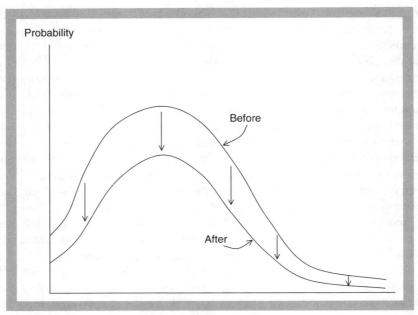

Figure 8.5 The effect of applying risk mitigators and controls
on the total loss distribution

time. Examples include property coverage, fire, workers compensation, employers liability, and professional indemnity. Insurance provides firms with the means of taking risk off their balance sheets and avoiding the significant costs of capital associated with the provision for risk. Demand for insurance coverage has increased dramatically in recent times as senior executives have realized the consequences of operational risk. A special case of risk transfer is risk sharing, where the underlying idea is to transfer risk from individual firms to a group of firms participating in the risk-sharing scheme. One example of such a scheme is the so-called mutual self-insurance pools, which is regarded as an alternative to insurance, as we are going to see later in this chapter.

However, it is arguable that taking insurance does not really amount to risk transfer because the insured would still be exposed to risk. This is like saying that by insuring your house against fire, it is the insurer's house that will catch fire, not yours, even though the fire is on a street that is 20 miles away from the insurer's house!! Risk transfer in the strict sense would occur only if the bank outsources the activity to the insurer, which does not sound a good idea. Insurance merely provides financial cover, should risk bearing leads to losses. In this sense, insurance provides risk financing (specifically, external financing) rather than risk transfer.

Strictly speaking, therefore, a firm cannot transfer risk to an insurance company by taking insurance. However, an insurance company can transfer the risk of insuring another firm through reinsurance, whereas a firm can transfer the risk to another firm via outsourcing. We will have more to say about reinsurance later on, which allows us to concentrate on outsourcing here. Outsourcing enables firms to select the various business processes or functions that are non-core and high risk to a third party. Examples are the IT and HR functions. In addition to risk transfer, Mestchian (2003) argues that outsourcing has the following advantages: cost control, access to best practice tools and methodologies, freeing up capital and resources to focus on core business, and reduction in bureaucracy and administrative burden. The problem here is that transferring a specific operational risk may lead to the emergence of other operational risks (for example, legal risk invariably arises from outsourcing and insurance). A firm may choose to manage the risks that arise in the transfer process so that it achieves an overall net reduction in the risk profile. Again, it is a matter of balancing costs and benefits.

Opposite to risk avoidance is risk assumption, which is the action of taking on risk either through proactive decision or by default. In this case, the risk is supported by the firm's capital (hence, the Basel II Accord). In practice, a firm may use a combination of risk reduction, risk transfer and risk assumption, depending on the frequency and severity of the underlying risk. Figure 8.6 displays a risk map showing the zones where various actions are taken. A firm would therefore avoid high-frequency, high-severity risks, assume low-frequency, low-severity risks, transfer low-frequency, high- severity risks and avoid high-frequency high-severity risks. The question mark in Figure 8.6 represents the "grey" areas that, depending on the circumstances, can be reclassified to be in one of the four zones. Similarly, Figure 8.7 shows the distinction between expected loss and unexpected loss at a given confidence level. The expected loss, which is the mean of the loss distribution, is assumed. Unexpected loss can be severe (between the mean and a certain percentile corresponding to the confidence level) and catastrophic (above the percentile corresponding to the confidence level). Severe operational risk is typically covered by regulatory (or economic) capital, whereas catastrophic risk is avoided (if possible) or insured.

8.4.4   Process assessment and evaluation

The final step in the process component is assessment and evaluation, which is used to determine how well the firm is controlling and managing risk, the potential weaknesses, scope for improvement, etc. It is some sort of performance evaluation in relation to operational risk management,

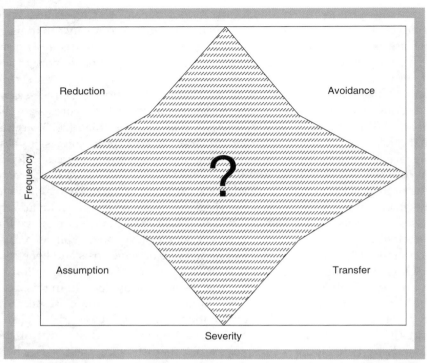

Figure 8.6 A risk map showing risk control/mitigation action

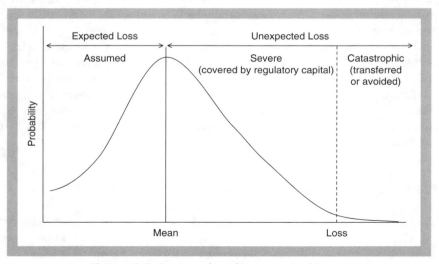

Figure 8.7 Expected and unexpected losses

where performance is measured against set standards to reveal when and where improvement is needed. This exercise also involves the measurement of the risk remaining after the risk controls and mitigation measures have been implemented. The amount of risk that remains is compared with the level of risk that the controls and mitigation were expected to achieve and also with the standards and objectives.

The internal audit function plays a role here, but as operational risk management becomes more explicit, the role of internal audit should change. In traditional models, the audit function is responsible for assessing controls, but now the primary responsibility for assessment is shifting to the business areas under the co-ordination of the operational risk management department. The role of audit should refocus on evaluating how well the overall risk management framework is functioning and on the testing of controls. Sharon (2006) argues that confusing the risk management function with the internal audit function amounts to confusing compliance with risk management and that merging the two essentially means that there is no oversight over the risk management function.

The role of the internal audit in operational risk management is made explicit by the BCBS (2004a). For example, one of the requirements for eligibility to use the standardized approach is effective risk management and control, in which internal auditors must regularly review the operational risk management process. In fact, banks are encouraged to establish independent internal audit and operational risk management groups in the structural hierarchy. The problem is that some firms place operational risk management within audit, claiming that it is the operational risk management department. However, Basel II suggests that for firms expecting (or required to) use the more sophisticated approaches, traditional decentralized business line management should be complemented by independent internal audit and corporate risk management departments. Kennett (2003) believes that there is perceived overlap of responsibility as far as the audit function is concerned. Audit, he argues, can feel threatened by the operational risk team, who may in turn view audit as being out of touch and not adding much value. Uncertainty about who is responsible for what leads to confusion and reduces the effectiveness of both. In an ideal world, they should be complementary.

8.5 THE RISK MANAGEMENT FRAMEWORK: INFRASTRUCTURE AND ENVIRONMENT

Infrastructure refers to the tools used to facilitate the entire risk management process, including systems, data, methodologies as well as policies and procedures. Mestchian (2003) refers to technology risk management by arguing that all successful risk management projects share a strong emphasis on complete management of input data and computed results. Data in this sense include self-assessment data, internal event/loss data, operational data, and external loss data.

On the other hand, the environment refers to the surroundings that set the tone and behavior of the firm, including culture and external factors. Culture, which refers to the involvement and support of senior management and the related values and communication that set the tone for decision making, is a component of the process because it supports the risk management objectives. Culture is the set of shared attitudes, values, goals, and practices that characterize how a firm considers risk in its daily activities. Kennett (2003) argues that operational risk management becomes embodied in the culture of the firm, in the sense that every decision must involve an explicit review of the underlying operational risk. The environment is also about communications, accountability, and reinforcement. People are another component, as there should be adequate and trained people to do the job. The external component of the environment includes competitors, customers, regulators, the economy, and the law.

Hubner et al. (2003) discuss cultural drivers, suggesting that the experience of implementing credit and market risk management frameworks leads one to think that operational risk management will in time become an intrinsic part of a corporate culture. Incorporating awareness of operational risk into a firm's culture is an important part of prevention, so the question is how to promote this culture. This is why education and training are important. Because operational risk is present across the entire firm, every employee should be made aware of the issue and related management processes. There is a tendency to associate operational risk management with the control environment, which may make the framework appear as a source of additional bureaucratic burden. One thing that can be done is to include operational risk in performance measurement and in the basis of bonus calculation.

Mestchian (2003) discusses people risk management, suggesting that three sets of human factors affect operational risk, the first of which is that of organizational factors. Firms need to establish a risk management culture that promotes employee involvement and commitment at all levels. The culture should emphasise that deviation from established risk management standards is unacceptable. The second set is that of job factors, as mismatch between job requirements and an individual's capabilities strengthens the potential for human error. Finally, there are the personal factors, because people need to be matched to their jobs through appropriate selection techniques, taking into account such attributes as habits, attitudes, skills and personality. While skills and attitude can be modified by training and experience, others (such as personality) are difficult to modify.

8.6   WHAT MAKES A SUCCESSFUL RISK MANAGEMENT FRAMEWORK?

Swenson (2003) describes what he calls a "well-crafted corporate operational risk policy" as a policy that should strive to: (i) define operational risk and its components; (ii) identify the roles, responsibilities and inter-relationships between the business units, internal audit, business line-resident risk management and firm-wide risk management; (iii) provide guidance commensurate with the size, complexity and the risk profile of the firm; (iv) document the process whereby risk self-assessment is completed; (v) establish templates for a risk-focused operational risk reporting package that includes risk and control self-assessment, key indicators and loss tracking; and (vi) address and/or cross-reference corporate and business activity guidance in selected areas (for example, loss escalation, separation of duties, and conflict of interest).

In general, a successful operational risk management framework requires the following:

1. Senior management support. Kennett (2003) argues that without senior management support, the operational risk team will "plough a lonely and ultimately unsuccessful furrow". After all, it is senior management that provides support, financially and visibly (for example, by ensuring that operational risk management is part of the appraisal process). Naturally, senior management needs to be persuaded that the operational risk management framework will deliver value. However, senior management support does not guarantee success (a necessary but not a sufficient condition for success).

2. The framework must be implemented in such a way as to provide direct value to the business units. Direct value may take the form of low regulatory capital, reduced losses, improved risk awareness, and the ability to price risk.

3. Incentives should be built into the system.

4. Consistency must be ensured in the system because it is the foundation for everything else that risk managers do. Consistency pertains to things like the definition of operational risk, risk categories, and key risk indicators.

5. The right people (in terms of right training, motivation and cultural fit) should be brought into the process.

6. The process should be dynamic, seeking improvement in measures and controls.

7. The results must be shared with all business areas.

8.7   THE ROLE OF INSURANCE IN OPERATIONAL RISK MANAGEMENT

Insurance has always been used to mitigate various kinds of operational risk, such as the risk of fire (damage to physical assets). As Young and Ashby (2003) put in reference to banking, "insurers have, for decades, played a role in financing the banking industry's operational risk by providing [insurance] products". Actually, insurance companies have been lobbying regulators to accept the idea of replacing (at least in part) regulatory capital with insurance or what they call the idea of "lightening the capital charge that banks must bear for operational risk".

8.7.1   Insurance products

Currently, a wide variety of insurance products (policies) are available to banks, which (as shown in Table 8.2) include peril-specific products (such as electronic computer crime cover) and multi-peril products (such as the all-risk operational risk insurance), as well as the traditional deposit insurance. The protection offered by an insurance policy is defined in terms of the maximum amount of cover and a deductible excess. Hadjiemmanuil (2003) considers in detail insurance and the mitigation of losses from legal risk and fraud.

Culp (2001) argues that the emergence of multi-peril products can be attributed to both demand and supply factors. On the demand side, these products provide a bank with a more comprehensive cover than the peril-specific products, which eliminates any gaps or overlaps that may exist when peril-specific products are used. They are also conducive to enterprise-wide or integrated risk management. On the supply side, the insurers benefit from the exploitation of risk correlations, which enables them to charge a lower price than the sum of the equivalent peril-specific products. There are, however, problems with the multi-peril products, such as the lack of critical mass and the lack of data. The lack of critical mass means that a large number of banks and insurance companies must be present for the product to be successful. Insurers need a large number of banks to spread risk, whereas a large number of insurance companies are required to spread the risk through reinsurance. The lack of data on all kinds of risk makes it difficult for insurers to assess the underlying risk and price the product correctly. Young and Ashby (2003) argue that the divergence of views on multi-peril products is like the S-shaped curve for the adoption of a new product, consisting of laggards, followers and early adopters. There are the skeptics, who question the viability of multi-peril products as a solution for operational risk; those who are indifferent, viewing multi-peril products as no more than an addition to the existing set of products; and the enthusiasts, who have already acquired the products.

Table 8.2 Operational risk insurance products

Product	Providing Cover Against
Fidelity/Banker's Blanket Bond	Employee dishonesty, fraud and forgery. Cover is also provided against office damage, in-transit loss and some forms of trading loss.
Electronic Computer Crime Cover	Computer failure, viruses, data transmission problems, forged electronic fund transactions.
Professional Indemnity	Liabilities to third parties for claims arising from employee negligence while providing professional services to clients.
Directors' and Officers' Liability	Expenses that might be incurred due to the legal actions arising from the performance of their duties.
Employment Practices Liability	Liabilities that may arise from infringements of the employment law, such as harassment, discrimination, and breach of contract.
Nonfinancial property	Property risks such as fire and weather.
Unauthorized Trading Cover	Unauthorized trading that is either concealed or falsely recorded.
General and other Liability	Public liability, employer's liability, motor fleet, etc.
All-Risk Operational Risk Insurance	Losses arising from internal fraud, external fraud, rogue trading, and many other forms of general liability.
Deposit Insurance	Losses incurred by depositors resulting from operational and non-operational risks faced by banks.

On the other hand, deposit protection schemes are typically government-run, as the government requires banks to acquire deposit insurance. Deposit insurance is not linked to a specific cause of bank failure, which makes it a multi-peril product in some sense. It is, however, rather controversial. On the one hand, consumer protection groups view these schemes as providing a "failsafe" for depositors against bank insolvency. Furthermore, Hadjiemmanuil (1996) argues that deposit insurance provides regulators with the option to refuse to bail out ailing banks, particularly if they are small or new. On the other hand, deposit insurance has been criticized severely, particularly by the proponents of free banking. For example, Karels and McClatchey (1999) attribute the high rate of failure of US savings and loans institutions in the 1980s to the use of "non-experience-rated, full-cover deposit protection schemes", which they explain in terms of moral hazard. In this case, moral hazard is manifested as the incentive for insured depositors to place their funds in banks that take large risks in an attempt to offer high returns (Hadjiemmanuil, 1996).

8.7.2 The role and limitations of insurance

Leddy (2003) argues that the insurer's impact on risk management may be both direct and indirect. In the first instance, the insurer is likely to accept only good risks. Insurers also take into account distinguishing factors in pricing risks, thus forcing the insured to upgrade their risk management systems. He also identifies the steps of which the process of entering a contract with an insurer consists. These steps are illustrated in Figure 8.8. One advantage of insurance is that when a bank takes insurance, it can utilize the expertise of the insurer that covers many fields. Insurance also provides monitoring by the insurer on behalf of the stakeholders, including customers and the government. However, there are problems with insurance, starting with moral hazard considerations that may make it difficult or infeasible to insure low-frequency, high-severity events.

There are also doubts about the role of insurance. For example, one of the reasons suggested in Chapter 3 for the special importance of banks is their sheer size, which makes them too big for insurance companies, and hence they cannot use insurance effectively to cover all elements of

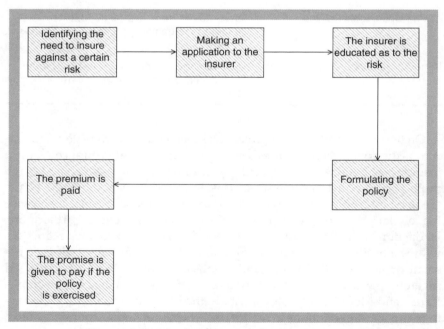

Figure 8.8 Entering a contract with an insurer

operational risk. Cruz (2003a) reiterates this point by arguing that the insurance industry is not well-capitalized vis-à-vis the banking industry, which makes a typical bank seeking insurance better capitalized than the insurance company. Furthermore, he identifies other pitfalls with insurance for operational risk, including the following:

1. Limiting conditions and exclusion clauses lead to doubt regarding payment in the event of failure.

2. Delays in payment could result in serious damage to the claimant.

3. It is difficult to determine the true economic value of insurance in the absence of sufficient and appropriate data.

Brandts (2005) casts doubt on the ability of insurance to provide a "perfect hedge" for operational risk, arguing that insurance compensation is often subject to a range of limitations and exceptions. Specifically, he identifies three problems (risks) with insurance. First, there is payment uncertainty resulting from mismatches in the actual risk exposure and the insurance coverage, as well as incompleteness of the compensation claims (insurance companies are notorious for telling customers that their latest mishap is not covered by the insurance policy). The second problem is delayed payment, which may result in additional losses. Third is the problem of counterparty risk resulting from the possibility of default by the insurance company.

Young and Ashby (2003) also cast doubt on the ability of the insurance products to go far enough in the current operational risk environment. The Basel Committee (BCBS, 2001b) has expressed doubts about the effectiveness of insurance products, stating that "it is clear that the market for insurance of operational risk is still developing". And although Basel II allows banks using the AMA to take account of the risk mitigating impact of insurance in their regulatory capital calculations, some conditions must be satisfied:

1. The recognition of insurance is limited to 20 percent of the regulatory capital held against operational risk.

2. The insurance providers must be A rated.

3. The insurance policy must have an initial term of at least one year and there must be a minimum notice period for cancellation or non-renewal.

4. There must be no mismatch between the insurance cover and the operational risk exposure.

5. Insurance must be provided by an independent insurer.

6. Banks must provide a documented insurance strategy.

7. Banks must disclose the extent by which regulatory capital has been reduced by insurance.

In general, regulators have a problem with the proposition that regulatory capital can be replaced (at least partially) with insurance. This is mainly because regulators are skeptical about the feasibility of immediate payouts (which is not what insurance companies are known for). There is also fear about the ability of the insurers to get off the hook (completely or partially) through some dubious clauses in the insurance policy.

Reinsurance, which is typically portrayed to be a means of spreading risk and the true means of risk transfer, has its own problems. Young and Ashby (2003) point out that the practice of reinsurance may create further problems for the insured, as it produces lack of transparency in the insurance industry to the extent that a firm holding an insurance policy finds itself dependent in recovering a claim on the weakest link in the reinsurance chain. The problem within insurance arising from payment delays may be accentuated by reinsurance, as an insurer or a reinsurer may not meet their obligations until they have secured payment from the next reinsurer in the chain. Reinsurance invariably results in the addition of further terms and conditions to the original insurance contract, again accentuating another problem of insurance. Reinsurance also creates counterparty risk that is unknown to the insured.

8.7.3 Determinants of the insurance decision

What determines whether or not a bank decides to acquire an insurance cover against operational risk? Some of these factors are bank size, the risk profile, the time horizons of managers/shareholders, and the attitude of stakeholders to risk and credit rating (Young and Ashby, 2003). The relation between bank size and the decision to insure is not clear-cut: small banks may be more inclined to acquire insurance than large banks because the former are more vulnerable to operational losses, a characteristic resulting from the fact that they do not have the spread of risks needed to pool the risk management benefits of insurance (Williams, Smith, and Young, 1998). On the other hand, a large bank might want to cover less-common, high-severity risks and may find it cost-effective to pass the day-to-day administration of common smaller risks to an insurer.

The risk profile affects the ability of a bank to acquire a cost-effective operational risk cover. As far as the time horizon is concerned, a longer-term horizon (of managers and shareholders) is more conducive to the acquisition of an insurance cover (Mayers and Smith, 1982). The effect of the risk attitude is clear, as risk aversion is more conducive to the acquisition of insurance (Schrand and Unal, 1998). Finally, credit rating is a determining factor because a high credit rating is associated with a lower cost of debt financing, in which case a bank with a high credit rating may choose to protect itself against operational losses through borrowing rather than insurance (Doherty, 2000).

8.7.4   Alternatives to insurance

If insurance against operational risk is not viable, what are the alternatives? Young and Ashby (2003) suggest three alternatives: mutual self-insurance pools, securitisation and finite risk plans. A mutual self-insurance pool is a group of banks that pool in resources to cover the operational losses incurred by any member of the pool. The problem here is that banks typically think that they are better-run than the others, in which case they will not venture into a scheme like this.

The second alternative, securitization, is the use of derivatives to cover the risks that have traditionally been insured, such as the risk of weather-related losses (weather derivatives). One advantage of securitization is that the risk is (transferred?) to investors in the global capital market, which reduces the counterparty risk of the insurer. One possible means of securitizing operational risk is the creation of bonds similar to catastrophe bonds (see, for example, Lalonde (2005)). The problem here is that data on operational risk is so limited that the pricing of these bonds becomes a big problem. The third alternative to insurance is the finite risk plans, which are designed to help banks structure the financing of their retained risks, and so they are not comparable to insurance as such (Williams et al., 1998).

8.7.5   Incorporating insurance in regulatory capital

The last point to discuss in this section (and this chapter) is the incorporation of insurance as a risk mitigator in the calculation of regulatory capital as required by the Basel II Accord. In general, the effect of insurance can be calculated either separately or incorporated in a Monte Carlo simulation exercise. The first approach is suitable for the basic indicators approach and the standardized approach, which are not based on actual loss data. While this approach solves the problem of unavailability of reliable loss data, it has the problem of the neglect of potential overlaps or gaps in the insurance cover. The second approach is used with the AMA, which requires as a first step the mapping of loss events to insurance policies. This is important because a loss event may be covered by more than one insurance policy, whereas one insurance policy may cover more than one event type. Having done that, Monte Carlo simulations are conducted on gross losses to obtain a distribution of these losses.

Figure 8.9 shows 37 simulated gross loss observations and the effect of three insurance policies (or groups of policies) affecting certain loss events. It is assumed in this illustrative exercise that policy 1 affects loss events 1–24, policy 2 affects loss events 24–37, whereas policy 3 affects loss events 11–37. What is shown in Figure 8.9 is the compensation received form the insurer associated with various loss events (in no case is it assumed that any policy gives full compensation, hence the argument that insurance does not provide a perfect hedge against operational risk). When the effect of insurance is taken into account, net losses can be simulated as shown in Figure 8.10. The regulatory capital is calculated from the distribution of the net loss as described in earlier chapters.

Bazzarello et al. (2006) show formally how to incorporate the effect of insurance in an LDA model of operational risk by taking into account the AMA requirements that include: (i) appropriate haircuts reflecting the policy's declining residual term; (ii) the payment uncertainty due (for example) to mismatches between insurance policy coverage and the analyzed operational risk class; and (iii) the recognition of counterparty risk in the creditworthiness of the insurers and potential concentration of risk of insurance providers. The term "haircuts" reflects the requirement that the insurance policy must have an initial term that is longer than one year. This means that for policies with initial terms of less than one year,

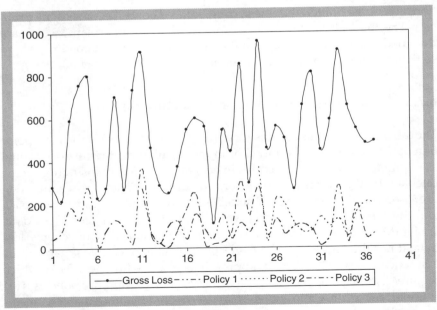

Figure 8.9 Gross losses and the effect of three insurance policies

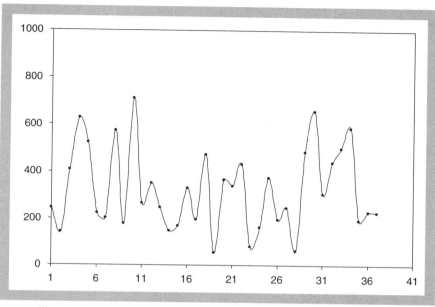

Figure 8.10 Net losses after the application of the insurance

haircuts should be introduced to reflect the shorter policy time horizon, up to 100 percent for policies lasting 90 days or less.

8.8 WHAT IS NEXT?

So far, we have covered aspects of Basel I and Basel II, then we moved on to the analysis of operational risk, starting with its description, definition and classification. Having done that, we moved on to the technical aspects of the topic, describing the general principles of modeling operational risk before going through a detailed description of the implementation of the AMA. In this chapter, we discussed the ultimate objective, which is the management of operational risk.

As we went through these topics, we came across a number of controversial issues that relate to operational risk as well as the Basel II Accord in general. What remains to be done is to come up with a view on the issues discussed so far in this book. This is the objective of Chapter 9, which starts with a recapitulation of the issues discussed in the previous chapters. Having done that, and before expressing a view on the Basel II Accord, the desirability (or otherwise) of banking regulation is discussed, since Basel II is a form of banking regulation.

Summary and Conclusions

9.1 RECAPITULATION

In any study of operational risk, and the Basel II Accord that elevated it to explicit prominence, we are bound to encounter a number of critical questions pertaining to highly controversial issues encompassing a multitude of debatable topics. What we try to do in this chapter is to recount these questions, issues, and topics to find out how much we have learned by going through the previous eight chapters.

The issues that we intend to summarize our thoughts on in this chapter pertain to (i) the definition of operational risk; (ii) misconceptions about operational risk; (iii) the problems of modeling operational risk; and (iv) the pros and cons of Basel II, including the problems of implementation. These issues will be dealt with in separate sections. Then we consider the desirability or otherwise of Basel II as a form of banking regulation, which has been a controversial issue for a while. The final section of this chapter (and this book) presents some final thoughts.

9.2 DEFINING OPERATIONAL RISK: PICK AND CHOOSE FROM AN EXOTIC MENU

The official definition of operational risk adopted by the BCBS (which forms the basis of the regulatory capital requirements) is that it is "the risk of loss arising from inadequate or failed internal processes, people and systems or from external events". This definition is not universally acceptable and has been subject to criticisms, mainly because of what it includes (for example, legal risk) and what it excludes (most notably business risk and reputational risk). The main feature of this definition is that it is based on pragmatism (to facilitate the measurement of operational risk) as opposed to comprehensiveness (including all risks arriving from the failure of people, processes, systems and external events). As a result of the historical development of this definition and the criticism directed at it, a large number of definitions have been suggested. An attempt has been made in this book to collect most of these definitions, which amounts to an exotic menu. Although attempting to pick the favorite "dish" out of this menu is hazardous, some comments are made on these definitions, as shown in Table 9.1.

Table 9.1 Definitions of operational risk

Definition	Comment
Any risk that cannot be classified as market risk or credit risk.	This is the negative definition of operational risk, which is hardly informative.
Uncertainty related to losses resulting from inadequate systems or controls, human error or management.	Are we mixing risk and uncertainty here? They are supposed to be different.
The risk encompassing all dimensions of the decentralized resources-client relationship, personnel, the physical plant, property and other assets, as well as technology resources.	The definition excludes external sources of operational risk.
Fraud, failures in controls and the like.	A definition that has the words "the like" can hardly be useful.
The risk arising from activities associated with fiduciary dealings, execution, fraud, business interruption, settlement, legal/regulatory and the composition of fixed costs.	Reference to "fixed costs" may imply that operational risk is one-sided, which is a disputable proposition.
All risks, other than credit and market risk, which could cause volatility of revenues, expenses and the value of the business.	Although this definition is somewhat negative, its strength is that it refers to costs as well as revenues, implying correctly that operational risk is two-sided.
A general term that applies to all the risk failures that influence the volatility of the firm's cost structure as opposed to its revenue structure.	This definition again implies that operational risk is one-sided.

(Continued)

Table 9.1 (*Continued*)

Definition	Comment
The risks associated with human error, inadequate procedures and control, fraudulent and criminal activities, technological shortcomings, and system breakdowns.	No mention of external factors, which can cause massive operational losses.
The direct or indirect loss resulting from inadequate or failed internal processes, people and systems, or from external events.	This is probably the broadest and conceptually most correct definition of operational risk. One weakness of the BCBS's definition of operational risk is that it excludes indirect losses.
Operational risk is the risk of operational loss.	This must be the least-informative definition.
The risk associated with operating a business.	This definition is rather vague and perhaps inaccurate. Market risk and credit risk are also associated with operating a business.
The risk that there will be a failure of people, processes or technology within the business unit.	No mention of external factors.
Every type of unquantifiable risk faced by a bank.	Describing operational risk as "unquantifiable" is controversial and the antithesis of the AMA.
A loose-limbed concept that includes potential losses from business interruptions, technological failures, natural disasters, errors, lawsuits, trade fixing, faulty compliance, fraud and damage to reputation, often intangible fallout from these events.	Perhaps the word "diverse" is more appropriate than "loose-limbed".
The risk that deficiencies in information systems or internal controls will result in unexpected loss.	This definition excludes the risk arising from the failure of people and from external events.
The risk that a firm will suffer loss as a result of human error or deficiencies in systems or controls.	Unlike the previous definition, this definition includes human errors but excludes external factors.
The risk run by a firm that its internal practices, policies, and systems are not rigorous or sophisticated enough to cope with untoward market conditions or human or technological errors.	A rather comprehensive definition.

(*Continued*)

Table 9.1 (*Continued*)

Definition	Comment
The risk of loss resulting from errors in the processing of transactions/ breakdown in controls/errors or failures in system support.	No mention of external factors.
The risk that the operation will fail to meet one or more operational performance targets, where the operation can be people, technology, processes, information, and the infrastructure supporting business activities.	No mention of external factors.
The risk of business disruption, control failures, errors, misdeeds, or external events, and is measured by direct and indirect economic loss associated with business interruption and legal risk costs, and also by "immeasurable" such as reputation risk costs.	A rather comprehensive definition.
The excess of allocation of capital in the firm after market and credit risk capital have been eliminated.	The problem with this definition is its implication that the absence of capital allocation means the absence of risk.
The uncertainty of loss in the book value of the firm due to failures in the manufacturing of the firm's goods and services.	A rather restrictive definition.

Having gone through the menu of definitions, it may not be that hard to pick the worst definition, which is that operational risk is the risk of operational loss. This is no more than describing water as water, as an old Arabic proverb says. A view on the issue of defining operational risk that seems to make sense is that being too fussy about the definition of operational risk does not serve any purpose. Right, provided that the definitions that tell us nothing useful are excluded.

9.3 THE PROBLEMS OF MEASURING OPERATIONAL RISK

One of the definitions of operational risk, as every type of unquantifiable risk faced by a bank excludes the possibility of measuring operational risk, casting doubt on the feasibility of implementing the AMA. Sometimes, difference is made between the measurement and assessment of operational risk on the grounds that measurement is a quantitative exercise whereas assessment is a qualitative exercise. A middle-of-the-road view on this issue is that both approaches must be used to get a feel of a firm's exposure to operational risk.

If we discard the extreme views that operational risk cannot be measured, the problems associated with the measurement of operational risk can be stated as follows:

■ The absence of a universally-acceptable definition of operational risk.

■ The scarcity of hard loss data and the subjectivity of soft data (external loss data or those obtained from scorecards and scenario analysis).

■ The cyclicality of loss events, which casts doubt on the feasibility of extrapolating the past to measure future risk.

■ The difficulty of assessing the level of correlation between operational risks of different kinds and/or those arising in different business lines.

These are the problems associated with the AMA, which require measuring operational risk by modeling it (basically fitting a distribution to operational losses). As crude as they may appear to be, no such problems arise in the case of the less sophisticated basic indicators approach and the standardized approach. So, do we forget completely about the measurement of operational risk because of these problems? An attempt will be made to answer this question in the final section of this chapter.

9.4   MISCONCEPTIONS ABOUT OPERATIONAL RISK

Operational risk is frequently portrayed to be one-sided, idiosyncratic, indistinguishable, and transferable via insurance. These arguments are disputable and can be discarded without much effort. This is how:

■ Operational risk is not one-sided in the sense that there is no risk-return trade off. One-sidedness means that bearing operational risk could result in losses but it produces no returns. This is nonsense, as no firm will bear any kind of risk if there is no anticipation of return. Financial institutions bear the risk of rogue trading because trading is profitable. Firms in general bear the risk of fire in conducting their daily business because the conduct of daily business brings in profit.

■ Operational risk is not idiosyncratic in that it affects only one firm and not other firms in the system like credit risk. This is a rather strange view, given that the very establishment of the Basel Committee came as a result of the Herstatt Bank crisis: one bank's failure, as a result of an operational loss event, adversely affected many banks world-wide. Operational risk is definitely not idiosyncratic, particularly in the banking industry where banks do a lot of business in the interbank market.

This, however, does not mean that every operational loss event experienced by a firm affects other firms in the industry.

■ Operational loss events are not indistinguishable from credit or market loss events. What matters is the cause of the loss, not how the loss is incurred. If a trader breaches trading guidelines, then a market downturn produces losses, this would be an operational loss event (not a mixture of operational and market loss events). If there is no breach of trading guidelines (and other operational failures), then it is a loss associated with market risk.

■ Operational risk cannot be transferred through insurance. A bank taking insurance against rogue trading will not transfer the risk of rogue trading to the insurance company unless the bank outsourcers its trading activity to the insurance company, which does not make any sense. Insurance provides (external) risk financing, not risk transfer.

9.5   THE PROS AND CONS OF BASEL II

Basel II has been described as "probably the most ambitious regulatory reform program any group of regulators has ever attempted". It is definitely an improvement over Basel I in that (i) it includes a more sophisticated measurement framework for evaluating capital adequacy; (ii) it provides incentives for better corporate governance and fostering transparency; (iii) it deals explicitly with operational risk; (iv) it is more risk-sensitive than Basel I; and (v) its application would narrow the gap between economic capital and regulatory capital. However, the Accord has been subject to severe criticism that can be summarized in the following points:

■ Risk measurement depends heavily on the VAR methodology, which has been found to be unreliable and destabilizing.

■ VAR-based regulatory regimes (including Basel II) may lead to lower systemic risk at the cost of poor risk sharing, an increase in risk premia and other adverse consequences. Furthermore, the reduction in systemic risk may not materialize if too many firms are left outside the regulatory regime.

■ Reliance on credit rating agencies is misguided.

■ Operational risk modeling is problematic (as we saw in a previous section).

■ Basel II will exacerbate procyclical tendencies, making the financial system more susceptible to crises. Business cycles will be more severe because banks will tighten credit too much during recessions and loosen it too much during booms.

- The definition of capital for the purpose of implementing Basel II is not clear-cut.

- Disclosure and transparency constitute a necessary but not a sufficient condition for effective market discipline.

- Certain elements of Basel II will pose difficulties for banks and supervisors in emerging economies.

- Regulatory capital will not prevent extreme loss events, which are due to the failure of internal controls.

- Neither the BIA nor the STA provides a persuasive way of relating regulatory capital to operational risk, whereas the AMA is problematical.

- Reliance on regulatory capital to mitigate unexpected losses undermines pillars 2 and 3 of the Accord.

- The connection between gross income and operational risk is loose.

- Regulatory capital may lead to complacency with respect to risk.

- Basel II does not deal with business and reputational risks, which can be more detrimental than the types of operational risk included in the BCBS's definition.

- Disclosures will create an uneven playing field between banks and their non-bank competitors and between small banks and big banks.

There are also problems with the implementation of Basel II. One must not forget that the Basel Committee only has an advisory role, without any power when it comes to the implementation of the Accord. The power of implementation lies with the national regulators, which creates discrepancies in implementation. Take, for example, the difference in implementation between the U.S. and the EU. US supervisors maintain that Basel II will be mandatory for only ten internationally active banks (the big and complex banking organizations), another ten may adopt the Accord voluntarily, and the rest will be supervised in accordance with Basel I. In a more recent report, it is stated that the number of U.S. banks that will implement Basel II is around 26, whereas all other banks will be regulated by Basel 1A (The Economist, 2006). By contrast, the EU has passed a legislation requiring all banks and investment firms, irrespective of size, to be Basel II-compliant.

Having said that, there could still be inconsistency within the EU, as some regulators may be tempted to manipulate the Basel regulations in accordance with the objectives of domestic macroeconomic policy. For example, regulators may twist the rules in order not to jeopardize lending to retail and small-business customers. And even within the U.S., some big banks are not happy about the change from Basel I to Basel II. Big banks are complaining that the switch will cost them million of dollars and benefit their smaller competitors, but smaller banks are also complaining that Basel II will benefit the big banks at their expense, because the latter will hold lower regulatory capital. The Economist (2006) reports that "big American banks are annoyed at having their wings clipped in this way" and that "smaller European banks are annoyed because their American equivalents do not have to spend time and money with Basel 2 at all". It is truly a dilemma: flexibility in implementation is necessary for a worldwide acceptance of the Accord, but it also means the adoption of inconsistent versions of the Accord.

9.6   BASEL II AS A FORM OF BANKING REGULATION

Basel II is a form of banking regulation, hence it takes us back to the basic question of why we need banking regulation. The compelling reason is that banks are too important to be left for themselves and because banking is a rather risky business, particularly due to the mismatch between the maturities of assets and liabilities. Banks are also believed to be inherently unstable because they are structurally fragile (fragility resulting from fractional reserves and high leverage). In a study of banking crises, the BCBS (2004b) points out that many highly developed economies with long-functioning banking systems and sophisticated financial markets have had significant bank failures or banking crises over the past 30 years. Several studies have shown that poor management played a key role in banking crises. Dziobek and Pazarbasioglu (1997) found that inadequate management and deficient controls were contributory factors in the 24 banking crises they studied. Likewise, Caprio and Kingebiel (1996) found that a combination of micro and macro factors were involved: recession and terms of trade on the macro side and poor supervision, weak regulation and deficient bank management on the micro side.

If a big bank fails, its depositors lose their money and the bank cannot meet its obligations to other banks, which may in turn fail and ruin their depositors. The creditors of the depositors of the failed banks will be hurt consequently. Even worse is that the mere fear that a bank may fail could spark a run that could spread to other banks, which may wreak economic havoc. The BCBS (2004b) argues in its study of banking crises that widespread bank failures exacerbate cyclical recessions and may trigger a financial crisis (on the differences among banking crises, financial crises, currency crises and foreign debt crises, see Moosa, 2004, p 151). This is why, according to the study, bank capital is needed to be a "buffer during periods of economic instability". Hence, the argument goes, "making capital more sensitive to the risks in banks should help stabilise the banking system, decreasing the incidence and cost of bank failures". Yes, banks are significantly different from (in the sense of being more important than) department stores, and this is where the need for banking regulation comes from.

However, there is significant skepticism about the role of regulation as a means of achieving financial stability. For example, Kaufman and Scott (2000) argue that regulatory actions have been double-edged, if not counterproductive. Koehn and Santomero (1980) suggest that regulation does not necessarily accomplish the declared objective of reducing the probability of bank failure and that a case could be argued that the opposite result can be expected. Benston and Kaufman (1996) assert that most of the arguments that are frequently used to support special regulation for banks are not supported by either theory or empirical evidence. They also share the view that an unregulated system of enterprise tends to achieve an optimal allocation of resources. They go as far as arguing that one reason for bank regulation is the provision of revenue and power for government officials. Indeed, there is a significant volume of literature on free banking, which is the ultra-extreme view of banking regulation skeptics (see, for example, Dowd, 1993, 1996; Glasner, 1989; Horwitz, 1992; Rockoff, 1975; Sechrest, 1993). For some classic work on free baking and related issues, see Hayek (1976); Meulen (1934) and Friedman (1960).

Barth, Caprio, and Levine (2002, 2006) present an extensive examination of the issue of banking regulation, emphasizing the difficulty of getting governments to control themselves, which amounts to regulatory failure. They argue that while banking regulation is intended for good purposes (for example, to avoid bank runs or other forms of market failure), it is designed without due consideration given to the risk of regulatory failure. This argument is similar to the normative microeconomic argument that market failure should not be replaced with government failure. As a result, the argument goes, regulatory failure (which is often worse than the market failure it is designed to deal with) occurs. By analyzing banking regulation in more than 150 countries, they reach the conclusion that so much banking regulation has been introduced without a sense of what actually works in practice. This conclusion is based on an analysis of the relation between different kinds of regulations and indicators of the health of the banking system, including the efficiency of banks, the extent of corruption, how developed the system is and the likelihood of a crisis.

The Barth et al. (2006) book also deals with the three pillars of Basel II, describing them as three broad categories of regulation (capital adequacy, supervisory requirements and disclosure). Their overall conclusion on Basel II is that it is some sort of "one size fits all" kind of regulation, which they seem to be very skeptical about. Their empirical results reveal that raising regulatory capital bears no relation to the degree of development of the banking system, the efficiency of banks, and the possibility of experiencing a crisis. They express the view that policies aimed at boosting the private sector monitoring of banks tend to make the banking system more developed and the banks more efficient, as well as reducing the likelihood of a crisis. They also put forward the idea that generous deposit insurance schemes are more conducive to the onset of a crisis because of the moral hazard problem: depositors become careless about the banks they deal with. The most surprising of their results is that strengthening supervision has a neutral or negative effect on banking development, reduces the efficiency of banks and boosts the likelihood of a crisis, particularly in countries where the legal systems are weak. Hence, they conclude that pillar 2 of the Basel II Accord may cause a lot of damage or, as they put it, "the overriding message is that simply strengthening direct official oversight of banks may very well make things worse, not better, in the vast majority of countries". They, therefore, provide a clear message on the dangers of regulation.

Risk-based regulation (including Basel II) has been criticized severely. Danielsson, Shin, and Zigrand (2002) demonstrate that, in the presence of risk regulation, prices and liquidity are lower, whereas volatility is higher, particularly during crises. They attribute this finding to the underlying assumption of the regulator that asset returns are exogenous, which fails to take into account the feedback effect of trading decisions on prices. Danielsson (2003) argues that while the notion that bank capital be risk sensitive is intuitively appealing, the actual implementation (in the form of Basel II) may boost financial risk for individual banks and the banking system as a whole. Danielsson and Zigrand (2003) use a simple equilibrium model to demonstrate "what happens when you regulate risk", showing that even if regulation lowers systemic risk (provided that not too many firms are left out by the regulatory regime, which is what will happen under Basel II), this can only be accomplished at the cost of significant side effects.

9.7 THE VERDICT

So, where do we stand on Basel II? In attempting to reach a verdict, three principles must be observed: (i) the importance of judging costs against benefits; (ii) the importance of striking balance as opposed to taking extreme positions; and (iii) the judgment must be ideology-free.

Ideology invariably drives the extreme positions taken with respect to the desirability or otherwise of regulation. Those who believe in financial *laissez-faire* argue strongly against banking regulation and for free banking. Those on the other extreme might believe that banks are too important to be left to the private sector and the tyranny of the market. Taking an ideology-free stance puts us somewhere in between these two extremes. Regulation (not excessive regulation) is needed because we have learned from history how damaging to the economy bank failures can be. Thus, this is a balanced view between the total abolition and total adoption of regulation.

Is Basel II worthwhile in terms of costs and benefits? We should not talk about Basel II as providing better ways of measuring regulatory capital and incentives for better risk management practices without asking about the costs, financial and otherwise, of being Basel II-compliant. Banks have been spending huge amounts of money on, and allocating resources to, efforts aimed at achieving the objective of being Basel II-compliant. Is this worth it, in the sense that this spending will produce some positive return in terms of risk reduction or reduction in the likelihood of a financial crisis? Our belief is that holding capital against operational risk is a useful "shock absorber". Our belief is also that allocating resources to the improvement of risk management techniques is justifiable. However, what may not be effective, in terms of costs and benefits, is the millions of dollars spent on the development of internal models of operational risk (and other kinds of risk for that matter) only for regulatory purposes.

Banks, and even some regulators, have been complaining about this point in particular, perhaps justifiably so. The Economist (2006) reported that "a succession of American bank regulators each cautioned against the sophisticated methods of Basel 2". This is also why the bankers surveyed by the Centre for the Study of Financial Innovation (2002) think that Basel II is complex (and dangerous). It is the belief of this author that the AMA is not a worthwhile exercise in terms of costs and benefits if internal models are developed for regulatory purposes only and if banks choose not to develop them otherwise. Banks should not spend millions of dollars on the development of these models just to be Basel II–complainant, then pass the cost on to customers. How about holding capital against operational risk based on the simpler and cheaper basic indicators approach and standardized approach, while still benefiting from the basic principles of pillars 2 and 3 of the Accord? This will definitely be more cost effective than the development of internal models.

Perhaps banks can spend millions of dollars on the development of internal models for regulatory purposes because it will result in them holding less capital against operational risk (and other kinds of risk). In this case, there is net benefit for the banks, which means that they will not pass on the costs of developing internal models to customers (one should at least hope so). The BCBS (2004a) seems to suggest that the AMA would lead to a lower capital charge, but why? One explanation is that the effect of insurance is considered only under the AMA, which means that the capital charge is calculated on the basis of net risk under the AMA and gross risk under the other two approaches. The other reason is that using gross income to calculate the capital charge implies that there is a linear relation between size and risk, which may not be so, as bigger banks may have more powerful risk controls and better risk management systems. If this is taken account of in the construction of internal models, banks using the AMA will have proportionately lower capital requirements. But this is not necessarily the case. Pezier (2003b) casts doubt on the assumption of linearity but in the opposite sense, questioning the proposition that larger firms are expected to have better operational risk management and hence they should be subject to less operational risk.

It seems that the AMA would produce lower capital charges only because the internal models can be manipulated in a large number of ways to produce the lowest capital charge. For example, Kalyvas and Sfetsos (2006), who consider the issue of whether the application of "innovative internal models" reduces regulatory capital, find that the use of extreme value theory produces a lower estimate of VAR than the variance-covariance, historical simulation, and conditional historical simulation methods. Another reason why results may differ from one case to another is the assumptions made about correlations among risk types/business lines.

It is true that the internal models have to be approved by the regulators. With respect to correlations, for example, the BCBC will allow the use of certain correlation assumptions (which will reduce regulatory capital) if it can be demonstrated that these assumptions are "soundly determined and implemented with integrity". However, it is not that difficult (by employing top-notch statisticians) to make the internal model that produces the lowest regulatory capital acceptable to the regulators. This may explain why small banks complain about the possible competitive disadvantage resulting from the use of the AMA by the big banks, but it does not explain why big banks complain about using the AMA.

It could be that banks view the development of internal models less favorably when the objective is regulatory compliance (when they are told what to do and how to do it) as opposed to risk management. If banks themselves believe that modeling operational risk is useful for non-regulatory purposes (as we saw in Chapter 6), they should feel free to engage in the development of operational risk models, just like they feel free to develop exchange rate forecasting models and model-based trading rules. What is important in this case is that banks should not be told to develop these models in a way that is acceptable to the regulators. If banks want to allocate resources for the development of these models, because they believe that these models are useful for the running of their business, this means that the banks believe that the models are effective in terms of costs and benefits. Banks do not complain about the development of models if it is their choice, but they do complain if they are told that this is something that they must do and that they should do it in a particular way. This is precisely the attitude of some large American banks, which is understandable.

Let us conclude by going back to the millennium bug fiasco. In the run up to 2000, we were told that if nothing was done about the millennium bug, then starting in the early hours of 1 January 2000, planes would fall from the sky, fires would start everywhere, power plants would shut down and we would have no water supply, no money, etc. It was a bonanza for IT specialists, as firms hired their services to protect themselves from the catastrophic consequences of the bug. The cost of this exercise, which turned out to be money not well spent, was naturally passed on to consumers. I can only hope that the Basel Committee is not telling us that, without sophisticated internal models, banks will fail and we will lose our money. As a bank customer, I think that I will be better off taking that chance than having banks passing to me (and other customers) the costs of developing operational risk models, which will most likely do nothing better than any basic method to determine the amount of regulatory capital. So, the verdict is: yes to regulatory capital, no to measuring regulatory capital by the AMA, yes to the development of internal models for non-regulatory processes, and yes to the basic principles of pillar 2 and 3 of Basel II.

References

Alexander, C. (2003a) Managing Operational Risks with Bayesian Networks, in Alexander, C. (ed.) *Operational Risk: Regulation, Analysis and Management*, London: Prentice Hall-Financial Times.

Alexander, C. (2003b) Statistical Models of the Operational Loss, in Alexander, C. (ed.) *Operational Risk: Regulation, Analysis and Management*, London: Prentice Hall-Financial Times.

Allen, L. and Bali, T.G. (2004) Cyclicality in Catastrophic and Operational Risk Measurements, Working Paper, City University of New York, September.

Allen, L. and Saunders, A. (2002) Cyclical Effects in Credit Risk Ratings and Default Risk, in Ong, M. (ed.) *Credit Ratings: Methodologies, Rationale and Default Risk*, London: Risk Books, 45–79.

Allen, L. and Saunders, A. (2004) Incorporating Systemic Influences into Risk Measures: A Survey of the Literature, *Journal of Financial Services Research*, 26, 161–91.

Altman, E. and Saunders, A. (2001) Credit Ratings and the BIS Reform Agenda, NYU Working Papers, March.

Anders, U. (2003) The Path to Operational Risk Economic Capital, in Alexander, C. (ed.) *Operational Risk: Regulation, Analysis and Management*, London: Prentice Hall-Financial Times.

Artzner, P., Delbaen, F., Elber, J.M. and Heath, D. (1999) Coherent Measures of Risk, *Mathematical Finance*, 9, 203–28.

Atkins, H.I. (2003) Letter to Basel Committee on Banking Supervision, 18 August, http://www.bis.org/bsbs/cp3/wellsfago.pdf

Bakker, M.R. (2005) Quantifying Operational Risk within Banks According to Basel II, in Davis, E. (ed.) *Operational Risk: Practical Approaches to Implementation*, London: Risk Books.

Barth, J., Caprio, G. and Levine, R. (2002) Bank Regulation and Supervision: What Works Best? NBER Working Papers, No 9323.

Barth, J., Caprio, G. and Levine, R. (2006) *Rethinking Bank Regulation: Till Angels Govern*, New York: Cambridge University Press.

Baud, N., Frachot, A. and Roncalli, T. (2002) How to Avoid Over-Estimating Capital Charge for Operational Risk? Working Paper, Credit Lyonnais.

Bawa, V.S. (1975) Optimal Rules for Ordering Uncertain Prospects, *Journal of Financial Economics*, 2, 95–121.

Bazzarello, D., Crielaard, B., Piacenza, F. and Soprano, A. (2006) Modeling Insurance Mitigation on Operational Risk Capital, *Journal of Operational Risk*, 1, 57–65.

BBA/ISDA/RMA (1999) *Operational Risk: The Next Frontier*, London: BBA/ISDA/RMA.

BCBS (1988) *International Convergence of Capital Measurement and Capital Standards*, Basel: Bank for International Settlements, July.

BCBS (1998) *Operational Risk Management*, Basel: Bank for International Settlements, September.

BCBS (1999) *Update on Work on a New Capital Adequacy Framework*, Basel: Bank for International Settlements, November.

BCBS (2001a) *Working Paper on the Regulatory Treatment of Operational Risk*, Basel: Bank for International Settlements, September.

BCBS (2001b) *Basel II: The New Base Capital Accord-Second Consultative Paper*, Basel: Bank for International Settlements, January.

BCBS (2002a) *Sound Practices for the Management and Supervision of Operational Risk*, Basel: Bank for International Settlements, July.

BCBS (2002b) *The Quantitative Impact Study for Operational Risk: Overview of Individual Loss Data and Lessons Learned*, Basel: Bank for International Settlements.

BCBS (2003a) *Basel II: The New Basel Capital Accord-Third Consultative Paper*, Basel: Bank for International Settlements, April.

BCBS (2003b) *Continued Progress Towards Basel II*, Press Release, 15 January.

BCBS (2003c) *The 2002 Data Collection Exercise for Operational Risk: Summary of the Data Collected*, Basel: Bank for International Settlements.

BCBS (2004a) *Basel II: International Convergence of Capital Measurement and Capital Standards: A Revised Framework*, Basel: Bank for International Settlements, June.

BCBS (2004b) *Bank Failures in Mature Economies*, Basel: Bank for International Settlements, April.

BCBS (2005a) *The Application of Basel II to Trading Activities and the Treatment of Double Default Effects*, Basel: Bank for International Settlements, July.

BCBS (2005b) *Basel II: International Convergence of Capital Measurement and Capital Standards: A Revised Framework*, Basel: Bank for International Settlements, November.

BCBS (2006a) *Basel II: International Convergence of Capital Measurement and Capital Standards: A Revised Framework- Comprehensive Version*, Basel: Bank for International Settlements, June.

BCBS (2006b) *Home-Host Information Sharing for Effective Basel II Implementation*, Basel: Bank for International Settlements.

BCBS (2006c) *Observed Range of Practice in Key Elements of Advanced Measurement Approach (AMA)*, Basel: Bank for International Settlements, October.

BCBS (2006d) *Results of the Fifth Quantitative Impact Study*, Basel: Bank for International Settlements.

Beales, R. (2006) Errors in Complex Trading, *Financial Times*, 31 May, 19.

Benston, G.J. and Kaufman, G.G. (1996) The Appropriate Role of Bank Regulation, *Economic Journal*, 106, 688–97.

Berkowitz, J. and O'Brien, J. (2002) How Accurate are Value-at-Risk Models at Commercial Banks?, *Journal of Finance*, 58, 1093–111.

Berens, C. (2004) Warning on Basel II Conformance, *Financial Management*, May, 4.

Bliss, C. and Flannery, M.J. (2002) Market Discipline in the Governance of U.S. Bank Holding Companies: Monitoring vs. Influence, *European Finance Review*, 6, 361–95.

Blunden, T. (2003) Scoreboard Approaches, in Alexander, C. (ed.) *Operational Risk: Regulation, Analysis and Management*, London: Prentice Hall-Financial Times.

Bocker, K. and Kluppelberg, C. (2005) Operational VAR: A Closed-Form Approximation, *Risk*, December, 90–3.

Borio, C., Furfine, C. and Lowe, P. (2001) Procyclicality of the Financial System and Financial Stability: Issues and Policy Options, in Bank for International Settlements, *Marrying the Macro- and Microprudential Dimensions of Financial Stability*, BIS Papers, No 1, March.

Brandts, S. (2005) Reducing Risk Through Insurance, in Davis, E. (ed.) *Operational Risk: Practical Approaches to Implementation*, London: Risk Books.

British Bankers' Association (1997) *Operational Risk Management Survey*, London: British Bankers' Association.

Buchelt, R. and Unteregger, S. (2004) Cultural Risk and Risk Culture: Operational Risk after Basel II, Financial Stability Report 6, Available on http://www.oenb.at/en/img/fsr_06_cultural_risk_tcm16-9495.pdf

Cagan, P. (2001) Seizing the Tail of the Dragon, *FOW/Operational Risk*, July, 18–23.

Calomiris, C.W. and Herring, R.J. (2002) The Regulation of Operational Risk in Investment Management Companies, *Perspective*, September, 1–19.

Capco Research (2002) Understanding and Mitigating Operational Risk in Hedge Fund Investments, Capco Research Working Papers.

Caprio, G. and Kingebiel, D. (1996) Bank Insolvencies: Cross Country Experience, *World Bank Policy and Research*, WP 1547.

Centre for the Study of Financial Innovation (2002) *Banana Skins*, London: CSFI.

Chavez-Demoulin, V., Embrechts, P. and Neslehova, J. (2006) Quantitative Models for Operational Risk: Extremes, Dependence and Aggregation, *Journal of Banking and Finance*, 30, 2635–58.

Chen, Y. (1999) Banking Panics: The Role of the First-Come, First-Served Rule and Information Externalities, *Journal of Political Economy*, 107, 946–68.

Coles, S. (2001) *An Introduction to Statistical Modeling of Extreme Values*, London: Springer.

Commonwealth Bank of Australia (1999) *Annual Report*, Sydney: Commonwealth Bank of Australia.

Consiglio, A. and Zenios, S.A. (2003) Model Error in Enterprise-wide Risk Management: Insurance Policies with Guarantees, in *Advances in Operational Risk: Firm-wide Issues for Financial Institutions* (second edition), London: Risk Books.

Cooke, R.M. (1991) *Experts in Uncertainty*, New York: Oxford University Press.

Crooke, A. (2006) Asia's Erratic Approach to Basel II, *Aisalwa*, 20 January, 1.

Crouchy, M. (2001) *Risk Management*, New York: McGraw Hill.

Crouhy, M., Galai, D. and Mark, R. (2003) Model Selection for Operational Risk, in *Advances in Operational Risk: Firm-Wide Issues for Financial Institutions* (second edition), London: Risk Books.

Cruz, M. (2002) *Modelling, Measuring and Hedging Operational Risk*, Chichister: Wiley.

Cruz, M. (2003a) Operational Risk: Past, Present and Future, in Field, P. (ed.) *Modern Risk Management: A History*, London: Risk Books.

Cruz, M. (2003b) Developing an Operational VAR Model Using EVT, in *Advances in Operational Risk: Firm-Wide Issues for Financial Institutions* (second edition), London: Risk Books.

Culp, C. (2001) *The Risk Management Process: Business Strategy and Tactics*, New York: Wiley.

Cummins, J.D., Lewis, C.M. and Wei, R. (2006) The Market Value Impact of Operational Loss Events for US Banks and Insurers, *Journal of Banking and Finance*, 30, 2605–34.

Currie, C.V. (2004) Basel II and Operational Risk: An Overview, in Cruz, M. (ed.) *Operational Risk Modelling and Analysis*, London: Risk Books.

Danielsson, J. (2001) The Emperor has no Clothes: Limits to Risk Modelling, Working Paper, London School of Economics (www.riskresearch.org).

Danielsson, J. (2003) On the Feasibility of Risk Based Regulation, Working Paper, London School of Economics (www.riskresearch.org).

Danielsson, J. and Shin, H.S. (2003) Endogenous Risk, in Field, P. (ed.) *Modern Risk Management: A History*, London: Risk Books.

Danielsson, J. and Zigrand, J.-P. (2003) What Happens when You Regulate Risk? Evidence from a Simple Equilibrium Model, Working Paper, London School of Economics (www.riskresearch.org).

Danielsson, J., Embrechts, P., Goodhart, C., Keating, C., Muennich, F., Renault, O. and Shin, H.S. (2001) An Academic Response to Basel II, LSE Financial Markets Group, Special Paper No 130.

Danielsson, J., Jorgensen, B.N. and Sarma, M. (2005) Comparing Downside Risk Measures for Heavy Tailed Distributions, Working Paper, London School of Economics (www.riskresearch.org).

Danielsson, J., Jorgensen, B.N., Sarma, M., de Vries, C.G. and Zigrand, J-P (2006) Consistent Measures of Risk, Working Paper, London School of Economics (www.riskresearch.org).

Danielsson, J., Shin, H.S. and Zigrand, J-P (2002) The Impact of Risk Regulation on Price Dynamics, Working Paper, London School of Economics (www.riskresearch.org).

de Fountnouvelle, P. (2003) Using Loss data to Quantify Operational Risk, Working Paper, Federal Reserve Bank of Boston.

de Fontnouvelle, P., DeJesus-Rueff, V., Jordan, J. and Rosengren, E. (2003) Capital and Risk: New Evidence on Implications of Large Operational Losses, Working Paper, Federal Reserve Bank of Boston, September.

de Fontnouvelle, P., Rosengren, E. and Jordan, J. (2004) Implications of Alternative Operational Risk Modeling Techniques, Working Paper, Federal Reserve Bank of Boston, June.

Dhane, J., Goovaerts, M.J. and Kaas, R. (2003) Economic Capital Allocation Derived from Risk Measures, *North American Actuarial Journal*, 7, 44–56.

Diamond, D.W. and Dybvic, P.H. (1983) Bank Runs, Deposit Insurance, and Liquidity, *Journal of Political Economy*, 91, 401–19.

Doherty, N. (2000) *Integrated Risk Management: Techniques and Strategies for Reducing Risk*, New York: McGraw Hill.

Dowd, K. (1993) *Laissez-Faire Banking*, London: Routledge.

Dowd, K. (1996) *Competition and Finance: A New Interpretation of Financial and Monetary Economics*, London: Macmillan.

Dowd, K. (1998) *Beyond Value at Risk: The New Science of Risk Management*, Chichester: Wiley.

Dowd, K. (2002) *Measuring Market Risk*, Chichester: Wiley.

Dowd, V. (2003) Measurement of Operational Risk: The Basel Approach, in Alexander, C. (ed.) *Operational Risk: Regulation, Analysis and Management*, London: Prentice Hall-Financial Times.

Ducot, C. and Lubben, G.H. (1980) A Typology for Scenarios, *Futures*, 12, 51–7.

Duffie, D. and Pan, J. (1997) An Overview of Value at Risk, *Journal of Derivatives*, 4, 7–49.

Dziobek, C. and Pazarbasioglu, C. (1997) Lessons from Systemic Bank Restructuring: A Survey of 24 Countries, *IMF Working Papers*, No 97/161.

Economist, The (2003) Deep Impact, *The Economist*, 8 May.

Economist, The (2005) Who Rates the Raters?, *The Economist*, 26 May, 61–3.

Economist, The (2006) A Battle over Basel 2, *The Economist*, 4 November, 83.

Edelson, D.B. (2003) Letter to Basel Committee on Banking Supervision, 31 July, http://www.bis.org/bcbs/cp3/citigroup.pdf

Ellis, E. (2006) A Fridge Full of Dollars, *The Bulletin*, March, 31–2.

Embrechts, P., Kaufmann, R. and Samorodnitsky, G. (2004) Ruin Theory Revisited: Stochastic Models for Operational Risk, Mimeo.

Embrechts, P., Kluppelberg, C. and Mikosch, T. (1997) *Modelling Extreme Events for Insurance and Finance*, Berlin: Springer-Verlag.

Embrechts, P., Resnick, S.I. and Samorodnitsky (1999) Extreme Value Theory as a Risk Management Tool, http://www.gloriamundi.org/picsresources/pesrgs.pdf

Evans, A. (2004) Operational Risk Management, *Risk Management*, 51, 50.

Everts, H. and Liersch, H. (2006) Diversification and Aggregation of Risks in Financial Conglomerates, in van Lelyveld, I. (ed.) *Economic Capital Modelling: Concepts, Measurement and Implementation*, London: Risk Books.

Fama, E.F. and French, K. (1993) Common Risk Factors in the Returns on Stocks and Bonds, *Journal of Financial Economics*, 33, 3–56.

Fayol, H. (1949) *General and Industrial Management*, New York: Pitman Publishing Corporation.

Federal Reserve System (1997) *Framework for Risk-Focused Supervision of Large Complex Institutions*, Washington, DC: Federal Reserve System.

Fischer, S. (2002) Basel II: Risk Management and Implications for Banking in Emerging Market Countries, The William Taylor Memorial Lecture at the International Conference of Banking Supervisors, Cape Town, 19 September.

Fishburn, P.C. (1977) Mean-Risk Analysis with Risk Associated with Below Target Returns, *American Economic Review*, 67, 116–26.

Foot, M. (2002) Operational Risk Management for Financial Institutions, *Journal of Financial Regulation and Compliance*, 10, 313–6.

Frachot, A. and Roncalli, T. (2002) Mixing Internal and External Data for Managing Operational Risk, Working Paper, Credit Lyonnais.

Frachot, A., Moudoulaud, O. and Roncalli, T. (2004) Loss Distribution Approach in Practice, in Ong, K. (ed.) *The Basel Handbook*, London: Risk Books.

Frachot, A., Roncalli, T. and Salmon, E. (2004) The Correlation Problem in Operational Risk, Working Paper, Credit Lyonnais.

Friedman, M. (1960) *A Program for Monetary Stability*, New York: Fordham University Press.

Fujii, K. (2005) Building Scenarios, in Davis, E. (ed.) *Operational Risk: Practical Approaches to Implementation*, London: Risk Books.

Gallagher, R.B. (1956) Risk Management: A New Phase of Cost Control, *Harvard Business Review*, September–October.

Gelderman, M., Klaassen, P. and van Lelyveld, I. (2006) Economic Capital: An Overview, in van Lelyveld, I. (ed.) *Economic Capital Modelling: Concepts, Measurement and Implementation*, London: Risk Books.

Geschka, H. and Reibnitz, U. (1983) Die Szenario-Technik-ein Instrument der Zukunftsanalyse und der Strategischen Planning, in Tlpfer, A. and Afheldt, M. (eds) *Parxis der Unternehmrnsplanung*, Frankfurt.

Giraud, J.-R. (2005) Managing Hedge Funds' Exposure to Operational Risks, in Davis, E. (ed.) *Operational Risk: Practical Approaches to Implementation*, London: Risk Books.

Glasner, D. (1989) *Free Banking and Monetary Reform*, Cambridge: Cambridge University Press.

Glosten, L.R., Jagannathan, R. and Runkle, D.E. (1993) On the Relation between the Expected Value and the Volatility of the Nominal Excess Return on Stocks, *Journal of Finance*, 48, 1779–801.

Goodhart, C., Hofmann, B. and Segoviano, M. (2004) Bank Regulation and Macroeconomic Fluctuations, *Oxford Review of Economic Policy*, 20, 591–615.

Grange, J.S. (2000) Risk Management and the 'Rogue Trader': Trading-Related Losses, Director and Officer Liability, Prudent Risk Management, Insurance Risk Transfer, and the Role of the Foundation, *Fordham Law Review*, 69, 329–44.

Groenfeldt, T. (2006) Opportunities in Risk, *Institutional Investor*, March, 1.

Group of Thirty (1993) *Derivatives: Practices and Principles*, Washington DC: Group of Thirty.

Gumbel, E.J. (1958) *Statistics of Extremes*, New York: Columbia University Press.

Gup, B. (2000) *New Financial Architecture for the 21st Century*, Westport (CT): Greenwood Books.

Haas, M. and Kaiser, T. (2004) Tackling the Inefficiency of Loss Data for the Quantification of Operational Loss, in Cruz, M. (ed.) *Operational Risk Modelling and Analysis: Theory and Practice*, London: Risk Books, 13–24.

Haas, M. and Kaiser, T. (2005) Prerequisites for Effective Operational Risk Management and Efficient Risk-Based Decision Making, in Davis, E. (ed.) *Operational Risk: Practical Approaches to Implementation*, London: Risk Books.

Hadjiemmanuil, C. (1996) *Banking Regulation and the Bank of England*, London: LLP.

Hadjiemmanuil, C. (2003) Legal Risk and Fraud: Capital Charges, Control and Insurance, in Alexander, C. (ed.) *Operational Risk: Regulation, Analysis and Management*, London: Prentice Hall-Financial Times.

Halperin, K. (2001) Balancing Act, *Bank Systems and Technology*, 38, 22–5.

Hand, D.J. (2005) Good Capital Practice in Retail Credit Scorecard Assessment, *Journal of the Operational Research Society*, 56, 1109–17.

Haubenstock, M. (2003) The Operational Risk Management Framework, in Alexander, C. (ed.) *Operational Risk: Regulation, Analysis and Management*, London: Prentice Hall-Financial Times.

Haubenstock, M. (2004) Constructing an Operational Event Database, in Ong, K. (ed.) *The Basel Handbook*, London: Risk Books.

Haubenstock, M. and Hardin, L. (2003) The Loss Distribution Approach, in Alexander, C. (ed.) *Operational Risk: Regulation, Analysis and Management*, London: Prentice Hall-Financial Times.

Hayek, F.A. (1976) *Choice in Currency: A Way to Stop Inflation*, Occasional Paper No 48, London: Institute of Economic Affairs.

Hendricks, D. (1996) Evaluation of Value-at-Risk Models Using Historical data, *Federal Reserve Bank of New York Economic Policy Review*, April, 39–46.

Herring, R.J. (2002) The Basel 2 Approach to Bank Operational Risk: Regulation on the Wrong Track, Paper Presented at the 38th Annual Conference on Bank Structure and Competition, Federal Reserve Bank of Chicago, 9 May.

Herring, R.J. and Litan, R.E. (1995) *Financial Regulation in the Global Economy*, Washington DC: The Brookings Institution.

Hills, S. (2004) Explaining the Credit Risk Elements in Basel II, in Ong, K. (ed.) *The Basel Handbook*, London: Risk Books.

Horwitz, S. (1992) *Monetary Evolution, Free Banking and Economic Order*, Boulder: Westview.

Hirtle, B. (2003) What Market Risk Capital Reporting Tell Us about Bank Risk, *Federal Reserve Bank of New York Economic Policy Review*, September, 37–54.

Ho, H. (2006) Timetable Trouble, *Asia Risk*, March, 36–8.

Holmes, M. (2003) Measuring Operational Risk: A Reality Check, *Risk*, 16.

Hubner, R., Laycock, M. and Peemoller, F. (2003) Managing Operational Risk, in *Advances in Operational Risk: Firm-Wide Issues for Financial Institutions*, London: Risk Books.

Hughes, P. (2005) Using Transaction Data to Measure Operational Risk, in Davis, E. (ed.) *Operational Risk: Practical Approaches to Implementation*, London: Risk Books.

Huisman, R., Koedijk, K. Kool, C. and Palm, F. (2001) Tail-Index Estimates in Small Samples, *Journal of Business and Economic Statistics*, 19, 208–16.

IFCI Financial Risk Institute (2000) *Sources of Risk*, May. Available from http://risk.ifci.ch/00007127.htm

Imeson, M. (2006a) Operational Risk—A Problem Shared, *The Banker* (Special Supplement), 1 January, 1.

Imeson, M. (2006b) Basel II: Capital Accord or Capital Discord?, *The Banker*, 1 March, 1.

Jameson, R. (1998) Playing the Name Game, *Risk*, 11, 38–42.

Jorion, P. (1996) Risk^2: Measuring the Risk in Value at Risk, *Financial Analysts Journal*, November/December, 47–56.

Jungermann, H. and Thuring, M. (1987) The Use of Mental Models for Generating Scenarios, in Wright, G. and Ayton, P. (eds) *Judgmental Forecasting*, Chichister: Wiley.

Kalhoff, A. and Haas, M. (2004) Operational Risk: Management based on the Current Loss Data Situation, in Cruz, M. (ed.) *Operational Risk Modelling and Analysis: Theory and Practice*, London: Risk Books, 5–12.

Kalyvas, L. and Sfetsos, A. (2006) Does the Application of Innovative Internal Models Diminish Regulatory Capital? *International Journal of Theoretical and Applied Finance*, 9, 217–26.

Kalyvas, L., Akkizidis, I., Zourka, I. and Bouchereau, V. (2006) *Integrating Market, Credit and Operational Risk: A Complete Guide for Bankers and Risk Professionals*, London: Risk Books.

Karels, G. and McClatchey, C. (1999) Deposit Insurance and Risk-Taking Behaviour in the Credit Union Industry, *Journal of Banking and Finance*, 23, 105–34.

Kaufman, G.G. (2003) Basel II: The Roar that Moused, Mimeo, Federal Reserve Bank of Chicago, October.

Kaufman, G.G. and Scott, K. (2000) Does Bank Regulation Retard or Contribute to Systemic Risk? Mimeo, Loyola University Chicago and Stanford Law School.

Kedar, B.Z. (1970) Again: Arabic Risq, Medieval Latin Risicum, Studi Medievali, Centro Di Studi Sull Alto Medioevo, Spelto.

Kennett, R. (2003) How to Introduce an Effective Risk Management Framework, in *Advances in Operational Risk: Firm-wide Issues for Financial Institutions* (second edition), London: Risk Books.

Keynes, J.M. (1936) the *General Theory of Employment, Interest and Money*, London: Macmillan.

Khan, H. (1965) *On Escalation: Metaphor and Scenarios*, New York: Praeger.

King, J. (1998) Defining Operational Risk, *Algo Research Quarterly*, 1, 37–42.

King, J. (2001) *Operational Risk: Measurement and Modelling*, Chichister: Wiley.

Klugman, S.A., Panjer, H.H. and Willmont, G.E. (1998) *Loss Models: From Data to Decisions*, New York: Wiley.

Knight, F. (1921) *Risk, Uncertainty and Profit*, Boston: Houghton Mifflin Co.

Knot, K., Bikker, J., van Broekhoven, H., Everts, H., Horsmeier, H., Klassen, P., van Lelyveld, I., Monnik, R., Ruijgt, F., Siegelaer, G. and Wanders, H. (2006) Risk Measurement within Financial Conglomerates: Best Practices by Risk Type, in van Lelyveld, I. (ed.) *Economic Capital Modelling: Concepts, Measurement and Implementation*, London: Risk Books.

Knowledge@Wharton and Aon Corporation (2003) Corporate Reputation: Not Worth Risking, in *Advances in Operational Risk: Firm-Wide Issues for Financial Institutions* (second edition), London: Risk Books.

Koehn, M. and Santomero, A.M. (1980) Regulation of Bank Capital and Portfolio Risk, *Journal of Finance*, 35, 1235–44.

KPMG-Risk (1997) VAR: *Understanding and Applying Value-at-Risk*, London: Risk Books.

Kritzman, M. and Rich, D. (2002) The Mismeasurement of Risk, *Financial Analysts Journal*, May/June, 91–8.

Kulp, C.A. (1956) *Casualty Insurance* (3rd edition), New York: Ronald Press.

Kuritzkes, A. and Scott, H. (2002) Sizing Operational Risk and the Effect of Insurance: Implications for the Basel II Capital Accord, Working Paper, Harvard Law School.

Laeven, L. and Majnoni, G. (2003) Loan Loss Provisioning and Economic Slowdown: Too Much, Too Late?, *Journal of Financial Intermediation*, April, 178–97.

Lalonde, D. (2005) Financing Risk, in Grossi, P. and Kunreuther, H., *Catastrophe Modeling: A New Approach to Managing Risk*, New York: Springer.

Lam, J. (2002) The Ten Requirements for Operational Risk Management, *Risk Management*, 48, 58.

Lam, J. (2003a) Enterprise-Wide Risk Management, in Field, P. (ed.) *Modern Risk Management: A History*, London: Risk Books.

Lam, J. (2003b) A Unified Management and Capital Framework for Operational Risk, *RMA Journal*, 58, 26.

Lawrence, M. (2000) Marking the Cards at ANZ, *Operational Risk Supplement*, London: Risk Books.

Leddy, T.M. (2003) Operational Risk and Insurance, in Alexander, C. (ed.) *Operational Risk: Regulation, Analysis and Management*, London: Prentice Hall-Financial Times.

Lewis, C.M. and Lantsman, Y. (2005) What is a Fair Price to Transfer the Risk of Unauthorised Trading? A Case Study on Operational Risk, in Davis, E. (ed.) *Operational Risk: Practical Approaches to Implementation*, London: Risk Books.

Llewellyn, D.T. (ed.) (2001) *Bumps on the Road to Basel: An Anthology of Basel 2*, London: Centre for the Study of Financial Innovation.

Lopez, J.A. (2002) What is Operational Risk?, *Federal Reserve Bank of San Francisco Economic Letter*, January.

Lopez, J.A. (2003) Disclosure as a Supervisory Tool: Pillar 3 of Basel II, *FRBSF Economic Letter*, August.

Lynn, B. (2006) Operational Risk: Are You Prepared?, *AFP Exchange*, 26, 40–5.

Marshall, J. and Heffes, E.M. (2003) Study Faults Bank Risk Management, *Financial Executive*, 19, 11.

Matten, C. (2003) Changing of the Guard, *The Business Times* (Singapore), 21 May.

Mayers, D. and Smith, C. (1982) On the Corporate Demand for Insurance, *Journal of Business*, 55, 281–96.

McConnell, P. (2003) The Use of Reliability Theory in Measuring Operational Risk, in *Advances in Operational Risk: Firm-Wide Issues for Financial Institutions* (second edition), London: Risk Books.

McDonough, W.J. (2003) Implementing the New Basel Accord, Speech Given at the Global Association of Risk Professionals, New York, 11 February.

McLorrain, C. (2000) Managing Risk—The Natural Way, *Oil and Gas Journal*, Fall, 16–7.

Medova, E.A. and Kyriacou, M.N. (2001) Extremes in Operational Risk Management, Working Paper, Centre for Financial Research, University of Cambridge.

Mengle, D. (2003) Risk Management as a Process, in Field, P. (ed.) *Modern Risk Management: A History*, London: Risk Books.

Mestchian, P. (2003) Operational Risk Management: The Solution is in the Problem, in *Advances in Operational Risk: Firm-Wide Issues for Financial Institutions*, London: Risk Books.

Metcalfe, R. (2003) Operational Risk: The Empiricists Strike Back, in Field, P. (ed.) *Modern Risk Management: A History*, London: Risk Books.

Milligan, J. (2004) Prioritizing Operational Risk, *Banking Strategies*, 80, 67.

Mitchell, R.B., Tydeman, J. and Georgiades, J. (1979) Structuring the Future Application of a Scenario Generation Procedure, *Technological Forecasting and Social Change*, 14, 409–28.

Meulen, H. (1934) *Free Banking: An Outline of a Policy Individualism*, London: Macmillan.

Moosa, I.A. (2003) *International Financial Operations: Arbitrage, Hedging, Speculation, Investment and Financing*, London: Palgrave.

Moosa, I.A. (2004) *International Finance: An Analytical Approach* (second edition), Sydney: McGraw Hill.

Moosa, I.A. (2007) Misconceptions about Operational Risk, *Journal Of Operational Risk* (Forthcoming).

Moosa, I.A. and Bollen, B. (2002) A Benchmark for Measuring Bias in Estimated Daily Value at Risk, *International Review of Financial Analysis*, 11, 85–100.

Moscadelli, M. (2005) The Modelling of Operational Risk: Experience with the Analysis of the Data collected by the Basel Committee, in Davis, E. (ed.) *Operational Risk: Practical Approaches to Implementation*, London: Risk Books.

Mowbray, A.H. and Blanchard, R.H. (1961) *Insurance: Its Theory and Practice in the United States* (5th edition), New York: McGraw Hill.

Muzzy, L. (2003) The Pitfalls of Gathering Operational Risk Data, *RMA Journal*, 85, 58.

Nash, R. (2003) The Three Pillars of Operational Risk, in C. Alexander (ed.) *Operational Risk: Regulation, Analysis and Management*, London: Prentice Hall-Financial Times.

Neil, M., Fenton, N. and Tailor, M. (2005) Using Bayesian Networks to Model Expected and Unexpected Operational Losses, *Risk Analysis*, 25, 963–72.

Neslehova, J., Embrechts, P. and Chavez-Demoulin, V. (2006) Infinite-Mean Models and the LDA for Operational Risk, *Journal of Operational Risk*, 3–24.

Ong, M. (2002) The Alpha, Beta and Gamma of Operational Risk, *RMA Journal*, 85, 34.

Peccia, A. (2003) Using Operational Risk Models to Manage Operational Risk, in Alexander, C. (ed.) *Operational Risk: Regulation, Analysis and Management*, London: Prentice Hall-Financial Times.

Peccia, A. (2004) An Operational Risk Ratings Model Approach to Better Measurement and Management of Operational Risk, in Ong, K. (ed.) *The Basel Handbook*, London: Risk Books.

Pezier, J. (2003a) Operational Risk Management, in Alexander, C. (ed.) *Operational Risk: Regulation, Analysis and Management*, London: Prentice Hall-Financial Times.

Pezier, J. (2003b) A Constructive Review of the Basel Proposals on Operational Risk, in Alexander, C. (ed.) *Operational Risk: Regulation, Analysis and Management*, London: Prentice Hall-Financial Times.

Postlewaite, A. and Vives, X. (1987) Bank Runs as an Equilibrium Phenomenon, *Journal of Political Economy*, 95, 485–91.

Powojowski, M., Reynolds, D. and Tuenter, H.J.H. (2002) Dependent Events and Operational risk, *Algo Research Quarterly*, 5, 65–73.

Pritsker, M. (1997) Evaluating Value-at-Risk Methodologies: Accuracy versus Computational Time, *Journal of Financial Services Research*, 12, 201–42.

Prouty, R. (1960) *Industrial Insurance: A Formal Approach to Risk Analysis and Evaluation*, Washington DC: Machinery and Allied Products Institute.

Raft International (2002) *Emerging Trends in Operational Risk within the Financial Services Industry*. Available from www.raft.co.uk

Regulation (2001) Basel Capital Accord, *Regulation*, 24, 9.

Resti, A. and Sironi, A. (2004) Loss Given Default and Recovery Risk: From Basel II Standards to Effective Risk Management Tools in Basel II, in Ong, K. (ed.) *The Basel Handbook*, London: Risk Books.

Risk Management (2002) Operational Risk Management, Controlling Opportunities and Threats, *Risk Management*, 49, 69–71.

Robert Morris Associates, British Bankers' Association and International Swaps and Derivatives Association (1999) *Operational Risk: The Next Frontier*, Philadelphia: RMA.

Rockoff, H. (1975) *The Free Banking Era: A Re-examination*, New York: Arno.

Roehr, A. (2002) Modelling Operational Losses, *Algo Research Quarterly*, 5, 53–64.

Rowe, D. (2004a) Op Risk and Black Swans, *Risk*, 17, 114.

Rowe, D. (2004b) Basel II and Economic Capital, *US Banker*, 114, 72.

Rowe, D. (2005) A Step to Basel 1.5, *Risk*, December 2005, 80.

Roy, A.D. (1952) Safety First and the Holding of Assets, *Econometrica*, 20, 431–49.

Saita, F. (2004) Risk Capital Aggregation: The Risk Manager's Perspective, NEWFIN Working Papers.

Sanghera, S. (2005) How to Avoid Kicking up a Stink over an Offensive Odour, *Financial Times*, 14 October, 9.

Saxton, K. (2002) Banks Face Risky Business of Basel, *Euromoney*, January, 131.

Schofield, P. (2003) Reputational Risk, in *Advances in Operational Risk: Firm-Wide Issues for Financial Institutions* (second edition), London: Risk Books.

Schrand, C. and Unal, H. (1998) Hedging and Co-ordinated Risk Management: Evidence from Thrift Conversions, *Journal of Finance*, 53, 979–1013.

Sechrest, L.J. (1993) *Free Banking: Theory, History and a Laissez-Faire Model*, Westport (CT): Quorom Books.

Servaes, H. and Tufano, P. (2006) Ranking Risk and Finance According to a Survey of Chief Financial Officers at Non-Financial Companies, *Financial Times*, 9 June, 4.

Shadow Financial Regulatory Committee (2000) *Reforming Bank Capital Regulation*, Washington DC: American Enterprise Institute.

Shadow Financial Regulatory Committee (2001) The Basel Committee's Revised Capital Accord Proposal, Statement No 169, February.

Shadow Financial Regulatory Committee (2002) The Basel 2 Approach to Bank Operational Risk: Regulation on the Wrong Track, Statement No 179, May.

Sharon, B. (2006) Operational Risk Management: The Difference between Risk Management and Compliance, *Business Credit*, 108, 12–3.

Shepheard-Walwyn, T. and Litterman, R. (1998) Building a Coherent Risk Measurement and Capital Optmisation Model for Financial Firms, *Federal Reserve Bank of New York Economic Policy Review*, October, 171–82.

Shewhart, W.A. (1980) *Economic Control of Quality of Manufactured Product*, Milwaukee (WI): ASQ Quality Press.

Shih, J., Samad-Khan, A. and Medapa, P. (2000) Is the Size of an Operational Loss Related to Firm Size? *Operational Risk*, January.

Shirreff, D. (2005) Open Wider, *The Economist* (A Survey of International Banking), 21 May, 3–4.

Smithson, C. (2000) Quantifying Operational Risk, *Risk*, March.

Sobehart, J. (2006) A Model of Op Risk with Imperfect Controls, *Risk*, 19, 90.

Societies of Actuaries (2004) Specialty Guide on Economic Capital, Societies of Actuaries: Schaumburg (Ill).

Structured Finance International (2004) ABS is Dead! Long Live ABS, *Structured Finance International*, July/August, 1.

Stulz, R.M. (1996) Rethinking Risk Management, Mimeo.

Swenson, K. (2003) A Qualitative Operational Risk Framework: Guidance, Structure and Reporting, in Alexander, C. (ed.) *Operational Risk: Regulation, Analysis and Management*, London: Prentice Hall-Financial Times.

Thirlwell, J. (2002) Operational Risk: The Banks and the Regulators Struggle, *Balance Sheet*, 10, 28–31.

Thirlwell, J. (2003) Building and Running an Operational Loss Database, in *Advances in Operational Risk: Firm-Wide Issues for Financial Institutions* (second edition), London: Risk Books.

Thomson, T.S. (2003) Letter to Basel Committee on Banking Supervision, 29 July, http://www.bis.org/bcbs/cp3/jpmorgan.pdf

Tripe, D. (2000) Pricing Operational Risk, Paper Presented at the 13th Australasian Finance and Banking Conference, Sydney, December.

Turing, D. (2003) The Legal and Regulatory View of Operational Risk, in *Advances in Operational Risk: Firm-Wide Issues for Financial Institutions* (second edition), London: Risk Books.

van Lelyveld (2006) A Supervisory View on Economic Capital Models, in van Lelyveld, I. (ed.) *Economic Capital Modelling: Concepts, Measurement and Implementation*, London: Risk Books.

Vaughan, E.J. (1997) *Risk Management*, New York: Wiley.

Vinella, P. and Jin, J. (2005) A Foundation for KPI and KRI, in Davis, E. (ed.) *Operational Risk: Practical Approaches to Implementation*, London: Risk Books.

Wei, R. (2003) Operational Risk in the Insurance Industry, Working Paper, The Wharton School.

Wei, R. (2006) *An Empirical Investigation of Operational Risk in the United States Financial Sectors*, University of Pennsylvania (AAT 3211165).

White, L. (2004) Market Discipline and Appropriate Disclosure in Basel II, in Ong, K. (ed.) *The Basel Handbook*, London: Risk Books.

Willett, A.H. (1951) *The Economic Theory of Risk and Insurance*, Philadelphia: University of Pennsylvania Press.

Williams, C., Smith, M. and Young, P. (1998) *Risk Management and Insurance* (eighth edition), New York: McGraw Hill.

Young, B. and Ashby, S. (2003) New Trends in Operational Risk Insurance for Banks, in *Advances in Operational Risk: Firm-Wide Issues for Financial Institutions* (second edition), London: Risk Books.

Index